The High Court: A User's Guide

SECOND EDITION

The High Court

A User's Guide

SECOND EDITION

KIERON WOOD
Barrister-at-Law

With a foreword by
HUGH O'FLAHERTY
formerly Judge of the Supreme Court

FOUR COURTS PRESS

Set in 10.5 on 12.5 Ehrhardt by
Carrigboy Typesetting Services for
FOUR COURTS PRESS LTD
Fumbally Lane, Dublin 8, Ireland
e-mail: info@four-courts-press.ie
and in North America for
FOUR COURTS PRESS
c/o ISBS, 5824 N.E. Hassalo Street, Portland, OR 97213.

© Kieron Wood 1998, 2001
e-mail: kieronwood@hotmail.com

A catalogue record for this title
is available from the British Library.

ISBN 1–85182–588–6
First edition 1998
Second edition 2002

Printed in Ireland
by ColourBooks Ltd, Dublin

Foreword to the First Edition

In a previous existence Kieron Wood was legal affairs correspondent for RTÉ, the national broadcasting authority. I was always struck by his ability to summarise in a manner of minutes quite complex cases decided in the courts. And, of course, he was obliged to cover simultaneously the proceedings of different courts – and to have the law and his facts right. I am delighted to report that Kieron has brought the adroitness that he displayed on the box to the book.

As he says, *The High Court: A User's Guide* has the modest but important aim that it will be a practical guide to help practitioners overcome the more common problems that they will have to face day in and day out. A good working knowledge of the Rules is absolutely necessary for any practitioner, barrister or solicitor. William Binchy (father of Maeve and Professor William) had two precepts that he would put before the young practitioner. He would invite him or her to say whether he had checked the rule in its entirety and, as to the construction of any document, he would enjoin that it should be read in its entirety – to find out its true purport. Even after nearly forty years, when I first heard these two pieces of advice, I attempt to observe them.

The modern rules have a distinguished ancestry. Ever since the abandonment of the old forms of action, the rules have been refined and updated from time to time so as to be as much help as possible to the litigant and to the practitioner. Indeed they are intended to smooth the path for the litigant and practitioner. It is remarkable how many of the rules go back for so long and have stood the test of time.

Further, the practitioner who has a good knowledge and respect for the rules is likely to be one whose presentation of his case in court is also well ordered and to the point. If a case once gets off the track it is difficult to get it back on the rails – without going back to the original point of departure. It is a great joy and pleasure to recommend this work by Kieron Wood. One hopes that, like the Rules, it will continue to be updated over the years. I know the venture is deserving of support from judges and practitioners – and a lay litigant will, I am sure, find it most helpful too.

HUGH O'FLAHERTY
Supreme Court, Four Courts, 29 May 1998

To my children
Tabitha, Laura, Sarah and Timothy

PLAN OF THE FOUR COURTS

GROUND FLOOR

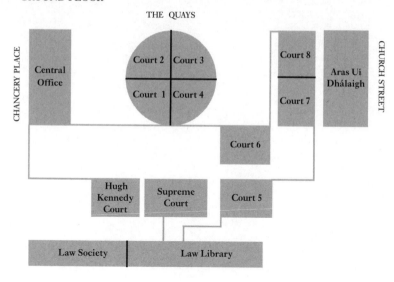

FIRST FLOOR

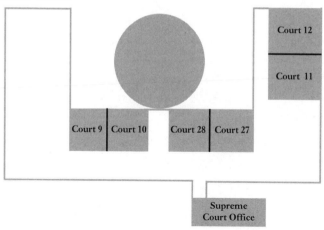

SECOND FLOOR

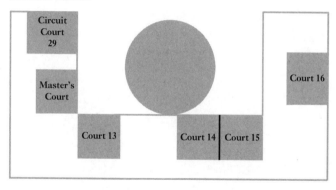

Preface to the Second Edition

Since the publication of the first edition of this book in 1998, there have been substantial changes to the rules of practice and procedure – notably in the areas of discovery, judicial review and disclosure of expert reports in personal injuries cases. Without doubt, the advent of computerisation will lead to further developments, as electronic communication, storage and retrieval of information become the norm.

Judgments, for example, are now becoming widely available on the internet. The British and Irish Legal Information Institute site (www.bailii.org) provides a range of Irish High Court and Supreme Court judgments within a short time of delivery and without charge to the user. Most statutes are available from the Attorney General's site at www.irlgov.ie/ag/

But, despite the rapid development of technology, a sound knowledge of the existing rules still remains a prerequisite for practitioners and lay litigants alike. As Mr Justice O'Flaherty warned in *AE Dawson & Sons* v. *Irish Brokers' Association*, Supreme Court, 6 November 1998: "(W)e extend as much understanding as we can to lay litigants in regard to technical aspects of any given litigation but, if there is a breach of the law or of some essential procedural matter, the consequences should be the same whether the person is represented or not."

Given the House of Lords decision in *Hall & Co.* v. *Simons*, 20 July 2000 that barristers in that jurisdiction may now be sued for negligence, it is all the more important that legal advisers should have a firm grasp of the rules.

I hope this second edition will continue to help lay litigants and practitioners to avoid what Mr Justice Carney described in *Breathnach* v. *Lindsay* [2001] IESC 14 as "inappropriate pseudo-legal verbiage".

Kieron Wood

4 August 2001
Feast of St Dominic

Preface to the First Edition

The rules of Court practice and procedure in Common Law jurisdictions have evolved over many centuries. Knowledge of those rules is vital to all who practise in our Courts. In the case of *Lee* v. *Morrissey-Murphy*, Supreme Court, 22 November 1996, O'Flaherty J warned:

> "(T)his Court has repeatedly said that the rules are there to be servants of the law, rather than that the law should be subservient to the rules. However, there comes a time when it is absolutely critical from the point of view of the proper administration of justice, and in order for justice to be done to all parties, that there has to be compliance with the rules."

His Supreme Court colleague, Barrington J, agreed:

> "The Courts have repeatedly stated that rules of procedure exist to serve the administration of justice, and must never be allowed to defeat it. Nevertheless those who ignore the rules run the risks of finding themselves on an uncharted sea." (*Murphy* v. *Donohoe and Fiat* [1996] 1 ILRM 481)

Traditionally, the navigational chart of practitioners in the Irish High Court has been the Rules of the Superior Courts, drawn up by the Rules of Court committee and published in 1986 by the Stationery Office. The alphabetical index lists everything from "Abatement, certificate of solicitor" to "Witness, evidence; Companies (winding up)". But, with more than 1,000 pages and weighing in at three-and-a-half pounds, the RSC doesn't exactly make for lightweight reading. Subsequent changes and additions, such as those introduced by SI 348 of 1997 or SI 265 of 1993, make adherence to the Rules even more problematical. Hence the need for a simplified guide.

This book does not pretend to be a comprehensively updated version of the Rules. It is intended to be a practical guide to some of the more common problems faced by practitioners. My hope is that it will help remove some of the mystique from the subject of practice and procedure – and that it will contribute to easing the lot of judges, practitioners and law students.

My thanks are due, in particular, to Brian Spierin, whose lectures at the Kings Inns inspired this book, and to Mr Justice Hugh O'Flaherty for his kind foreword and help with the section on Supreme Court appeals. I am also grateful to Mr Justice Declan Costello, Mr Justice Frederick Morris, Mr Justice Peter Kelly, former Master Harry Hill, Ben Ó Floinn, Nuala McLoughlin, Debbie Wheeler, Bernard Barton, Brendan Reedy, Ciaran Kelly, Kevin O'Neill, Elizabeth Lyne, Anne Ross in the Probate Office, and all my other lecturers and colleagues in the Kings Inns and Law Library who urged me not to give up. This volume would never have been finished without the support and encouragement of Michael Adams and all at Four Courts Press. Any errors are mine; any corrections or proposed improvements must be the task of the reader.

Kieron Wood
27 May 1998
Feast of St Bede

Contents

Table of Cases

Table of Statutes

Table of Rules of the Superior Courts

Order	Rule	Page	Order	Rule	Page
15	20	44	22	1(8)	105
15	22	165	22	1(10)	105
15	37	33, 177	22	4	106
16		78, 79	22	6	104, 105
16	1(2)	81, 82	22	10	106
16	1(3)	80	22	13	107
16	5	82	23	1	57
16	12	80	23	3	58
17	1	177	25	1	6
18	1	32	26	2	61
19	1	42, 46	27	5	20
19	3	42, 47	27	7	169
19	3A	70	27	9	5, 11
19	5	49	27	9(2)	11
19	6(1)	169	27	14	13
19	7	5	28		43
19	7(3)	5	28	1	38
19	9	43	29		128
19	13	55	29	2	129
19	15	54	29	3	63, 129
19	17	54	29	6	130
19	19	55	30		30
19	22	54	31	2	103
19	27	54	31	6	103
19	28	16	31	11	103
20	1	18, 19, 46	31	12	84, 86, 88
20	2	4	31	12(1)	89
20	4	4	31	12(4)	86
20	7	46	31	17	92
21	2	5	31	21	86, 101
21	7	170	31	29	83, 90
21	8	54	31	12	6, 77
21	14	57	31	20(2)	93
21	15	57	31	20(3)	100
21	17	169	31	21	91, 101
22	1(2)	104	32	1–9	102
22	1(3)	104	32	2	58
22	1(5)	104	32	4	58
22	1(6)	104	32	9	58

⟶

Court Fees

Fees must be paid on a large range of documents used in Court. The documents are stamped to indicate that the correct fee was paid. A Court may refuse to admit a document which is incorrectly or insufficiently stamped. In 1998, the Courts collected £11 million in fees.

The constitutionality of Court fees was tested in the case of *Murphy* v. *Minister for Justice, Equality and Law Reform* [2001] IESC 20. The applicant claimed that fees were unconstitutional because they could impede an impecunious applicant from proceeding with his case. Murphy J agreed that the fees could present a "significant burden" to a person on social welfare, but he said it would be impossible to consider the impact of particular fees without knowing the full circumstances of the plaintiff and the options or facilities available to him.

No fees are payable in the Central Office or Supreme Court office for any application, order, judgment or report (nor for the filing of any notice of motion, affidavit or other document) in cases relating to *habeas corpus*, extradition, bail, family law proceedings and matters where a party is represented by the Chief State Solicitor.

With those exceptions, the fees payable are set out in SI 251 of 2001. From January 1 2002, all fees are payable in euros. Article 14 of EU Council Regulation (EC) No. 974/98 of 3 May 1998 on the introduction of the euro says: "Where reference is made to the national currency units in legal instruments existing at the end of the transitional period, these references shall be read as references to the euro unit according to the respective conversion rates. The rounding rules laid down in Regulation (EC) No. 103/97 shall apply."

The current fees include:

Copy judgments £8 (plus £1 per 5 pages copied)
Attested copy documents £4 per page
Supreme Court notice of appeal £60
Supreme Court case stated £24
High Court summons £72
Concurrent summons £18
High Court petition £48
High Court *ex parte* application £24

Third party notice £8
Appearance £8
Affidavit £8
Script £8
Notice of motion £12
Notice of appeal from Master £12
Notice of appeal from Circuit Court £30
Other notices £4
Setting down for trial £60
High Court case stated £36
Subpoena £8
Default judgment in Central Office £8
Power of attorney £8
Bankruptcy petition £48
Probate officer's order £4
Probate Court order £4
Entry of *caveat* £4
Inspection of will £1
Copy of will £2.50

1. Summonses

Under the Irish Constitution, the High Court has "full original juris-diction in and power to determine all matters and questions whether of law or fact, civil or criminal."

The procedure governing the Court's determination of those matters is set out in the Rules of the Superior Courts (RSC), which were origi-nally drawn up in 1986 by the eleven members of the Superior Courts Rules Committee. Order 124 of the Rules makes clear that failure to comply with the Rules will not, of itself, invalidate any proceedings. But the Court may order that faulty proceedings be set aside or amended on specified terms, so it is in the interests of barristers, solicitors and lay litigants to adhere to the Rules as closely as possible.

Civil proceedings in the High Court are begun by petition, origi-nating notice of motion or summons. Matters which begin by petition include matrimonial, bankruptcy, revenue and Companies Acts cases. The most common use of originating motions is in the area of judicial review.

A summons is basically a written demand for a person to attend court at a certain time. The three types of originating summons are:

1 **Plenary** (where there is to be oral evidence or a full plenary hearing),
2 **Summary** (for a liquidated sum, or where there are no pleadings and the matter is to be heard on affidavit, with or without oral evidence), and
3 **Special** (in actions such as administration suits and mixed common law/equity matters. There are no pleadings and the matter is usually heard on affidavit.)

The form of the three types of summons is set out in Appendix A of the Rules of the Superior Courts. Anyone who chooses to use a different form of application may be penalised in costs (O. 1 rule 5 RSC). If the summons is issued in Irish, an English copy must be provided – and *vice-versa*, if the summons is served personally in the Gaeltacht (O. 120 rules 2–3 RSC).

PLENARY SUMMONS

The **plenary summons** is used in all cases which don't require the use of a special summons or summary summons (except taking a minor into wardship – O. 1, rule 6 RSC). It's most frequently used in cases involving personal injuries, breach of contract, specific performance, declaratory relief and the Constitution. The name of the summons reflects the fact that there will eventually be a full hearing of the case with oral evidence, as distinct from a hearing based on affidavit only.

Unlike other summonses, which may change course during the progress of an action, **plenary summonses** normally follow the same course throughout the proceedings. The President of the High Court assigns certain judges to deal with certain types of summons (O. 5 rule 4 RSC)

A **plenary summons** is a document under the seal of the High Court. Even the shape, size and quality of the paper and details of printing are regulated by the President of the High Court (O. 117 rule 3 RSC). The summons contains the names of the plaintiff and defendant and a series of formal details which appear on all **plenary summonses** (Appendix A Part I No. 1 RSC). It normally requires the defendant to enter an appearance within eight days, and includes a **general endorsement of claim** (O. 4 rule 2 RSC) which sets out concisely the plaintiff's cause of action (O. 4 rule 3 and Appendix B Part II RSC). This is not as extensive as a **special endorsement of claim** in a special or summary summons, because it is supplemented by a more detailed **statement of claim**.

There is space on the summons for the solicitor to give details of service. Counsel usually drafts the **title** and **general endorsement of claim**, while the solicitor deals with the formal elements and service.

The **plenary summons** is issued by filing it in the Central Office of the High Court (High Court documents must be filed in person, not by post). All summonses are given a reference number (preceded by "P" for a plenary summons and "Sp" for a special summons) and entered consecutively in a cause book (O. 5 rule 7 RSC). The Central Office will mark the original summons with a seal and return it to the plaintiff or his solicitor. A copy signed by the plaintiff's solicitor (or the plaintiff in person) will be stamped and kept on the Court file. The office will frank as many duplicates as there are defendants.

Like all summonses, a **plenary summons** remains in force for 12 months. It may be extended "for good reason" by the Master – or, after the 12-month period, by the Court (O. 8 rule 1 RSC). The summons may be renewed for six months at a time, for as long as necessary to prevent an action becoming statute-barred.

In *Foran* v. *O'Connell*, High Court, 6 May 1997, Morris J said the test to be applied was whether the renewal of the summons would work an injustice on the defendant.

A summons may only be renewed if reasonable efforts have been made to serve the defendant or for some other good reason. In *Roche* v. *Clayton* [1998] 1 IR 596, Mr Justice O'Flaherty said the High Court had a wide discretion to renew a summons, but there had to be some good reason. He said it was not a good reason simply to prevent the defendant availing of the Statute of Limitations.

If the original summons has been destroyed or lost, the Court may order that a copy be sealed and served in its place (O. 8 rule 4 RSC).

Proceedings are deemed to be instituted in the High Court when the summons is *issued* – that is sealed and marked with the record number. (In the Circuit Court, proceedings were formerly instituted when the Civil Bill was *served* by registered post or summons server, but Circuit Court proceedings are now deemed instituted when *issued*, as in the High Court).

Once proceedings have been instituted, they must be served *personally* "if reasonably practicable" by showing the **original sealed summons** to the defendant and handing him a **copy**. (The Companies Acts allow service by delivering the summons to the company's registered office, or by post.) The **affidavit of service** should say when, where, how and by whom the summons was served and state that the person serving the summons was acquainted with the appearance of the defendant at the time the summons was served.

A summons need not be served if the defendant's solicitor accepts service and undertakes in writing to enter an appearance. If he fails to enter an appearance, he may be attached for contempt (O. 12 rule 12 RSC). A summons should not be served in the precincts of the court, on Sundays or on a person aged under 16. **Particulars of service**, including the day and date of service, should be endorsed on the summons within three days of service, as an *aide-memoire* to the person swearing the **affidavit of service** (O. 9 rule 12 RSC). If the wrong date is endorsed by mistake, the Court has power to amend it.

The defendant must **enter an appearance** in the Central Office within eight days, exclusive of the day of service (O. 12 rule 2(1) RSC) unless the Court orders otherwise (or unless the defendant is a lunatic or minor, when the appearance is entered in the Office of Wards of Court). This is done by delivering a **memorandum in writing,** in the form set out in Appendix A, Part II, Form No. 1 RSC, dated the day of delivery, and containing the name and address for service of the solicitor for the defendant(s) or the defendant(s) in person. (If the address is false, the appearance may be set aside – O. 12 rule 8 RSC.)

If a **statement of claim** is required, the defendant's solicitor should say so. A duplicate of the memorandum of appearance is stamped and returned by the Central Office. The duplicate should be served or posted the same day to the plaintiff or his solicitor.

Alternatively, a defendant wishing to appear in person may enter an appearance by registered letter, enclosing the memorandum of appearance and two duplicates, a postal order for the fee and two stamped envelopes, one addressed to the plaintiff (or his solicitor) and the other to the defendant himself. The Central Office then stamps and posts the duplicates. (O. 12 rules 4–5 RSC). The rules for appearance in relation to a claim for the recovery of land are somewhat more complicated (O. 12 rules 13–25 RSC).

If the defendant intends to contest the jurisdiction of the Court or service of the summons (O. 12 rule 26 RSC), he may enter a **conditional appearance** and bring a motion directing the **trial of an issue**, which will be dealt with at the appearance or at a later hearing. In *Short* v. *Ireland, Attorney General and British Nuclear Fuels* [1997] 1 ILRM 161, BNFL entered an appearance solely for the purpose of contesting an order allowing service of notice of a plenary summons on them out of the jurisdiction.

But in *McMahon* v. *Lynch*, High Court, 20 November 1996, Flood J refused an application for a preliminary trial of an issue, citing "the extreme unwisdom – save in very exceptional cases – of adopting this procedure of preliminary issues", and agreeing with the dictum of Lord Evershard MR that "the shortest cut so attempted inevitably turns out to be the longest way round."

If the defendant fails to enter an appearance, the plaintiff may bring **a motion for judgment in default of appearance**.

If the plaintiff has not already delivered a **statement of claim** (Appendix B Part IV No. 1 RSC), he should do so within 21 days of service of the summons (O. 20 rule 2 RSC). The statement of claim sets out the full facts of the claim, details the loss or damage suffered and claims the full relief sought. The **statement of claim** amplifies and supersedes the **general endorsement of claim**. If the plaintiff fails to deliver a **statement of claim** within a reasonable time, the defendant may bring a **motion on notice** to have the claim dismissed for want of prosecution. No **statement of claim** need be delivered where the defendant fails to request one in writing, or where he fails to enter an appearance (O. 20 rule 4 RSC).

During the **exchange of pleadings**, either side may seek further particulars of the other side's claim by sending a written **notice for further particulars**, requiring detailed answers to questions about the **statement of claim, defence** and/or **counterclaim** (O. 19 rule 7 RSC). If the **statement of claim** contains full details of the alleged injury, **notices for particulars** should *not* be delivered as a matter of course.

Particulars are, strictly speaking, not part of the pleadings, but ancillary to them. The Court will not order delivery of particulars before the **defence** or **reply** unless necessary or desirable to enable a party to plead (O. 19 rule 7(3) RSC). In *Cooney* v. *Browne* [1986] ILRM 444, the Supreme Court said a party would only be compelled to give further particulars *during* the exchange of pleadings where absolutely necessary to enable the other side to plead. *After* the close of pleadings, particulars would only be compelled where necessary for a fair trial.

In the case of *Church & General v. Moore* [1996] 1 ILRM 202, the defendant failed to give adequate replies to a notice for particulars and the plaintiff obtained a High Court order for further particulars. Three years later, the defendant had still failed to comply with the order, so his defence was struck out. Execution of the order was stayed for two weeks on condition that the defendant complied with the order and paid £50,000 into Court to the credit of the action.

On appeal, the Supreme Court said the inherent power given to the Court to order a further and better statement of the nature of any pleading (O. 19 rule 7 RSC) was intended to ensure compliance with Court orders. The payment of money into Court was not necessary for that purpose, and could only be regarded as a penalty for failure to obey the Court order. The Court had no jurisdiction to impose such a penalty.

After a defendant has been served with the **statement of claim**, he delivers his **defence** to the plaintiff (Appendix B Part V No. 1 RSC). The **defence** may be a complete denial (or "traverse") of the plaintiff's claim, or liability may be admitted but the loss disputed ("confessing and avoiding"), and/or the defendant may make a **counterclaim**.

If the defendant fails to deliver his **defence** within 28 days of his entry of **appearance** or receipt of **statement of claim** (or the period specified by O. 21 rule 2 RSC), the plaintiff may issue a motion for **judgment in default of defence**. But first, the defendant must formally be given a 21-day extension of time in which to deliver his defence if the claim is for unliquidated damages in tort or contract – O. 27 rule 9 RSC).

On receipt of the defence, the plaintiff decides whether a **reply** needs to be delivered (Appendix B Part VI No. 1 RSC). A **reply** is only required where *new matter* is raised on the **defence** or where there is a **counterclaim**.

The **reply** incorporates the **defence to a counterclaim**. (New matter might include, for example, a claim of contributory negligence, that the matter is statute-barred or the discovery of relevant new facts not set out in the **statement of claim**). Alternatively, the plaintiff may raise **particulars on the defence**.

Any **reply** must be delivered within 14 days of the delivery of the defence and the pleadings close with the **reply**. If there is no need for a **reply**, the **pleadings** close with the **defence**. The **originating summons**, **statement of claim, defence, counterclaim** and **reply**, (or **petition** and **answer**), constitute the **pleadings**.

If a point of law arises in the pleadings, the Court may deal with it before the trial of the action, if both sides agree or if the Court so orders (O. 25 rule 1 RSC).

Interlocutory applications

Before the action comes to Court, either side may apply for **interlocutory** relief, such as an **interim** or **interlocutory injunction**, a **Mareva order**, liberty to **amend pleadings**, or joinder of a **co-defendant**. On the filing of a **defence**, an application may be made by the defendant to **join a third party** from whom the defendant claims indemnity. Any of these applications may be brought before or after the close of pleadings.

After the pleadings have closed, the parties may seek voluntary discovery of documents from each other. If either party is dissatisfied with the **discovery** volunteered, he may apply to the Master for an order for discovery from the other side (or even from someone who is not a party to the action). The subject will be required to swear an **affidavit** setting out details of any relevant documents he has in his **possession, custody or power**.

In *Bula Ltd* v. *Tara Mines Ltd* [1994] 1 IR 493, O'Flaherty J said that those three concepts must be "considered disjunctively." He said a document was within the power of a party "if he has an enforceable legal right to obtain from whoever actually holds the document inspection of it without the need to obtain the consent of anyone else." That view was reinforced by the Supreme Court in *Quinlivan* v. *Conroy* [1999] 1 IR 271.

Exceptionally, discovery may be sought *before* the **statement of claim** is issued or the **defence** delivered (for example in medical negligence cases, where an application may be made for discovery of medical notes relating to the plaintiff's complaint – O. 31 rule 12 RSC)

In *Law Society of Ireland* v. *Rawlinson* [1997] 3 IR 592, the plaintiff had obtained an order for discovery from the Master before delivering a statement of claim, on the grounds that discovery was necessary for a properly particularised statement of claim. The defendant appealed on the grounds that discovery was only available after a statement of claim had been filed, and should not be granted to allow a plaintiff to establish a basis for making a claim. Morris J held that an order for discovery could be made where the application was not a "fishing expedition" and where the order was merited by the unusual or peculiar nature of the cause of action.

Interrogatories are questions which may be formally put to the defendant to relieve the plaintiff of proof in matters which may be difficult or expensive to prove. They should take the form of leading questions (which can only be answered yes or no) and must be answered under oath. The answers to **interrogatories** may avoid the expense of unnecessary witnesses being called, even though they might not necessarily establish liability. A defendant may artificially deny matters in the **defence** (in order to "put the plaintiff on proof"), but may not do so under oath in answer to an interrogatory.

Motions

Interlocutory applications are based on a **notice of motion** and **affidavit**. A **motion** is a request to the Court issued through the Central Office (O52 rule 1 RSC). The **notice of motion** must have the title and record number of the action and include:

1   the **names** of the parties,
2   the **return date** for hearing ,
3   details of all orders or **reliefs sought**,
4   details of any relevant **documents or affidavits**,
5   the **date** of the motion,
6   name and address of the **applicant's solicitor**,
7   name and address of the **solicitor to be served** and
8   **signature** of the solicitor for the moving party.

If the **notice of motion** does not claim all the reliefs required, and later has to be amended, the applicant may be penalised in costs (O. 52 rule 5 RSC).

The **notice of motion** is addressed to the Chief Registrar and the parties (or their solicitors). The Central Office will specify the **date, time** and list in which the application will be heard. The stamped copy of the **notice of motion** which is lodged in the Central Office may indicate whether it relates to the motions (Common Law) list, the Chancery 1 list, the Chancery 2 list, the non-jury (Common Law) list or family law list. In the latter four cases, a full set of documents should be lodged in the Central Office with the copy notice. A book of documents should be prepared, indexed and paginated and handed up in court on the hearing of the application.

If the other side is represented by a solicitor, the **notice of motion** must be served (with any affidavits – O. 52 rule 15 RSC) *two clear days* before the hearing of the application (excluding the date of service, date of hearing, weekends and bank holidays). If the other side is not legally represented, at least *four clear days'* notice must be given (or more for certain types of application, such as judicial review). This is effectively a working week, so, if the application is to be heard on a Monday, the **notice of motion** must be served on the previous Monday – or the previous Wednesday if the notice party is represented. Saturdays, Sundays, Christmas Day and Good Friday are not taken into account in computing notice (O. 122, rule 2).

If the notice party is *not* represented, the **notice of motion** is called a **motion for the sitting of the Court**. In the case of Common Law reliefs (such as damages for negligence or personal injuries), the matter should appear in the Legal Diary in the **Common Law motion list** under the heading "**Motions for the sitting of the Court**". If *equitable relief*, such as an injunction, is sought, the case will appear in the Monday motion list in Chancery 1 or Chancery 2, where **motions for the sitting of the Court** are not separately listed.

When the Court sits, Counsel should ask for the notice party to be called. If the notice party appears, the application takes its place in the list and everyone should wait in court until the matter is called again. If the notice party does not appear, the matter should be put back to second calling, when he should be called again. If the notice party is not called, the judge may *strike out* the application, on the assumption that the party may have turned up in court at the required time, but left again.

Default of appearance

If a defendant fails to enter an **appearance** to a plenary summons, the claim will have to go to Court, so that a judge can assess damages. Where the claim is for a specific liquidated amount (on a plenary *or* summary summons), final judgment may be entered in the Central Office for the sum plus interest (if any) and costs, without going to Court – except in cases involving moneylenders, hire-purchase or credit sales (O. 13 rule 3 RSC).

If it is necessary to go to Court, the plaintiff brings a **motion on notice** to the defendant for liberty to enter judgment in default of appearance.

If the defendant is an infant or mentally ill, the plaintiff should first apply to the Master for the appointment of a guardian *ad litem* to defend the case (O. 13 rule 1 RSC).

The notice of motion must be served on the defendant (or any one of several defendants who may be in default) and the plaintiff must file an **affidavit of service** of the motion in the Central Office (O. 13 rule 2 RSC). The documents required for an **application for judgment in default of appearance** are:

1   **notice of motion,**
2   **affidavit of service** of the notice of motion,
3   original **plenary summons** with details of service,
4   **affidavit of service** of the summons, as filed in the Central Office,
5   any **order** relating to **substituted service** or **service outside the jurisdiction,**
6   copy **statement of claim,** certified as to no appearance (the original will have been filed in the Central Office in lieu of delivery) and
7   **certificate of no appearance,** issued by the Central Office.

In practice the **certificate of no appearance** will not be needed if the Court extends time to enter an appearance. But if time is not extended and judgment obtained, the registrar won't issue the order until he has seen the certificate.

As the defendant will be unrepresented, it will be a **motion for the sitting of the Court** and the defendant must be given at least *four* days' clear notice of the return date of the motion (or more, if he lives abroad).

If the **notice of motion** was served by registered post, the **affidavit of service** will exhibit the certificate of posting. If there's been a long delay between the date of service of the originating summons and the service of the **notice of motion,** the Court may require personal service, in case the defendant has changed address.

If the defendant doesn't appear at the sitting of the Court or at second calling, the Court will decide whether or not to deal with the matter. Such *ex parte* applications must be made *uberrimae fidei* (with the utmost good faith), so Counsel must indicate any difficulties or uncertainties about the proofs or service and offer to open the papers to the Court. The requirement for full and frank disclosure in *ex parte* applications was set out by Kelly J in *Adams* v. *DPP* [2001] 2 ILRM 401.

The Court may then give judgment against any defendant in default and direct that damages be assessed either by judge alone or by judge and jury (in, for example, a defamation action). The **judgment order** should be served *personally* on the defendant. If personal service is not possible, an application may be made for **substituted service**.

If the defendant appears and asks for extra time to enter an appearance, he may be granted an extension, but the costs of the motion will normally be awarded to the plaintiff. (O. 13 rule 13 of the RSC says a defendant may enter an appearance at any time before judgment, except in cases for the recovery of land). If the defendant appears and claims there was some defect in service, the Court may reserve the costs (which means that they will be ruled upon by the judge at the outcome of the substantive action). If the Court makes no order, each party bears his own costs.

A defendant who has been caught unawares may apply to have the judgment set aside by issuing a **notice of motion** to the plaintiff, grounded on an **affidavit** giving the reasons why the judgment should not be implemented (O. 124 rule 3 RSC).

In *Maher* v. *Dixon* [1995] 1 ILRM 218 Budd J said that an application to set aside a default judgment must be supported by an affidavit setting out the merits of the defence to the plaintiff's claim. If the affidavit discloses a defence, O. 13 rule 11 RSC gives the Court an untrammelled discretion to set aside the judgment.

In the case of *Petronelli* v. *Collins*, High Court, 19 July 1996, boxer Stephen Collins asked the Court to set aside a judgment for £166,000 on the basis that he had not been served with the summons. The judge ruled that he had been properly served but gave him liberty to enter an appearance to challenge the judgment, on condition that the full amount be lodged in Court within four weeks.

If the defendant fails to appear and the plaintiff is not entitled to enter judgment in the Central Office, but for some reason he does not need to proceed with the case, he may apply to the Master by **notice of motion** for his costs to date (O. 13 rule 13 RSC).

If the plaintiff or defendant fail to appear at the trial and the Court gives judgment, either party may apply to the Court within six days to set aside the judgment (O. 36 rule 33 RSC).

Default by foreign defendants

Where a summons has been served out of the jurisdiction under Order 11A of the Rules, the plaintiff may not enter judgment in default of appearance without leave of the Court (O. 13A rule 1 RSC). The plaintiff must prove (O. 11B rule 4 RSC) that the summons was

1 served in a way prescribed by the law of the recipient's State *or* actually delivered to the defendant (or his home) by another method
2 permitted under the 1965 Hague Convention *and*
3 that the defendant was given sufficient time to defend the matter.

If, despite every reasonable effort, no certificate of service or delivery is received from the Central Authority of the receiving State within six months, the Court may give leave to enter judgment. A certificate should first be obtained from the Master certifying the date of transmission of the request for service (O. 11B rule 5 RSC)

An application for leave to enter judgment is made by **motion on notice** with a **verifying affidavit** confirming that:

1 the Court has **power to hear and determine** each claim,
2 no other Court has **exclusive jurisdiction** to decide the claim and
3 **service of the summons** (or notice of summons) satisfies Article 15 of the Hague Convention

If the defendant fails to enter an appearance to a plenary summons within five weeks (or six weeks for non-European territories), the plaintiff must first file a statement of claim in the Central Office. In the case of a summary summons, the plaintiff must file a grounding affidavit in the Central Office. With a special summons, he files a verifying affidavit.

Default of defence

If the defendant enters an **appearance** but fails to deliver his **defence**, a **motion for judgment** may also be brought. But in actions for unliquidated damages in tort or contract, the defendant must first formally be warned about the consequences of failing to deliver his defence (O. 27, rule 9).

The plaintiff must send a warning letter, consenting to an extension of time of *21 days* in which to deliver the **defence** and warning that, if a **defence** is not filed within that time, a motion for **judgment in default of defence** will be issued.

After the 21 days, the plaintiff can issue the **notice of motion**. The Central Office will require to see a copy of the 21-day letter. A **return date** (for the hearing of the motion) will be given for at least 14 days thereafter, and the notice of motion is then served on the defendant. The notice of motion must be filed at least six days before the return date (O. 27 rule 9(2) RSC).

If a **defence** is delivered within seven days of service of the **notice of motion for judgment**, and a copy of the defence and notice of motion lodged in the Central Office, the plaintiff will only be entitled to £100 costs. If the defence is not delivered within that period, the motion goes into the Common Law motion list and, if the defendant then seeks an extension of time, he must pay the full costs of the motion.

A motion for **judgment in default of defence** appears in the Common Law motion list under *motions for judgment*. The proofs required are the:

1   **notice of motion**,
2   **affidavit of service** of notice of motion,
3   original **plenary summons**,
4   notice of **entry of appearance**,
5   **statement of claim** endorsed as to no defence and
6   copy of the 21-day **warning letter**.

A **certificate of no defence** (or **certificate of proceedings**) from the Central Office is no longer required. Details of service of the plenary summons are not necessary, as the defendant has entered an appearance.

If the defendant does not appear when the motion is called or at second calling, the Court should be asked to give judgment. If the defendant does appear, the Court will usually allow an extension of time for filing the **defence**, with costs to the plaintiff.

On a motion for **judgment in default of defence** in tort or contract actions for unliquidated damages, where the Court makes an order extending time for delivery of the defence, the applicant may also request the Court to adjourn the motion generally with liberty to re-enter. Then, if no defence is delivered within the time fixed, the motion may be brought back before the Court by serving a **notice of re-entry** and by lodging in the Central Office a copy of the notice of motion and of the original notice and order.

If the plaintiff is granted judgment in a **plenary summons** case, he no longer has to establish liability, but if damages have to be measured, the case will have to be sent to the list for **assessment of damages** by a judge alone (or, if appropriate, by a judge and jury). The case is set down by service of **notice of trial** and the filing of a **setting down docket**.

The order granting judgment should be served on the defendant as soon as possible. He may bring a motion to set aside the judgment, but if he has already entered an appearance, he will have to have a good explanation for not having delivered his defence. The judgment may be set aside on terms – for example, that the defendant pay all the costs to date or lodge a sum in Court (O. 27 rule 14 RSC).

If the defendant does not apply to set aside the judgment, he should be notified of the date of the hearing for assessment of damages. At that hearing, he will be allowed to cross-examine the plaintiff's witnesses on *quantum* but will not be allowed to lead any evidence. To succeed in an appeal against the quantum of damages, he would have to convince the Supreme Court that the amount of the award was perverse. The Supreme Court will not normally reconsider the facts of the case on appeal.

Delay

If a long time has elapsed since the **entry of appearance,** and the plaintiff has taken no further action for two or more years, the *defendant* may bring a motion on notice to dismiss the claim for want of prosecution. If more than one year has elapsed since the last service of a pleading or bringing of a motion as a result of which an order was made, one month's notice of **notice of intention to proceed** is required (O. 122, rule 11 RSC).

The plaintiff may ask the defendant to consent to late delivery of a **statement of claim**. If the defendant refuses – for example, on the grounds that he has been prejudiced by the delay – the plaintiff will have to bring a **motion on notice** to the Master seeking liberty for late delivery of the **statement of claim** (O. 63 rule 1(5) RSC).

The Supreme Court considered the issue of delay in *O'Domhnaill* v. *Merrick* [1985] ILRM 40. The plaintiff had been severely injured in a car accident in the 1960s when she was only three years old. Until the decision in *O'Brien* v. *Keogh* [1972] IR 144, she did not have a cause of action which was not, on the face of it, statute-barred. But the issue of proceedings in 1977 was followed by further delays in the **statement of claim**, which was never delivered.

The Supreme Court said the defendant car driver and witnesses would be unlikely to recall with any degree of reliability events which had happened a quarter of a century previously. The defendant brought a **motion to dismiss for want of prosecution**. The Supreme Court, granting the motion by a 2–1 majority, overruled the decision of Hamilton P in the High Court. The Court said it would be against the rules of natural justice to expect the defendant to defend herself in such circumstances.

In *Celtic Ceramics* v. *IDA* [1993] ILRM 248, the plaintiffs sued for negligence and breach of contract in relation to the building of a factory in 1982 and early 1983. The plenary summons was issued in February 1988 and served in October 1988. The defendant entered an appearance, but the plaintiff took no further steps until August 1989 when a statement of claim was delivered. In February 1992, the defendant applied to dismiss the case for want of prosecution.

O'Hanlon J agreed. He said there had been an "inordinate, inexcusable and unjustifiable" delay in commencing proceedings and there had been unjustifiable delay in prosecuting the action once it started. An appeal to the Supreme Court was dismissed

In *Hogan* v. *Jones* [1994] 2 ILRM 512, the plaintiffs had begun proceedings in 1982 in relation to the alleged negligent design and construction of the West Stand in Lansdowne Road rugby ground. The works had been finished in 1978. The certificate of readiness for trial was issued 15 years later! The following month, the builders issued a motion to dismiss the claim for want of prosecution.

But Murphy J refused the application. He said in deciding whether to dismiss a claim for want of prosecution, the Court should inquire whether the delay was inordinate and, if so, whether it was inexcusable. The onus of proof was on the party seeking the dismissal. He said the extent of the litigant's personal blameworthiness for the delay was material. In this case, the defendants had taken four years to deliver their defence. If proceedings were commenced late, but within the relevant limitation period, there was all the more reason for a plaintiff to move quickly.

In *Rainsford* v. *Limerick Corporation* [1995] 2 ILRM 561, the plaintiff's vehicle had collided with a heap of rubble in May 1971 and he'd been severely injured. A plenary summons seeking damages for negligence was issued in August 1973. After delays in the solicitor's office, the statement of claim was settled in March 1978. The defendants refused to consent to late filing of the statement of claim. The Master extended the time for delivery and filing of the statement of claim for seven days and the defendants appealed.

In the Supreme Court, Finlay CJ agreed with the criteria set out by Murphy J in *Hogan* v. *Jones*. He said that, where a delay was not inordinate and inexcusable, there were no real grounds for dismissing the proceedings. Even if the delay were inordinate and inexcusable, the Court should exercise its discretion, if the balance of justice was in favour of going on with the case.

In *Primor* v. *Stokes Kennedy Crowley* [1996] 2 IR 459, where the cause of action had occurred 17 years earlier, the Supreme Court said that, when deciding on the balance of justice, the Court should take into consideration:

1   implied Constitutional principles of fairness of procedures,
2   whether the delay and prejudice made it unfair to the defendant to
     allow the case to proceed,
3   any delay by the defendant,
4   whether delay by the defendant amounted to acquiescence in the
     plaintiff's delay
5   whether the defendant's conduct had put the plaintiff to further
     expense in pursuing the action,
6   whether the delay had given rise to a substantial risk of an unfair trial
     or was likely to cause serious prejudice to the defendant and
8   the fact that damage to the defendant, his reputation or business
     might be caused other than by mere delay.

In *Carroll Shipping* v. *Mathews Mulcahy and Sutherland*, High Court, 18 December 1996, McGuinness J struck out the plaintiff's claim for delay. As a result of a shipping accident in 1973, damages of £263,000 were awarded against the plaintiff shipping charter company. Only £50,000 of the claim was covered by the plaintiffs' insurance, and they brought an action against the defendant insurance broker for failing to provide full cover.

A plenary summons was issued in 1981 and a statement of claim delivered in 1985. The defence was delivered in 1988 and a notice of trial served in 1989. But in 1990 the plaintiff company was struck off the companies register. In 1993 the proceedings were struck out. Two years later, the plaintiff company was restored to the companies register and applied to have the proceedings reinstated. The defendants claimed they would be prejudiced because they only retained files for six years and an essential witness had died in 1986.

McGuinness J said the delay of more than 15 years since the issue of the summons was inordinate and inexcusable. She said that, if the issues could be decided solely on documentary evidence, then delay – however inordinate and inexcusable – could not prejudice a fair trial and the claim would not be struck out. But in this case the death of a vital witness prejudiced the defendants' case and the interests of justice required that the claim be dismissed.

In *Re Matthew Kelly* [2000] 2 IR 219, the High Court refused to extend time for the Revenue Commissioners to submit proof of back taxes of £1.8 million. Kelly, a bankrupt, had admitted the debt in his statement of affairs in 1984. The Official Assignee had fixed 31 July 1997 as the last date for proof of the debt to be received by him. In November 1999, the Revenue Commissioners sought an extension of time but Laffoy J said the delay had been inordinate and inexcusable, and the applicant's excuse of "administrative error" was inadequate.

Striking out

If, on the agreed facts, there appears to be no cause of action, the defendant may apply to strike out the pleadings (O. 19 rule 28 RSC). In *Sun Fat Chan* v. *Osseous Ltd* [1992] 1 IR 425, the Supreme Court ruled that a Court had an inherent jurisdiction to strike out a case where, on agreed facts, the plaintiff could not succeed. But McCracken J, in *Ruby Property Company* v. *Kilty*, High Court, 1 December 1999, said that, where there was a dispute on facts on affidavit, the Court would be most unlikely to strike out the proceedings, as to do so would limit the plaintiff's right of access to the Courts.

In the case of *Leinster Leader* v. *Williams Group Tullamore*, High Court, 9 July 1999, the judge said that, apart from the provisions of O. 19 rule 28 of the RSC, the Court had an inherent jurisdiction to stay proceedings if they were frivolous or vexatious or if they put forward a claim which must fail.

The same principles were applied by the High Court in *Ennis* v. *Butterly* [1997] 1 ILRM 28, and in *Supermac's Ireland and anor* v. *Katesan (Naas)*, High Court, 15 March, 1999.

If there have been errors in service, the Court may be asked to strike out pleadings. In the case of *Harrington* v. *JVC (UK)*, Supreme Court, 21 February 1997, the plaintiffs had sued the defendants in 1994 for negligence, breach of contract, unlawful interference with the plaintiffs' business and conspiracy.

There were irregularities in the service of notice of the proceedings outside the jurisdiction, but the High Court judge refused to set aside the proceedings for irregularity (under O. 124 rule 2 RSC) because there had been undue delay by the defendant – who had appeared and been represented in Court. The Supreme Court accepted that the High Court judge had properly exercised his jurisdiction, and disallowed the defendant's appeal.

Once proceedings have been properly issued, a Court will be reluctant to strike them out without a hearing where there is a conflict of fact. In *Mehta* v. *Marsh*, High Court, 5 March 1996, where the plaintiff had brought a "litany of applications" which the Court described as "vexatious", Carroll J said the Court's inherent jurisdiction could not be invoked because there were no agreed facts. She said conflicts of fact could only be resolved by a hearing and she knew of no way to short-circuit that.

SPECIAL SUMMONS

As a general rule, the **special summons** (Appendix A Part I No. 3 RSC) is used in cases involving purely legal questions. It allows matters to be dealt with speedily on affidavit, instead of going to full plenary hearing. Order 3 of the **Rules of the Superior Courts** lays down 19 specific situations for use of a **special summons**, and permits the use of the procedure where:

1   the Rules authorise or require the use of a **special summons**,
2   a statute authorises or requires the use of a **summary procedure**, and no other procedure is specified by the Rules and
3   the Court considers the **special summons** procedure to be suitable.

Examples of situations in which the **special summons** should be used include:

- family law,
- mortgage suits,
- extradition applications,
- Garda compensation cases,
- appeals relating to tour operators' licences,
- appeals from the Employment Appeals Tribunal,
- appeals from the Labour Court,
- declarations under the Trade Union Act 1971,
- trust applications,
- applications for a *cy-près* scheme,
- directions for the administration of a deceased's estate,
- payment into Court of money in the hands of trustees,
- relief under the Settled Land Acts or the Conveyancing Acts,
- matters in connection with the guardianship of infants,
- applications under s.117 of the Succession Act, 1965 and
- applications for a declaration under s. 9 of the Vendor and Purchaser Act, 1874.

The **special summons** is issued in the Central Office. At the time of issue, a return date (at least seven days later) will be given (O. 38 rule 1 RSC), at which time the matter will be listed in the Master's Court under *Summonses*. The Master's sole function with a **special summons** is administrative: checking that it was properly served, whether an appearance was entered and that all affidavits have been filed.

The summons has a **special endorsement of claim** (O. 4 rule 4 and Appendix B Part II No. 3 RSC) which performs the functions of both the **general endorsement of claim** and the **statement of claim** in a plenary summons case and sets out "specifically and with all necessary particulars" the facts relied on and the reliefs sought. No other pleadings are allowed, except by order of the Court. (O. 20 rule 1 RSC). A **verifying affidavit** (or schedule of affidavits) must be filed, exhibiting any documents necessary to prove the claim (Appendix A Part 1 No. 6 RSC). The **affidavit** should verify that the **special summons** has been read and that the facts in the **special endorsement of claim** are true and accurate. There is *no* **statement of claim, defence, counterclaim** or **reply** (that is, no **pleadings**, as such).

The **summons** must be served *four clear day*s before the return date in the Master's Court (excluding the day of service), otherwise an application must be made to the Master for a new return date. Particulars of service should be endorsed on the summons within three days.

The defendant may enter an appearance at any time (O. 12 rule 2 RSC). On the return date, he may seek time to put in a **replying affidavit**, which performs a similar function to the **defence** in a **plenary summons** application. If the plaintiff wants to respond to the defendant's replying affidavit, he will be granted time to do so.

If the Master is satisfied that the **special summons** is in order, he sends it to the judges' list which is taken in Chancery 1 or Chancery 2 every Monday (except in the case of a **mortgage suit**). But, unless the **special summons** is straightforward and can be disposed of in less than half an hour, the Chancery Court judge will send it to the list to fix dates, so that a date can be set down for a longer hearing in another court. The Thursday *before* the case is due to come on, it will be mentioned at callover. If Counsel is not there to confirm that the case is ready to proceed, it will be *struck out*.

Matters arising on **special summonses** can be complex, in which case legal argument can take some time. Conflicts of *fact* cannot be resolved on affidavit, but only by a full plenary hearing with oral evidence, in which case the Court will usually direct that the parties exchange pleadings – a full **statement of claim, defence** and **reply**. The **special summons** case thus effectively becomes a **plenary summons** action (O. 38 rule 9 RSC).

If the evidence in an affidavit needs expansion, an application should be made for an **order permitting oral evidence**. This may either be done when the case goes from the judges' list, in the list to fix dates or at the Thursday callover. Either side may serve notice on the other requiring them to be cross-examined on their affidavits (O. 38 rule 3 RSC). If the order is granted, the affidavit is taken as the direct evidence and the witness is then cross-examined on its contents (and possibly re-examined by his own Counsel).

SUMMARY SUMMONS

The **summary summons** procedure is designed to give a plaintiff a swift and summary method of recovering judgment – hence its name. Order 2 of the **Rules of the Superior Courts** sets out the circumstances in which a **summary summons** may be issued. It is *not* only used in claims for liquidated damages. In effect, the **summary summons** procedure is used where the defendant appears to have no *bona fide* defence to the claim (such as where someone has failed to repay a contract debt, where goods have been delivered but not paid for, or in the recovery of property for non-payment of rent.)

It may also be used in Revenue cases (O. 68 rule 3) and in *any* matter where all parties agree (O. 2 rule 2 RSC). Once a debt becomes payable, a **summary summons** may be served without further demand for the outstanding amount. Any issue of fact may be determined by the Master if both sides agree, but if there is a dispute, the Master will normally transfer the summons to the Court list (O. 37 rule 6 RSC). The Master may not transfer a claim which has been improperly brought by summary summons. All he can do is strike out the action (*Bank of Ireland* v. *Lady Lisa* [1992] IR 404).

The summons (Appendix A Part 1 No. 2 RSC) is issued and served personally and allows the defendant eight days to enter an appearance. The summons warns that, if no appearance is entered, the plaintiff may proceed to recover judgment without further notice. If the plaintiff chooses not to seek judgment, the defendant may enter an appearance at any time before judgment is obtained.

The summons contains a **special endorsement of claim** (O. 4 rule 4 RSC) which, like the **special summons** procedure, sets out all the necessary facts to justify the relief sought (Appendix B Part III No. 1 RSC). No other pleadings are allowed, except by order of the Court. (O. 20 rule 1 RSC). In the case of a dishonoured cheque, the **special endorsement of claim** would set out:

1 the **names** of the plaintiff and defendant,
2 that the defendant **owed money** to the plaintiff,
3 that **demand** had been made for payment,
4 that the defendant **paid the debt** by cheque,
5 that the cheque was **returned unpaid** by the bank,
6 that the defendant had failed, refused or **neglected to pay up**,
7 details of the **sum claimed**, showing any interest calculations,
8 a **claim for payment** with Courts Act interest (unless the debt already provided for payment of interest) and
9 claim for **costs**.

In the case of a bounced cheque, the **special endorsement of claim** must allege notice of dishonour (*Bank of Ireland* v. *Ryan* 29 ILTR 101). If the plaintiff is a moneylender, he must say so and set out further information, including the interest rate charged (O. 4 rule 12 RSC). The plaintiff's solicitor endorses the address and occupation of the plaintiff and his own name and registered address on the summons.

Where a **summary summons** claims a liquidated (specific) sum only, the special endorsement of claim must include an **endorsement for costs** (O. 4 rule 5 RSC) and state that, if the full amount and costs are paid within six days after service, the proceedings will be stayed. (Form 2 Appendix A Part 1 RSC). Costs are assessed according to a predetermined scale.

In the case of a demand for a specific sum, if the defendant does not enter an appearance within eight days, the plaintiff may **enter final judgment** in the Central Office (O. 13 rule 3 RSC). In the case of proceedings for the recovery of land, the landlord should file an affidavit stating that at least one year's rent is outstanding (O. 13 rule 4 RSC).

Judgment in the Central Office

Judgment may be obtained in the Central Office in the case of a claim for the recovery of land or a liquidated sum, whether by plenary summons or summary summons (except in the case of a moneylender, hire purchase or credit agreement – O. 13 rule 3 RSC). First, the solicitor must lodge a *judgment set* comprising the:

1   original **summons**, with endorsement of service,
2   **affidavit of service** of the summons (or notice of the summons for foreign citizens),
3   **affidavit of debt** and
4   **judgment form**, setting out the amount due.

The **affidavit** will exhibit any relevant documents, such as the bounced cheque, invoices or agreements and the letter of demand to the debtor. It will explain how the final figure was arrived at. The figures may be updated to include interest but any interest payment *must* be identified in all documents. If the claim is for recovery of land, the affidavit must state that at least one year's rent is due (O. 27 rule 5 RSC). When the papers have been checked by the Central Office, judgment is entered.

If the contract on which the debt is based allows interest, that is claimed as part of the debt. If the contract does *not* allow interest (for example, a sale of goods contract), interest may be claimed under the Courts Act 1981. The current rate is 8% per annum. Section 50(2) of the Courts and Court Officers Act 1995 allows the Master and the Registrar of the Central Office to award Courts Act interest.

If judgment is obtained in Court, it may be executed immediately. But if the Master grants *liberty* to enter judgment, it can't be executed until the plaintiff has entered it in the Central Office. The judgment will not be published in *Stubbs Gazette* until it has been entered in the Central Office and there will often be a stay on entry to allow the defendant to pay up without publication. Once the judgment is entered, it can be *registered* in the Court office.

If the defendant does enter an **appearance** in a **summary summons** case, the plaintiff should bring the **motion for judgment** in the Master's Court. (This is different from a motion for judgment in a **plenary summons** case where an application may be made in default of appearance or in default of defence.)

Order 37 Rule 1 of the RSC says the summons endorsed with a claim shall be set down before the Master by the plaintiff by way of **notice of motion for liberty to enter final judgment** for the amount claimed plus interest. The motion is heard on the first available day, not less than four clear days after service of the summons on the defendant. It is supported by an affidavit sworn by the plaintiff (or by anyone else who can verify the claim), stating that there is no defence to the action. A copy of the affidavit must be served with the **notice of motion**.

The motion will appear in the Master's list under the heading *Motions for judgment*. The proofs required are the:

1   original **summary summons**, endorsed as to service,
2   **notice of motion,**
3   **grounding affidavit,**
4   **affidavit of service** of the **notice of motion** and **grounding affidavit** and
5   notice of **entry of appearance.**

The grounding affidavit is similar to the affidavit of debt filed in the Court office, except that it should also say "*It is believed that the defendant has no bona fide defence to this claim and that he has entered an appearance solely for the purpose of delay.*" Since the **notice of motion** is not an originating document, it may be served by registered post, and the affidavit should exhibit the certificate of posting.

If the defendant does not appear when the case is called or at second calling, Counsel should move the application for judgment on affidavit (O.

37 rule 2 RSC). If the Master accepts that there is no *bona fide* defence, he will give **liberty to enter judgment** in the Central Office.

If Courts Act interest is claimed, the Master used to have to remit the case to the judges' list (the Common Law motion list). But, under the terms of the Courts and Court Officers Act 1995, he now has power to award Courts Act interest.

If the defendant *does* appear in the Master's Court, he may seek time to put in a **replying affidavit**. This may simply be a delaying tactic if the claim is for a large sum, and the defendant is unsecured or appears to be trying to remove his assets. (If this is the case, Counsel might oppose the application for extension of time *and* consider applying *ex parte* to the High Court for a **Mareva injunction** to preserve any assets pending the hearing of the action.)

The function of the **replying affidavit** is to satisfy the Master or the judge that there *is* a *bona fide* defence or counterclaim, as there should be no *bona fide* defence in **summary summons** cases. The affidavit might, for example, admit that a loan was made or goods provided, but dispute issues such as the amount owed, the term of the loan or the fitness of the goods. There might be a technical defence (such as the Statute of Limitations). If the defendant admits matters in this affidavit, he is not precluded from denying them in the **defence** later.

The defendant's replying affidavit would include:

1   reference to the **summary summons, notice of motion** and **grounding affidavit** when produced,
2   the general **nature and amount of the claim**,
3   the **defence**, exhibiting any relevant documents, and
4   a clause saying "*The defendant has a good defence (and/or counterclaim) to these proceedings and has not entered an appearance for the purpose of delay. The defendant therefore seeks liberty to defend the action*".

In *Bank of Ireland* v. *EBS Building Society* [1999] 1 IR 220, the Supreme Court said that, where issues of fact and law arose which could not be conclusively resolved, and unless the defendant's affidavits failed to disclose even an arguable defence, the matter should be sent for plenary hearing.

The affidavit is filed and served on the plaintiff. If there's a dispute about the contents of the affidavit, the case will probably have to go to plenary hearing, as a judge will not rule on a conflict of fact on affidavit.

When the matter comes back into the Master's Court, he can only decide whether or not a defence is open if both parties consent. If the parties disagree, the matter must be transferred to the judges' list (O. 37 rule 6 RSC).

If both sides do agree to let the Master decide, Counsel for the plaintiff opens *all* the documents, including the defendant's **replying affidavit**, then makes submissions. Counsel for the defendant responds, Counsel for the plaintiff replies and the Master adjudicates. He may:

1 remit the case to plenary hearing,
2 grant the plaintiff liberty to enter final judgment,
3 grant the plaintiff liberty to enter final judgment for an agreed part of the claim, and remit the balance for plenary hearing or
4 transfer the whole matter to the judges' list (O. 37 rule 12 RSC, rather like a **case stated**).

If the Master remits the case in full or in part for **plenary hearing**, he will normally:

1 order delivery of a **statement of claim** if the defendant asks for one (though the **special endorsement of claim** and **affidavit of debt** should fully detail the claim),
2 make orders relating to **discovery, pleadings, settlement of issues**,
3 fix time for delivery of the **defence** and
4 reserve costs.

Both sides may seek discovery at this stage to save having to return to the Master later. The Master will require the names of the deponents who will swear the affidavits. Six weeks is usually given for making discovery from the date of the filing of the **defence**. If the case is transferred for plenary hearing, it is dealt with as if it had been a **plenary summons** case from the start, and is set down in the non-jury list. Either side may appeal this order (or any order of the Master) to the High Court under s.25(5) of the Courts and Court Officers Act 1995.

Where a defendant does not have a genuine defence to a summary summons, he will not be allowed to defend the matter. In *First National Commercial Bank Plc* v. *Anglin* [1996] 1 IR 75, the Supreme Court upheld a High Court decision refusing the defendant permission to defend a summary summons under O. 37 rule 3 RSC.

The processing of a defended **summary summons** case through the Master's Court may take several months – time which is wasted if the case is eventually transferred for plenary hearing. So, if the plaintiff believes that the defendant may have a *bona fide* defence, it may save time to start the case by plenary summons in the first place.

2. Court Lists

Cases listed for hearing are all contained in the Legal Diary, which is published daily during term-time and is now available by electronic mail or on the internet at www.courts.ie

The Diary lists the cases due to be heard that day, Court by Court, and contains an advance warning list of cases due to be heard in the near future. The Diary may also contain practice directions, warning notices and details of future lists to fix dates (including jury and non-jury lists and uncertified cases lists).

On most days, the Diary includes the following lists:

- Supreme Court
- Central Criminal Court
- Court of Criminal Appeal
- personal injuries
- Chancery 1 and 2
- family law
- jury
- non-jury
- non-jury motions
- judicial review
- admiralty
- circuit appeals
- judgments
- Master's Court
- Taxing master
- Examiner's office
- Circuit Criminal Court
- Circuit Civil Court
- County Registrar
- Notices

PERSONAL INJURIES

Personal injuries list cases (which are all begun by plenary summons) are now heard by a judge alone (although actions for assault are heard with a jury). In an effort to shorten the lengthy waiting list, a practice direction was issued making changes in the Wednesday callover. The purpose of the direction was to remove settled cases from the list before they could be allocated a hearing date. Its result was to cut the waiting time for hearings from three years to just 12 months.

Applications to list cases for hearing may either be made on consent to the registrar at 9.30am or on notice to the other party to the Court at 10.30am. Any case set down for hearing may be listed on the application of one of the parties. If the matter is not on consent, 10 days' notice must be given of the application. Alternatively, the Court lists cases for hearing from the warning list. It is important to check the Legal Diary to see whether the case is in the list. If one of the parties does not wish the case to be listed for hearing, he should attend Court on the Wednesday morning and have it adjourned.

If Counsel needs an adjournment, he should apply on notice to the other side, otherwise the case will be fixed for hearing a week or two later. Normally adjournments won't be granted for less than two weeks without good reason. If the application for an adjournment is made after a date has been fixed, the case may go to the bottom of the list! Where everyone (including third parties) has agreed the terms of an adjournment (other than cases listed on specific days), Counsel should apply for an adjournment at 9.30am on Wednesday to the registrar in charge of the personal injury list.

After each Wednesday call-over, cases will be listed for the following week at a rate of about 25 cases a day. If witnesses are coming from abroad, Counsel may apply on notice to the other side to have the trial date specially fixed. If the client is, for example, very ill or very old, Counsel may ask the Court to give the case priority.

If an unlisted personal injuries action is settled, the chief registrar should be informed by letter. Naturally enough, some judges become very irritated if a case is listed for trial after it has been settled, and may call on Counsel and solicitors to explain the reason for the waste of the Court's time.

Applications to adjourn or specially fix cases which have actually been listed for hearing may be made on any day to the judge presiding over the personal injuries list.

If the defendant ordinarily lives or carries on his business, profession or occupation in one of the Circuit jurisdictions, the case may be set down for a venue outside Dublin. The High Court goes out on Circuit at least twice a year to Waterford, Cork, Limerick, Galway, Sligo and Dundalk. Cases will be listed in the legal diary two weeks beforehand, and a day fixed for applications relating to that list.

In an effort to provide speedy hearings for personal injury actions outside Dublin, the plaintiff may apply for it to be listed for trial on the

Wednesday, Thursday or Friday of the last week of each sitting. The case
does not have to have appeared in the published list, but it must have been
set down for trial, be expected to last one day or less and involve an
assessment of damages only. The application for listing must be made to
the presiding judge at the Dublin callover preceding the hearings in each
country venue.

NON–JURY

Non-jury list cases comprise Common Law actions, other than personal
injuries actions and those requiring juries. This list includes challenges to
wills where proof in solemn form of law is required, as well as cases for
damages for breach of contract, summary summons cases remitted for
plenary hearing, special summonses and extradition cases.

Before the cases enter the list to fix dates, they must be certified as
ready for hearing by Counsel for the plaintiff. Once certified, the case
joins the list of cases awaiting a date. Lists to fix dates in non-jury cases
are held at the end of Michaelmas, Hilary and Trinity terms. Uncertified
cases (which had been set down but not certified as ready for trial) are also
listed and the parties or their legal representatives are required to attend
Court and explain to the judge the reason for the delay in certifying the
case as ready for trial.

The judge dealing with the non-jury list also usually deals with the
judicial review list.

JURY

Jury list cases now include only a small number of civil matters, such as
defamation, false imprisonment and civil assault. Jury trials take up three
weeks in Michaelmas and Hilary terms and two weeks each in Easter and
Trinity terms. A list to fix dates is held (either at the beginning of the
term or the end of the previous term) and there is a callover on each day
of the of the civil jury list. Since January 2000, jurors in civil cases have
been entitled to a daily £10 luncheon voucher.

CHANCERY 1 AND CHANCERY 2

Chancery 1 and Chancery 2 lists include cases in which equitable relief
is sought. Such cases will have pleadings (except where begun by special

summons, in which case the summons and the affidavits take the place of pleadings – although it is possible to have pleadings if necessary). The moving party in all chancery motions must hand in to the judge a book of documents containing copies of all pleadings, affidavits, exhibits and relevant correspondence.

No case will be listed for hearing in the non-jury list or included in the list to fix dates for chancery actions in Chancery 1 or 2 until a certificate signed by Counsel has been filed in the Central Office, saying that the case is ready for hearing. Notice of the certificate must be served promptly on all parties to the action. If the certificate is not filed within a reasonable time after the service of the notice of trial, any party may apply to have the case listed for hearing on 14 days' notice to the other parties.

Special summonses are sent by the Master to the Chancery 1 or 2 judges' list and from there to the list to fix dates. (There is no setting- down procedure for a special summons case and, because the case will normally turn on a point of law, it will be ready for hearing once all the affidavits are filed. There is therefore no need to certify it as ready for hearing.)

The lists to fix dates takes place at the end of term on alternate days in Chancery 1 and 2. The registrar will call over the list, with the judge allocating dates in order of place in the list. A particular date may be requested, if available. If a case does not get a date, it goes into the next list, but keeps its place in the list. Because of the pressure on lists, Chancery 1 and 2 may offer provisional dates for hearing, on which the case queues behind another case listed for the same date.

From time to time, in the lists where cases must be certified as ready for hearing (non-jury and Chancery 1 and 2), the Court will list cases which have been set down but which are not certified as being ready to find out why the case is not ready for certification. If there is no adequate explanation for the delay, the case may be struck out of the list.

On the Thursday of the week before a case is due to be heard in Chancery 1 or 2, there is a call-over of all the following week's cases. If there is no appearance at the call-over, the case will be struck out and another case may be given the date.

Urgent *ex parte* applications for interim relief in chancery, family law, company law and judicial review matters should be made to the assigned judge during term. During vacation, applications should be made to the duty judge. In cases of urgency outside normal Court sitting times, the application may be made to any High Court judge, preferably in reverse order of seniority.

The **Chancery 1 and 2 motions** list includes all motions on notice in equitable actions, such as discovery, third party joinder and interlocutory injunctions. There are separate lists for Chancery Courts 1 and 2 and cases are assigned to each Court on an alternating basis at the date of the issue of the summons. There is no separate list for *ex parte* motions or motions for the sitting of the Court, so such applications should be made at the beginning of the list.

Also in the list are special summonses sent by the Master to the judges' list under the heading *Summonses* at the end of the list. In theory, matters raised by special summons should be capable of being dealt with on affidavit, so some procedural applications will be dealt with on the Monday. But many special summons cases, such as s.117 applications and construction of wills, may be contested. These applications will move from the judges' list to the next list to fix dates in Chancery 1 or Chancery 2 towards the end of each term.

An application to approve a *cy-près* scheme, which is dealt with by special summons, may fall into either category. (Cy-près applications are brought when the objects of a charitable trust have failed or become impracticable. The cy-près scheme provides for the application of the charity's funds or property to a similar purpose.) The Charity Commissioners have jurisdiction to deal with cases up to £25,000 but other cases must be submitted to the High Court. The defendant is the Attorney General, as the protector of charities in the State. Depending on the complexity of the scheme and the Attorney General's attitude, it may be dealt with on a Monday or remitted to the list to fix dates.

Mortgage suits by special summons are in a separate special summons list, taken each Monday. These include applications where the mortgagee seeks possession of a property for sale, or asks the Court to deem a judgment mortgage or an equitable mortgage by deposit well charged against the defendant's property.

Applications for interim injunctions and substituted service or service outside the jurisdiction in equitable cases may be made in this list.

COMMON LAW

The *ex parte* **Common Law list** is always taken on a Monday. All *ex parte* applications concerning Common Law actions (seeking damages in actions like personal injuries, defamation or breach of contract) are made in this list. Example of *ex parte* applications are applications for substituted service, for service outside the jurisdiction or for a conditional order of garnishee. (There is no list, as such, published of *ex parte* cases and there is no equivalent of the Master's Court *ex parte* docket.) If an action has been set down for a particular venue and both sides want it heard elsewhere, an application should be made to the judge dealing with the list. If the application is contested, it must be done by way of notice of motion.

The *ex parte* **Common Law list in which papers have been lodged** comprises fatal and infant rulings in personal injury actions. The papers are lodged in advance so the judge can read them. A list is published and the cases are usually taken on a Monday by the Common Law *ex parte* judge.

The **stateside** *ex parte* list includes applications for judicial review, *certiorari*, *mandamus*, prohibition and *habeas corpus*. This list is usually taken on a Monday by the Common Law ex parte judge, but it is a separate list and the Stateside applications are usually taken first. There is no published list and the papers are not lodged in advance.

The **Common Law motions** list is a published list of cases, taken each Monday, usually divided into two.

List 1 includes motions for the sitting of the Court (such as motions for judgment in default of appearance), returns for conditional orders of garnishee and motions for judgment in default of defence in Common Law actions.

List 2 includes other Common Law motions on notice, such as applications for security for costs, applications to join third parties and appeals from the Master's Court.

The **probate list** is divided into *ex parte* applications, motions on notice and motions for the sitting of the Court. *Ex parte* applications include cases where notice is not necessary, since nobody would be prejudiced by any order which the Court might make (such as applications for a s. 27(4) special grant, where nobody other than the applicant might apply, or an application to prove a copy of a will, where all interested parties have consented in writing). Papers are lodged in advance in the Probate Office. Unlike other types of *ex parte* application, a motion paper sets out the facts of the case and gives notice of the application. (No probate case is automatically a motion on notice or a motion for the sitting of the Court, as each case turns on its own facts.)

MASTER'S COURT

The **Master's Court**. Under Order 63 RSC, the Master of the High Court may make a number of orders including orders for:

- the appointment of a guardian *ad litem* of an infant or person of unsound mind not so found,

- enlargement of time,
- discovery, inspection of documents or interrogatories,
- dismissal of an action for want of prosecution or failure to make discovery,
- striking out a defence for failure to make discovery,
- taking evidence on commission,
- adding or substituting parties or correction of names,
- amending pleadings on consent,
- payment out of funds to an infant,
- lodgment of scripts.

On consent, the Master may assess damages or decide matters of fact. The powers of the Master were extended by s.24 to s.26 and s.50 of the 1995 Courts and Court Officers Act. Section 24 (1) authorises the Master to exercise limited judicial powers. Section 25 says the Master may exercise the powers of a High Court judge in *ex parte* applications, motions on notice and applications for judgment by consent or in default of appearance or defence. But the Master may not deal with:

- criminal matters,
- proceedings relating to a person's liberty,
- injunctions,
- bail,
- the trial of an issue before the hearing of an action,
- judicial review applications, except for abridgement or enlargement of time,
- wards of court or child custody matters,
- approval of infant settlements and
- applications under s.63 of the Civil Liability Act 1961.

In the case of a claim for a debt, the Master may award Courts Act interest in the case of judgment in default of defence. The Master may make side-bar orders (O. 30 RSC) including:

- to proceed with an action after the death of a party,
- to proceed against a new Attorney General,
- to confirm a sale of land absolutely and
- for tenants to pay their rents to a receiver.

All the orders of the Master are subject to appeal to the High Court within six days of perfection of the order. If the Master refuses to make an order, any application to the High Court must be made within six days of the refusal. (O. 63 rule 9 RSC).

The Master's list is divided into summonses, motions for judgment, motions on notice and *ex parte* applications. Normally the Master will deal with revenue, family law and garda compensation matters on Wednesday, and other matters on Tuesday, Thursday and Friday.

Special summonses dealt with in the Master's Court include most mortgage proceedings, s. 117 applications and applications such as those involving trustees and cy-près schemes. If there are problems with the service of the summons, a new return date should be sought. If there are several defendants and not all have been served, a return date may be sought in appropriate cases and adjournments in the others. These cases will eventually be transferred to the judges' list in Chancery 1 or 2, the non-jury list, the Garda compensation list, the family law list or the chancery special summons list (which takes place each Monday afternoon). If the matter is not ready to go on, the Master should be asked for an adjournment. It is the Master's function to ensure that all affidavits are properly filed in special summons cases, and he then sends the cases to the judges' list.

Motions for judgment are *only* in respect of summary summons cases and the Master may give liberty to enter final judgment if there is an appearance but the case is uncontested. (Judgment in default of *appearance* in a summary summons case may be entered in the Central Office.)

Motions on notice comprise all interlocutory applications which the Master has jurisdiction to hear, such as discovery, interrogatories, third party or co-defendant joinder, fixing mode of trial and the amount of security for costs. (The Master may only join a third party to proceedings if the third party consents.)

Ex parte applications, taken at the end of the Master's list, include applications regarding funds in Court for infants and amendment of summonses. On or before the day of the application, an *ex parte* docket should be completed and left with the registrar.

3. First Steps

When Counsel first receives papers from a solicitor in a High Court action, he should read them through carefully, noting any issues which require clarification by the solicitor or client. The first matters to be considered may include:

- On the given facts, does an action lie?
- If so, who should be the plaintiff(s) and defendant(s)?
- Is the action statute-barred or is time running out?
- Should the case be run in the High Court or in a lower Court?

Once Counsel has decided that there is a statable case, he must consider who should sue whom? In most cases, that will be obvious. But sometimes it will become apparent during the course of pleadings that other parties should be joined in the action. The Court has jurisdiction to add, strike out or substitute any number of plaintiffs or defendants. If such a decision would embarrass or delay the trial, the Court may order separate trials (O. 15 rule 1 RSC). Equally, the plaintiff may unite several causes of action in one, but, in the interests of "necessity or expediency", the Court may order that the matters be dealt with separately (O. 18 rule 1 RSC).

Counsel should note the date of the cause of action and ensure that it is not statute-barred. The limitation period for personal injuries is normally three years (but only two years where the action begins after the defendant is dead or where the injury comes within the Warsaw Convention).

If the defendant has died, his estate can't be sued until a grant of representation has been taken out, and a personal representative appointed. (A grant of representation is a document issued in the High Court allowing a person to represent the estate of a deceased person.) Until the grant is raised, nobody can defend proceedings against the estate, even though the Statute of Limitations continues to run, so citations should be issued through the Probate Office, in the form of Appendix Q Form 23 RSC, requiring anyone entitled to administer the estate to raise representations, so they can be sued.

If no appearance is entered to the citations, an application should be made in the Probate List by **motion on notice** to the persons entitled to raise representation, seeking a grant of representation to a nominated person, solely for the purpose of defending the proposed proceedings. If the defendant was alive when proceedings were instituted, the Court may appoint someone to represent the estate of the deceased (O. 15 rule 37 RSC).

LIABILITY

If there are several potential defendants and it's not clear which of them is liable, the plaintiff's solicitor should write to each of them *before* instituting proceedings, calling on each of them to exonerate the other potential defendants from liability for the plaintiff's injury, and pointing out that, if they do not admit liability between themselves, the plaintiff will sue *all* of them.

Without this so-called "O'Byrne letter", if *all* the potential defendants were sued, those found not liable would be entitled to costs against the plaintiff. But if the letter is sent, those costs will be awarded against the unsuccessful defendants.

If two defendants are liable under the same heading, one may be vicariously liable if he has some degree of *authority* or *control* over the other.

In *Moynihan* v. *Moynihan* [1975] IR 192, a two-year-old child visited her grandmother for tea. During tea there was a telephone call. The child's aunt, who was alone with her, left the room hurriedly to answer the phone. The child pulled at the bright tea-cosy and upset the teapot, scalding herself badly. The question referred to the Supreme Court after the High Court judge withdrew the case from the jury was "Was the grandmother vicariously liable for the negligence of her daughter?"

The Supreme Court decided there *was* vicarious liability, on the basis that the grandmother was responsible for hospitality in her own home and had delegated to her daughter a task which she would normally have undertaken herself.

In *Phelan* v. *Coillte Teo* [1993] 1 IR 18, the plaintiff was employed as a heavy machine operator by the defendant under a contract of service (as opposed to a contract for services). He was injured as a result of the negligence of an employee of the defendant. Barr J said that, in terms of an employer's vicarious liability to an injured third party arising out of the negligence of an employee, it was irrelevant whether the contract was specified to be a contract *for services* or a contract *of service*, if the evidence showed that the employer's right of control over the employee's work would have been the same, whatever the alleged nature of the contract.

In *Gaspari* v. *Iarnrod Eireann*, Supreme Court, 15 December 1993, the Supreme Court decided a landowner was *not* vicariously liable for a train accident because he did not have a sufficient degree of authority or control over someone else's cattle on his land.

The owner of a car may be vicariously liable for the driver or for any mechanical faults. Section 118 of the Road Traffic Act 1961 makes a car owner automatically liable for the negligence of the driver of the vehicle where it's driven with the owner's consent or knowledge. Also, where a person is injured by an uninsured or untraceable driver, the personal injury aspect of the claim will be met by the Motor Insurers' Bureau of Ireland.

The MIBI is a company set up by motor insurers to give effect to the second EC Directive on Motor Insurance 84/5 EEC of 30 December 1983. The Bureau covers certain uninsured road accidents occurring on or after 31 December 1988. The victim of an accident involving an uninsured vehicle may apply directly to the Bureau for compensation and may appeal to the Court if he is refused compensation or is dissatisfied with the award.

But it is a condition *precedent* to the liability of the MIBI that, *before* the issue of proceedings, the Bureau must be notified by registered post of the circumstances of the accident and the intention to sue to recover damages from the Bureau. Except in the case of an untraceable driver, the Bureau is not actually a party to the proceedings. (The driver of the vehicle would be the defendant.)

Where the driver of the other vehicle remains unidentified, untraced and unidentified, the plaintiff must sue the MIBI as a sole defendant, following the judgment of Morris J in *Kavanagh* v. *Reilly and MIBI*, High Court, 14 October 1996. The judge said that Clause 2(3) of the 1988 agreement did not permit the joinder of the MIBI as a co-defendant in such circumstances.

In *Bowes* v. *MIBI* [2000] 2 IR 79, a driver involved in a fatal accident involving an uninsured motorcyclist in November 1993 put the Bureau on notice of the claim in July 1994. The MIBI delayed in nominating a solicitor to accept proceedings so, in February 1996, the plaintiff sued the MIBI as sole defendant. When the MIBI delivered its defence a year later, it claimed that the matter was statute-barred as the plaintiff had failed to issue proceedings against the motorcyclist within two years of his death.

The High Court ruled that the proceedings were statute-barred. The Supreme Court, rejecting the appeal, said that, since the case did not involve an unidentified or untraced driver, any attempt by the plaintiff to be compensated for the motorcyclist's negligence must fail. In order for the claim to succeed, proceedings should have been brought to judgment against the identified driver or his estate.

Where an uninsured vehicle is leased and the leasing agreement specifies that the car must be insured to be driven with the lessor's consent, the leasing company will not be liable to the injured party (*Fairbrother* v. *MIBI* [1995] 1 IR 581)

Where an insurance company disclaims liability on a policy, s.76 of the Road Traffic Act 1961 says that, if the plaintiff serves a notice on the insurance company by registered post before proceedings are issued, any judgment may be executed directly against the insurance company, notwithstanding the company's repudiation of liability.

In *Troy* v. *CIE* [1971] IR 321 the plaintiff's husband, Thomas Troy, had been killed in a collision between his car and a bus. A car passenger, Declan Slattery, was injured. The widow and Mr Slattery sued CIE. The bus company claimed that Mr Troy had been guilty of contributory negligence and joined Mrs Joan Troy (as personal representative of her late husband's estate) as a third party.

The High Court ordered that the question of the vicarious liability of Mrs Troy be tried first – even though her action had been instituted *before* the third-party proceedings. But the Supreme Court on appeal ruled that the plaintiff was entitled to have her action for damages tried by a jury *before* the issue of vicarious liability was decided, and that the decision on the relative liability of CIE and the husband would bind the parties in the third-party proceedings. (Section 29(6) of the Civil Liability Act says a decision apportioning blame shall bind the same parties in a subsequent claim.)

In a typical case, such as a personal injury action, Counsel for the plaintiff should initially obtain from the instructing solicitor:

1   a **statement from the plaintiff** giving his account of the incident,
2   **statements from witnesses** (where liability is in issue),
3   where relevant, an **engineer's report**, establishing the cause of the accident,
4   if possible, **photographs** of the injuries and the scene of the accident and
5   **medical reports** to help evaluate the plaintiff's injuries.

Counsel acting for the *defendant* should ask his instructing solicitor to obtain:

1   **proceedings** as issued,
2   **statements** from the defendant and any witnesses,
3   **expert and technical reports** on behalf of the defendant and
4   **medical reports** on behalf of the defendant.

The practice and procedure in personal injuries actions was substantially changed by SI 391 of 1998 on *Disclosure of Reports and Statements*, which was deemed to have come into force on 1 September 1997. The new procedures were inserted as rules 45–51 of Order 39 of the RSC. ("Personal injuries actions" include claims for damages for personal injuries (including diseases and fatal injuries), except where jury trial is available.)

Rule 51 of Order 39 says that rules 45–50 shall not apply to proceedings instituted before 1 September 1997, nor to any report or statement coming into existence before that date for the purposes of such proceedings.

In all cases where proceedings were instituted after 1 September 1997, a plaintiff must – within one month of service of the notice of trial (or within one month of the transfer of the case from the Circuit Court to the High Court) – deliver to the defendant or his solicitor a schedule listing all reports from any expert witnesses who are intended to be called at the trial. Experts may include accountants, actuaries, architects, dentists, doctors, engineers, occupational therapists, psychologists, psychiatrists, scientists and "any other expert whatsoever".

In *Galvin* v. *Murray*, Supreme Court, 21 December 2000, the High Court had ruled that a local authority engineer who compiled a report for his employer could not be considered an expert. The Supreme Court held that engineers were undoubtedly experts and the fact that they wree employed by one of the parties did not change their status.

Within seven days of receiving the plaintiff's schedule, the defendant must deliver a similar schedule to the plaintiff and other parties. The parties must exchange copies of the reports listed in the schedules within seven days thereafter.

("Reports" include statements of any expert intended to be called, copies of reports, letters, statements, maps, drawings, graphs, charts, photographs, calculations and "like matter".)

The parties must also – within one month of service of the notice of trial – exchange the names and addresses of all proposed witnesses of fact, full details of all items of special damage – together with appropriate vouchers or witness statements – and a written statement from the Department of Social Welfare showing all payments made to a plaintiff subsequent to an accident (or an authorisation from the plaintiff for the defendant to apply for such information).

Where a party certifies in writing that no report exists which needs to be exchanged, any other party (including third parties, counterclaimants or notice parties) must deliver any relevant report to all the parties on the expiry of the relevant time limit.

If either side later receives further expert reports or intends to call further witnesses, the information must be given to the other side "forthwith".

Reports may be served by ordinary pre-paid post with an accompanying letter which should specifically state that the service is for the purpose of complying with s. 45 of the Courts and Court Officers Act 1995 and the Rules of the Superior Courts. If necessary, any party may apply to the Court requiring an affidavit to be filed relating to proof of disclosure or service.

At any stage, either side may inform the other side in writing that they do not intend to call any particular expert or witness, in which case any privilege which previously existed in relation to the report or statement is retrospectively restored.

Time limits may be extended by agreement between the parties. If either side fails to comply with the new rules on disclosure, the aggrieved party may issue a **motion for directions**, based on a **grounding affidavit**. The Court may at any stage:

1   direct the defaulting party to comply with the requirements immediately or within a fixed time limit,
2   prohibit certain evidence being given at the trial,
3   adjourn the matter pending compliance or
4   strike out the claim or defence, with an appropriate order for costs.

If either side believes that, in the interests of justice, a report should not be disclosed, he may apply for an order exempting him from the requirement to deliver the document.

If there is a good reason for non-compliance, either side may apply to the Court to allow the admission of evidence that has not been disclosed, and the Court may make whatever order seems just in the circumstances.

If Counsel is acting for more than one defendant and there's a potential conflict of interest, he should ask the instructing solicitor to decide which defendant he should represent.

Counsel should also consider any technical or special defences, including:

1   **delay** (or **laches** or **acquiescence** in equitable claims),
2   **faulty pleadings** (such as failure to make demand for goods allegedly retained by the defendant in a detinue case: *McCrystal Oil Co. Ltd* v. *Revenue Commissioners* [1993] ILRM 69) and
3   the **Statute of Limitations** 1957.

The Statute of Limitations is a complete defence where pleaded, although it does not prevent the *institution* of proceedings.

If the Statute is not pleaded, the Court may refuse to allow any subsequent amendment to the **defence**. But in *Palamos Properties Ltd* v. *Hickey Beauchamp Kirwan and O'Reilly*, [1996] 3 IR 597, Flood J did allow the defendants to amend their defence by pleading the Statute of Limitations. He said the facts on which the issues depended were known to the parties and could hardly be said by either party to come as a surprise, so the amendments were not prejudicial. But he said there must be evidence before the Court which explained – if not justified – the omission from the original pleadings.

In the case of *Ryan* v. *Connolly and Connolly*, Supreme Court, 31 January 2001, a plenary summons in a personal injuries case was not issued until three years and eight months after the accident. The plaintiff claimed that the delay was due to the actions of the defendant and the defence was therefore estopped from pleading the Statute of Limitations. The High Court agreed and struck out that part of the defence, but the Supreme Court said the defendants were entitled to rely on a defence under the statute and allowed the appeal.

In *Krops* v. *Irish Forestry Board* [1995] 2 ILRM 290, the plaintiff's wife was killed when a tree fell on their car. Proceedings were not instituted within two years of the wife's death. The plaintiff applied to amend his statement of claim to include a claim for nuisance, to bring it within the Statute of Limitations. Keane J allowed the amendment and said the High Court could allow a party to amend pleadings "in such manner and on such terms as may be just". He said where an amendment would not prejudice a defendant by new allegations of facts, no injustice was done. (O. 28 rule 1 RSC)

In *Tromso Sparebank* v. *Beirne (No. 2)* [1989] ILRM 257, Costello J said: "The Rules of Court are designed to further the rules of justice and they should be construed by the Court so that they assist in the achievement of this end."

In *County Meath VEC* v. *Joyce* [1997] 3 IR 402 at 407, Flood J. said that the rules of procedure "should always be regarded as the servants, and not the masters, of justice."

And in *Aer Rianta International* v. *Walsh Western International* [1997] 2 ILRM 45, the Supreme Court said that the aim of the Court was to decide the rights of the parties, not to punish them for mistakes made in the conduct of the case. At soon as it became apparent that the pleadings would not allow the Court to decide on the real matters at issue, then it was a matter of right to have the error corrected, if it could be done without injustice. The Court would not allow pleadings to be amended if the amendment would put the other party in a worse position than if the matter had been properly pleaded in the first place.

Counsel should decide whether liability should be admitted, denied or contested. If the defendant puts the plaintiff to unnecessary expense in proof, he may be penalised in costs. If the defendant is clearly liable, liability should be admitted and the case should continue on the basis of assessment of damages only.

CHOICE OF COURT

Once Counsel has considered the issue of liability and the value of the claim – as well as the level of any contributory negligence – he should decide in which court to issue proceedings. The 2001 jurisdiction of the Courts in civil actions was:

District Court	up to IR£5,000
Circuit Court	IR£5,000 to IR£30,000
High Court	over IR£30,000

The Courts and Court Officers Bill, 2001 proposed to increase the jurisdiction of the District Court to 20,000 euros (IR£15,751) with effect from 1 January 2002, and the jurisdiction of the Circuit Court to 100,000 euros (IR£78,756).

If, on the basis of the expected damages, the action has been started in too high a Court, either side may bring a **motion to remit** the case to a lower Court. The motion may be brought at any time between entry of appearance and service of notice of trial. Personal injuries actions may be transferred at any time before trial (O. 49 rule 7(2) RSC).

Section 14 of the Courts Act 1991 says that, where the plaintiff wins his action but fails to recover damages appropriate to the Court in which proceedings were issued, he may only recover the costs he would have received if the action had been started in the lower Court. The Act also gives judges power to order that the plaintiff pay the difference between the *defendant's* potential costs in the lower Court and his actual costs in the higher Court (although the plaintiff may plead that the defendant could have brought an action to remit the matter to a lower Court.)

Section 14 also says that, where damages recovered in the High Court are between £25,000–£30,000, the plaintiff is only entitled to Circuit Court costs, unless the High Court judge certifies that it was reasonable to issue the proceedings in the High Court because of their exceptional nature or the question of law involved. (Those figures are likely to change with the increased jurisdiction of the Circuit Court under the Courts and Court Officers Bill, 2001.)

In *O'Shea* v. *Mallow UDC* [1993] ILRM 884, the plaintiff brought a motion to remit his personal injuries action from the High Court to the Circuit Court when it became apparent that his injuries were not as serious as first thought. Counsel for the defendant said that s.11(2)(a) of the Courts of Justice Act 1936 meant the High Court should not remit an action where it was reasonable for the action to have been begun in the High Court. If the case were remitted, it followed that no award in excess of the Circuit Court jurisdiction could be made.

Morris J, remitting the action, said s.11(2)(a) related to a situation where – even though the action fell within the jurisdiction of the Circuit Court – it was reasonable to retain it in the High Court. He said he was confirmed in his view by s.20 of the 1936 Act which allowed the Circuit Court to make an award in excess of its jurisdiction where a case was remitted from the High Court.

If a defendant wishes to remit an action to a lower Court, it is done by **motion on notice** to the plaintiff, grounded on an **affidavit** sworn by a doctor giving his opinion (on behalf of the *defendant*) that the plaintiff's injuries are not as bad as they appeared. The defendant will also swear his own affidavit saying that he has been advised that case should be dealt with by a lower Court, on the basis that the plaintiff's injuries are not as serious as was thought.

The plaintiff should swear a **replying affidavit** – supported by an affidavit from his own doctor – saying he has been advised that his injuries are sufficiently serious for him to recover High Court damages.

Judges are reluctant to remit an action at the request of a *defendant*, but if the action is remitted to the Circuit Court at the defendant's request, the lower Court has unlimited jurisdiction. (If it were otherwise, it would be equivalent to the High Court judge deciding the issue of quantum before the hearing of the action.)

The main disadvantage of beginning an action in the Circuit Court is that, on a practical level, Circuit Court damages tend to be lower than those awarded by the High Court for similar injuries. The risk of losing an appeal from a lower Court is also greater, because there are more avenues of appeal in a case which starts in the District Court than in a case which begins in the High Court.

If a judgment is appealed, the appellate Court will not normally substitute its view of the facts for the view of the trial judge. In *Keenan* v. *Constant*, Supreme Court, 2 December 1993, in which there was a "complete conflict" between the evidence of the plaintiff and defendant, O'Flaherty J said a trial judge had the opportunity to assess witnesses in Court and an appellate Court had no jurisdiction to substitute its view for that of the trial judge on a question of primary fact.

If the proceedings were originally instituted in the High Court solely to prevent the matter becoming statute-barred, the *plaintiff* may wish to remit the action to a lower Court. (Formerly, time stopped running in the Circuit Court on the service of the Civil Bill, which could be delayed. Now, under SI 500 of 1997, the clock stops when the proceedings are issued.)

An application on consent may be brought in the Master's Court (O. 63 rule 1(33) RSC). In this case, the lower Court does *not* have unlimited jurisdiction because the plaintiff has chosen to limit damages to the Circuit Court level. If the defendant opposes the application, the motion must be brought in the Common Law list in the High Court.

The **order to remit** should state the appropriate circuit, county and town. (High Court cases are heard in Dublin unless otherwise ordered, or unless statute or the Rules of the Superior Courts provide otherwise (O. 36 rule 1 RSC).) If the *defendant* is seeking the order, costs are usually reserved to the judge in the lower Court at the end of the hearing. At the trial of the action, if the plaintiff recovers damages exceeding the jurisdiction of the lower Court, he will usually be awarded the costs of the motion; otherwise costs will go to the defendant.

4. Drafting

It is an important part of Counsel's role to draft pleadings. These relate to the particular circumstances of an action and so differ from case to case. Standard paperwork will normally be drafted by the solicitor. In a plenary summons case, the pleadings would comprise the:

1 **summons** with **general endorsement of claim,**
2 **statement of claim,**
3 **defence** and
4 **reply** (and **counterclaim,** if necessary)

(In a **summary summons** or **special summons** case, the summons itself comprises the pleadings. In, for example, a family law case, the **petition** and **answer** are the pleadings)

Pleadings are concerned with the *essentials* of the case and should avoid wordiness or irrelevant matters, otherwise the offending party may be penalised in costs (O. 19 rule 1 RSC). In *Bloomer and Ors* v. *Incorporated Law Society of Ireland*, Supreme Court, 6 February 1996, the Court said a successful litigant might not always be awarded costs if his submissions failed to deal objectively with the law and facts of the matter. In this case, where the successful plaintiff had used contemptuous language and made unfounded allegations, he was awarded only part of his costs.

Every pleading (O. 19 rule 3 RSC) must:

1 contain a short **statement of the relevant facts** of the claim or defence (but *not* details of evidence),
2 be divided into consecutively **numbered paragraphs** where necessary,
3 express dates, sums and numbers in **figures, not words,** and
4 be **signed by Counsel,** if settled by him.

The object of pleadings was set out by Fitzgerald J in *Mahon* v. *Celbridge Spinning Company Ltd* [1967] IR 1. He said: "The whole purpose of a pleading, be it a statement of claim, defence or reply, is to define the issues between the parties, to confine the evidence of the trial to the matters relevant to those issues and to ensure that the trial may proceed to judgment without either party being taken at a disadvantage by the introduction of matters not fairly to be ascertained from the pleadings. In other words, a party should know in advance, in broad outline, the case he will have to meet at trial."

The headings in Appendix B Part IV of the Rules must be used for all **pleadings**, where applicable. Every **pleading** must contain the record number of the action and the description of the pleading. Pleadings up to 15 folios long may be handwritten; any longer pleadings must be printed (O. 19 rule 9 RSC).

Pleadings – which are *never* sworn documents – are said to be "closed" when the last document is delivered, although they may be amended in certain circumstances (O. 28 RSC).

The only documents filed in Court nowadays are the **plenary summons** and the **appearance**. However, when the case is set down for hearing, the solicitor for the person setting it down should provide two books of pleadings – one for the judge and the other for the registrar. (Only one book of pleadings is necessary in personal injuries actions.) The book of pleadings, which should be indexed and paginated, should contain all the pleadings which have been exchanged between the parties and any relevant orders (such as consolidation or adoption of proceedings). A letter on headed paper from the solicitor is required, stating that the copies in the books of pleadings are true copies of the originals. The pleadings are lodged in the Central Office within 14 days of service of the notice of trial.

A **notice of trial** must be served in all actions involving a plenary hearing (O. 36 rule 3 RSC) within six weeks of the close of pleadings (O. 36 rule 12 RSC). In the case of *Lee* v. *Morrissey-Murphy*, Supreme Court, 22 November 1996, Morris J had stayed an order dismissing the plaintiff's action on condition that the plaintiff served a notice of intention to proceed within seven days and a **notice of trial** "as soon as is allowed thereafter by the Rules". The notice of trial was not served until four months after service of the notice of intention to proceed. The Supreme Court refused to extend time to appeal against the dismissal .

After service of the notice of trial, the matter must be "set down" in the Central Office (that is a date obtained for the trial of the action) within 14 days of service of the notice (O. 36 rule 18 RSC). The defendant must be given at least 21 days' notice of the trial date and the venue of the hearing. A personal endorsement of service is written on the back of the document by the server. The setting down docket, which contains details of the venue and date, is filed, not served. A motion to set aside a notice of trial must be brought within four days of service of the notice (O. 36 rule 3 RSC).

In civil proceedings where substantial legal issues are likely to arise and where there's likely to be legal argument at the hearing, both sides should exchange written summaries of the submissions at least seven days before the hearing and file the submissions in the Central Office. The submissions should refer briefly to the relevant statutes or statutory instruments, as well as to any text books or case law. Relevant passages may be photocopied, rather than included in the text of the submission. Costs may be awarded to the successful party for preparing the submission.

THE HIGH COURT

Record Number: 2001 P 4321
(The letter "P" indicates a plenary summons)

Between/

KENNETH MURPHY
Plaintiff

and

BRENDAN O'BRIEN
Defendant

PLAINTIFF'S DESCRIPTION

If the plaintiff is an adult, he is described by his full Christian name first and then his surname – not his initials. In the case of *Roe* v. *Blood Transfusion Board* [1996] 1 ILRM 555, the Court ruled that a plaintiff could not use a fictitious name. If the plaintiff is a limited liability company, the name must be given exactly as set out in the Certificate of Incorporation.

If the plaintiff is an infant (aged under 18), his name appears as *Kenneth Murphy* (*suing by his father Patrick Murphy and next friend*). The next friend (who cannot also be a defendant) must sign a written consent before the summons is issued, authorising the solicitor to institute the proceedings (O. 15 rule 20 RSC). A certified copy of the plaintiff's birth certificate must be produced at the trial (O. 66 rule 1 RSC).

If the plaintiff (or defendant) attains full age before the matter is heard, the next friend may apply on affidavit to the Registrar of the Central Office for a certificate that the plaintiff (or defendant) should proceed in his own name.

If the party is of unsound mind, not so found by inquisition, the form of citation is *Kenneth Murphy (a person of unsound mind not so found by inquisition) suing by his father Patrick Murphy and next friend*. If the person has been found of unsound mind by inquisition, he will be represented by a person known as a **committee**: *John Reilly, suing as committee of Kenneth Murphy, a person of unsound mind*.

If the plaintiff is a city corporation, the correct citation is *The Right Honourable The Lord Mayor, Aldermen and Burgesses of Dublin*. (See the decision in *Dublin Corporation* v. *Garland* [1982] ILRM 104). For a County Council, it's The County Council of the City of Dublin.

An unincorporated association (such as a club) will normally be cited as the names of the members of its committee *suing as the committee of the_____ Club*.

If, through a genuine mistake, an action is begun in the name of the wrong plaintiff, the Court may order that anyone be added or substituted for the original plaintiff, if necessary (O. 15 rule 2 RSC). But in *Southern Mineral Oil Ltd (in liquidation)* v. *Cooney (No. 2)* [1999] 1 IR 237, Shanley J said that, before substituting a plaintiff, the Court must be satisfied that the mistake to be corrected:

1   was a genuine mistake and
2   was not misleading or such as to cause any reasonable doubt about the identity of the intended plaintiff.

DEFENDANT'S DESCRIPTION

If the defendant is an infant, he should be sued in his own name (not through the next friend) and the parent or guardian enters an appearance as guardian *ad litem* ("for the suit"). If the parent fails to enter an appearance, Counsel should apply to have someone appointed as guardian *ad litem*.

Where a person of unsound mind with a committee is the defendant, the committee is sued. Otherwise he is sued in his own name, and there is a similar application for the appointment of a guardian *ad litem*.

Any two or more people claiming to be partners may be sued in the name of their company. If the proceedings concern the Constitutional validity of any law, notice should be served on the Attorney General, who is entitled to appear as a defendant (O. 60 RSC).

GENERAL ENDORSEMENT OF CLAIM

The **general endorsement of claim** (O. 4 rule 2 RSC) is headed "General endorsement of claim" and states the grounds of the claim in a manner "as brief as the nature of the case will admit" (O. 19, rule 1 RSC). The Rules say it is not essential to set forth the *precise* ground of complaint or the precise remedy or relief sought (O. 4 rule 3 RSC) as these may be clarified by the **statement of claim**.

There might also be a claim for declaratory relief in a **plenary summons** action claiming that parts of a statute are unconstitutional (O. 3 rule 7 RSC).

STATEMENT OF CLAIM

Except by Court order, a **statement of claim** is only delivered in a **plenary summons** action – not in the case of a **summary summons** or **special summons** (O. 20 rule 1 RSC). The **statement of claim** may alter, modify or extend the general endorsement of claim.

A **statement of claim** is broken down into the **essentials** of the case, and the **particulars** of negligence or breach of duty alleged. As a rule, the **statement of claim** only includes substantive reliefs (not ancillary reliefs, such as interim or interlocutory applications). Relief is claimed either simply or in the alternative, and it is not necessary to ask for general or other relief which "may always be given, as the Court may think just, to the same extent as if it had been asked for." (O. 20 rule 7 RSC).

The draft statement of claim has:

1   a **heading**,
2   a **delivery clause**,
3   a preliminary **description** of the parties and the events leading to the cause of action,
4   particulars of the **negligence**, breach of duty and/or statutory duty by each defendant,
5   an **establishment of the link** between the act or omission of the defendant(s) and the alleged injury,
6   particulars of **injuries**,
7   particulars of **special damages** suffered (such as out-of-pocket expenses) and
8   the **relief** claimed

The delivery clause gives the date of delivery and the name and address of the solicitor or litigant who delivered the statement of claim:

DRAFT STATEMENT OF CLAIM

Delivered on the ___ day of _____ 200__ by Kelly & Co. of 250 Grafton Street in the city of Dublin, solicitors for the plaintiff.

Pleading must be drafted in numbered paragraphs. Dates, sums and numbers should be expressed in figures, rather than words (O. 19 rule 3 RSC).

Paragraph 1 identifies and describes the plaintiff (or each of them, where more than one, in separate numbered paragraphs). If there are several plaintiffs, they are described in turn as *the first-named plaintiff, the second-named plaintiff* and so on, giving the name, address and occupation of each plaintiff. Women may be described by their occupation or their married status. If a man is employed, his job should be stated, rather than describing him as "gentleman".

If the plaintiff is a limited liability company, the document should say *The plaintiff is a limited liability company having its registered office at _____ in the City of _____ and carrying on the business of _____.* In the case of a local authority: *The plaintiff is the local authority (or corporation) for the city of _____, having its head office at _____.*

In the subsequent paragraphs(s), the defendants are described in the same way. Then the circumstances leading to the cause of action are detailed.

To establish a causal connection, the plaintiff must plead:

1 the **relationship** of the plaintiff to the defendant,
2 the resulting Common Law or statutory **duty of care** owed to the plaintiff by the defendant,
3 that the defendant was in **breach of that duty** of care and
4 that, as a result of that breach, the plaintiff has suffered **personal injury, loss, damage, inconvenience and expense**.

The basis of the cause of action must first be established in order to decide the category into which the claim falls – such as contract, tort, nuisance, road traffic accidents, industrial accidents, occupiers' liability or professional negligence. For example, with a **road accident**, all the basic, salient facts of the incident can be distilled into one brief paragraph:

On or about the   day of   2000, the plaintiff was
lawfully riding his bicycle and was stopped at traffic lights at the
junction of Morehampton Road and Waterloo Road in the City of
Dublin when the defendant so negligently drove his car that it
collided with the rear of the plaintiff's bicycle, causing him severe
personal injury, loss and damage.

A claim involving an industrial accident might say:

On or about the   day of   2000, the plaintiff in the
course of his employment at _____ timbermill in the City of
Limerick was cutting wood with a circular saw when his hand was
caught by the blade, thereby causing him severe injuries, loss and
damage.

If the claim involves **employers' liability**, it is essential to plead the
employer/employee relationship and, if appropriate, that the place in
which the injury occurred was a factory within the meaning of the Safety
In Industry Acts 1955–1982. The pleadings might read:

At all material times hereto, the plaintiff was employed by the
defendant at its timbermill at ____ in the City of Limerick. The
said premises are a factory within the meaning of the Safety In
Industry Acts.

In an employers' liability case, there may be statutory breaches of the
Safety, Health and Welfare at Work Regulations 1960–1993, which require
an employer to:

*   make the workplace as safe as reasonably practical
*   ensure that machinery is as safe as is reasonably practical
*   provide a safe means of entry and exit to and from the workplace
*   ensure that walkways, corridors and stairways are free from obstructions
*   provide a safe system of work
*   ensure adequate training and supervision
*   ensure that dangerous machinery is adequately fenced or guarded
*   provide competent fellow employees

The Occupiers' Liability Act 1995 changed the common law duties,
liabilities and rights of occupiers and users of property and premises.
("Premises" includes land, water, any fixed structures thereon or means

of transport.) So, in the case of **occupiers' liability**, the pleadings should now state:

> *At all material times the defendant was the occupier of the premises/property situated at _____and the plaintiff was an entrant/visitor/recreational user/trespasser on the premises/ property occupied, controlled and/or managed by the defendant, his servants or agents.*

NEGLIGENCE

With a claim for **professional negligence**, the pleadings might read:

> *The plaintiff retained the defendant as his dentist for reward to provide treatment in relation to the plaintiff's continuing toothaches. At all material times hereto the plaintiff relied on the skill and judgment of the defendant in relation to his dental treatment.*

Negligence should be specifically pleaded, if alleged:

> *The accident was caused by the negligence and breach of duty (including breach of statutory duty) of the defendant, his servants or agents (or the defendants and each of them, their respective servants and agents).*

The use of the phrase *his servants* or *agents* covers the possibility of *vicarious liability* – that is that the injury was attributable to somebody under the defendant's control or supervision.

In road accidents, the owner of a vehicle is vicariously liable for the negligence of a driver who is using the vehicle with the owner's consent or knowledge, so the plaintiff should sue both the driver and the owner.

The **Rules of the Superior Courts** require that the **particulars** of wrong, personal injuries suffered and any items of special damage must be set out. (O. 19 rule 5 RSC).

The **particulars of negligence and breach of duty** in an employer's liability case might say that a defendant:

1. *failed to provide a safe system of work*
2. *failed to ensure that the circular saw was adequately fenced*
3. *failed to provide any or any adequate training for the plaintiff in the correct use of the circular saw*
4. *failed to provide any or any adequate supervision for the plaintiff, who was inexperienced in using the circular saw*

5   *failed to provide the plaintiff with suitable protective gloves*
6   *failed to warn the plaintiff of the inherent dangers in using the circular saw*
7   *allowed the plaintiff to use the circular saw when he was not adequately instructed in its use*

In an action involving a road traffic accident, the particulars might say:

The defendant, his servant or agent, was guilty of negligence and breach of duty (including breach of statutory duty) in that he:

1   *drove at an excessive speed with regard to all the circumstances* (by reference to weather, traffic-flow, the condition of the vehicle or general conditions. It is not necessary to establish that the defendant was exceeding the speed limit.)
2   *drove without due care and attention*
3   *drove on the wrong side of the road*
4   *drove in a dangerous and/or negligent manner contrary to the provisions of the Road Traffic Acts as amended and the regulations made thereunder*
5   *failed to keep any or any proper lookout or to have any or any sufficient regard for other traffic*
6   *failed to stop when the traffic lights were showing red to the defendant*
7   *failed to see the bicycle ridden by the plaintiff*
8   *failed to stop, slow down, swerve or brake or otherwise manage or control his vehicle in such a way as to avoid the said collision*

Where one defendant is vicariously liable for the negligence of another (e.g. car owner/driver or employer/employee), it is not necessary to plead separate particulars of negligence against each defendant. But where one defendant owes a separate and distinct duty of care, that should be pleaded. For example, if two vehicles collide and the plaintiff is a passenger in one vehicle, the drivers of each vehicle owe separate duties of care to the plaintiff.

If the driver of a car is not the owner of the vehicle but is driving with the owner's knowledge and consent, the duty-of-care of the owner and driver run concurrently, and the owner is vicariously liable for the driver's negligence. Generally, parties which are vicariously liable are grouped together in the claim:

The first-named defendant and second-named defendant were guilty of negligence in that they_____

The **statement of claim** may end:

9   *By reason of the foregoing, the plaintiff has suffered personal injury, loss, damage, inconvenience and expense.*
10   *The plaintiff reserves the right to furnish further particulars of negligence in due course and will further rely on all particulars of negligence which may be adduced at the hearing.*
11   *The plaintiff will rely, as far as may be necessary, upon the doctrine of res ipsa loquitur.*

Personal injury and loss are detailed under separate subheadings of **particulars of injury** and **particulars of special damage**. The particulars of injury should be based on a detailed medical report. The particulars can be given either in separate lettered paragraphs or in one composite paragraph:

a)   *On the day of the accident, the plaintiff attended hospital where he underwent X-rays.*
b)   *Later the same day, the plaintiff attended his family doctor complaining of stiffness and soreness in his shoulder. The pain was increased on lying down or raising the shoulder.*
c)   *On examination, he was found to have a 50% reduction in movement in his shoulder in all directions. He had poor anterior elevation and pain in his right shoulder at the extremes of all movements. A diagnosis was made of frozen shoulder.*
d)   *The prognosis is that, in the absence of X-ray changes, recovery may take up to two years, but, as the plaintiff continues to suffer pain, further adverse sequelae cannot be ruled out.*
e)   *On receipt of further up to date medical reports, the above particulars will be updated*
f)   *The plaintiff's lifestyle and ability to enjoy life have been diminished by the reason of the injuries sustained, and evidence in relation to this aspect of the claim will be given at the hearing of the action.*

Details of acute or chronic disability are also set out. It is important to plead **particulars of special damage** because most torts are only actionable on proof of special damage. The particulars may claim liquidated sums or out-of-pocket expenses incurred by the plaintiff as a result of the accident, such as:

1   *Hospital fees*
2   *Doctors' bills*
3   *Medicines*
4   *Physiotherapy*
5   *Loss of earnings*
6   *Travel expenses*
7   *Damage to clothing*

The **claim** at the end of the **statement of claim** is largely a repetition of the **general endorsement of claim** on the **special summons**:

AND THE PLAINTIFF CLAIMS:

1   *Specific performance of the agreement in writing between the plaintiff and the defendant for the purchase of lands as set out in the schedule hereto for the sum of €250,000.*
2   *All necessary and consequential orders and reliefs*
3   *Damages for negligence and breach of duty (including breach of statutory duty).*
4   *Interest pursuant to the Courts Act 1981.*
5   *Costs*

In the lower Courts, damages must specifically be limited to the jurisdiction of the Court, but the High Court has unlimited jurisdiction, so no limit need be set. It is not strictly necessary to claim "any other order", although many pleadings do so.

In the case of an action for **specific performance** for the purchase of land, it should be specifically pleaded that the contract was evidenced in writing, to satisfy the requirements of the Statute of Frauds, 1695:

AND THE PLAINTIFF CLAIMS:

1   *Specific performance of the agreement in writing between the plaintiff and the defendant for the purchase of lands as set out in the schedule hereto for the sum of €250,000.*
2   *All necessary and consequential orders and reliefs.*
3   *Damages for breach of contract, instead of or in addition to specific performance.*

4   *Interest pursuant to the Courts Act, 1981.*
5   *Costs.*

SCHEDULE

*ALL THAT AND THOSE the premises situate at 25
O'Connell Street in the City of Dublin.*

A statement of claim is *not* sworn, but is signed by Counsel who drafted
it (or, if not drafted by Counsel, by the solicitor or lay litigant).

DRAFTING OF DEFENCE

Defences vary, depending on the **statement of claim**. A **defence** is
based on the **statement of claim**, but is generally shorter. The heading
will be the same as that of the **statement of claim**:

THE HIGH COURT

Record Number: 2001 P 4321

Between

KENNETH MURPHY

Plaintiff

and

BRENDAN O'BRIEN

Defendant

DRAFT DEFENCE

*Delivered on the ___day of _____200_ by Kelly and
Partners of 2 Dorset Road in the City of Dublin, solicitors for
the defendant*

The purpose of the **defence** is to put the plaintiff on proof of *all* the
allegations in the **statement of claim**. Any matter that is not denied in
the **defence** is taken to be admitted, so it is important to go through the
statement of claim carefully, separately denying any contested matters

of fact. But agreed facts should not be artificially denied, as a defendant may be penalised in costs for putting the plaintiff on proof of matters unnecessarily (O. 21 rule 8 RSC).

The **defence** deals specifically with every contested allegation of fact except for damages (O. 19 rule 17 RSC). Any claim that a contract was void or voidable, or any suggestion that a claim is out of time, fraudulent or illegal must be pleaded (O. 19 rule 15 RSC). In the case of a debt, the defence may not simply deny owing the money, but must deny some matter of fact, such as the receipt of the money, delivery of goods or the specific amount claimed.

In personal injuries actions, there is generally a denial that the accident happened, that a duty of care was owed by the defendant to the plaintiff, or that any loss or injury was caused to the plaintiff. This traverse may form the entire basis of the **defence**.

A defendant may also allege that, if injury *was* caused, it was due wholly to the negligence of the plaintiff, or that there was contributory negligence on the part of the plaintiff. In a road accident case, for example, the **defence** might claim that the plaintiff was not looking where he was going, or in an industrial accident case, that the plaintiff was misusing the machinery.

Alternatively the **defence** may state that a third party, rather than the defendant, was liable for the injury (for example, in a road accident). The **defence** may also plead that the claim is statute-barred under the Statute of Limitations 1957 (for example, if the injury occurred more than three years ago). If the plaintiff is seeking equitable relief, the Statute of Limitations does not apply, but the **defence** may plead acquiescence or *laches* (that is equitable delay).

If the **defence** alleges fraud, malice, undue influence or some other condition of a plaintiff's mind, it is sufficient to allege that as a fact, without setting out the surrounding circumstances (O. 19 rule 22 RSC). Allegations or implications relating to documents or letters or conversation may be set out as a fact, without the necessity to give all the details in full.

Where specific performance is sought in relation to the sale of land, the **defence** may claim there is no adequate note or memorandum for the purpose of the Statute of Frauds 1695.

In *Phonographic Performance Ltd* v. *Cody* [1998] 4 IR 504, Keane J said a defendant was entitled to raise alternative defences which were inconsistent with one another, as long as they did not cause prejudice, embarrassment or delay to the plaintiff within the meaning of O. 19 rule 27 RSC.

Generally the **defence** follows the style of the **statement of claim** in a rather artificial manner. The denial of events obliges the plaintiff to produce witnesses to prove that the events alleged in the **statement of claim** actually did happen.

Paragraphs should be numbered, as in the **statement of claim**, but the defence does not repeat the names and details of the parties. The **defence** will not take issue with the description of the plaintiff and defendant in the **statement of claim**, unless they are inaccurate. Otherwise, the paragraphs to be contradicted will be repeated more or less verbatim, preceded by "*It is denied that*", and followed by the words "*or at all*". If a fact is admitted, the **defence** need not refer to it, because a claim that is not denied is *automatically* admitted (O. 19 rule 13 RSC).

The **defence** must not be evasive, but must answer the point of substance. For example, if a plaintiff claims the defendant received a certain amount of money, it is not enough for the **defence** to deny receipt of that particular amount. It must deny that the defendant received the sum *or any part of it*, or set out exactly how much was received (O. 19 rule 19 RSC).

If issue is taken with only part of a paragraph, the **defence** might admit elements of the paragraph:

> *It is admitted that at all material times the defendant was the occupier of the premises as set out in paragraph 3 of the statement of claim, but it is denied that the premises are a factory within the meaning of the Factories Acts*

Particulars are normally denied generally, rather than individually:

> *The particulars of negligence and breach of duty are denied as if they were set out here and traversed seriatim.*
> *The particulars of personal injury are denied as if they were set out here and traversed seriatim.*

The **defence** may plead contributory negligence:

> *If the plaintiff suffered the alleged or any personal injury, loss, damage or expense (which is denied) the same was caused or wholly contributed to by the negligence and/or contributory negligence of the plaintiff.*

> PARTICULARS OF NEGLIGENCE AND CONTRIBUTORY NEGLIGENCE

> *The plaintiff was guilty of negligence and contributory negligence in*

*(a) failing to have any or any adequate regard for his own
    safety*
*(b) failing to fit the guard provided on the circular saw
    failing to follow the safety directions for use of the*
(c) circular saw
(d) using the circular saw when not authorised to do

If the **defence** is alleging that the accident was caused by the negligence
of a third party, it continues:

> *If the plaintiff suffered the alleged personal injury, loss, damage or
> expense (which is denied), the same was not caused by the
> negligence and breach of duty of the defendant, but was caused by
> the negligence and breach of duty of XYZ Saw-Guards Ltd.*

The claim of third-party negligence should not be particularised, and an
application should be made to join XYZ Saw-Guards as co-defendants.
    If alleging that the claim is statute-barred, it is not necessary to refer
to any particular section of the Act:

> *The plaintiff's claim herein is barred by reason of the provisions of
> the Statute of Limitations, 1957.*

The final paragraph of the **defence** will read:

> *The plaintiff is not entitled to the relief claimed nor any relief.*
>
> *Signed A. Barrister*

Like the **statement of claim**, the **defence** is signed but *not* sworn, as it
is a pleading, rather than evidence.

COUNTERCLAIM

If a defendant decides to make a **counterclaim** in his **defence**, the cause
of action must derive from the *same set of facts*. An independent cause of
action would *not* give rise to a **counterclaim**. The **counterclaim** is an
additional section which is added to the end of the defence and headed:

COUNTERCLAIM

WITHOUT PREJUDICE TO THE FOREGOING:

The facts giving rise to the **counterclaim** are set out, using numbered paragraphs as in the **statement of claim**, but following on the numbering of the **defence**. The **counterclaim** ends with "*And the defendant claims* ..." Even if the original claim is dismissed, stayed or discontinued, the **counterclaim** remains alive, as it is a *new and separate action* between the parties (O. 21 rule 15 RSC). All the same interlocutory applications may be brought on the **counterclaim** as on the original claim. If a claim is settled, the settlement should also deal with the **counterclaim**.

If a plaintiff believes that a counterclaim does not arise out of the same facts and should be dealt with as a completely independent action, he may apply to the Court to exclude the counterclaim (O. 21 rule 14 RSC). In *Re MV Anton Lopatin* [1995] 3 IR 503, Barr J said the Court had discretion to decide whether a counterclaim should be permitted and whether it was proper to bring the claim in the action. In making its decision, the Court must review the situation and try to do justice to both parties, having regard to all the circumstances.

REPLY

If there is a **counterclaim**, the plaintiff may draft a **reply**. As the **counterclaim** performs the function of a **statement of claim**, the **reply** must contain a **defence** to the counterclaim and must deny each point of the counterclaim that is not admitted.

A **reply** is not necessary where there is merely a joinder of issue (that is where the defendant raises no new issue, where the **defence** is a full denial of the plaintiff's claim or where liability is admitted, but it is denied that loss has been sustained – O. 23 rule 1 RSC). But a **reply** *will* be required when the **defence** raises new matters, such as:

1   an allegation of **contributory negligence**,
2   a plea that the claim is **statute-barred** (or barred by **acquiescence** or *laches* in the case of equitable proceedings) or
3   a **counterclaim**.

In the first two instances, the **reply** simply denies the **defence** claim. The **reply** is drafted in the same way as the **defence** and starts with a delivery clause. It continues:

1   *The plaintiff joins issue with the defendant on his defence,
     save insofar as the same contains admissions.*

2   *The plaintiff denies that he was guilty of the alleged or any
     negligence or contributory negligence*

3   *By way of special reply to paragraph ( ) of the defence, the
     particulars of negligence as set out therein are denied as if the
     same were set out here and traversed seriatim*

4   *By way of special reply to paragraph ( ) of the defence, it is
     denied that the plaintiff's claim is statute-barred by virtue of
     the provisions of the Statute of Limitations, 1957 (or barred
     by reason of acquiescence or laches).*

A **counterclaim** should be dealt with as if drafting a **defence** and may
raise new facts (*Kidd* v. *Kidd* 18 ILTR 5). The **defence to the counterclaim** ends with the formula:

> *The defendant is not entitled to the relief claimed in his counterclaim
> nor any relief.*

> *Signed: A Barrister*

The **reply** should be delivered within 14 days of delivery of the **defence**.
If a **reply** is not filed, the pleadings close when the **defence** is filed (O. 23
rule 3 RSC) and the matter can then be set down for trial. If, exceptionally, the Court permits any further pleadings, they must be delivered
within *four days* of delivery of the previous pleading.

At any time up to nine days before the date of trial, any party may call
on any other party in writing to admit any documents or facts in the pleadings. The request should be made in the form of Appendix C Forms 14 and
16 RSC. If unnecessary documents are demanded, the party giving notice
will bear the cost (O. 32 rule 9 RSC). If a party unreasonably fails to admit
documents or facts, he will be penalised in costs (O. 32 rules 2 and 4 RSC).

If the issues are not sufficiently clearly defined at the close of
pleadings, the Court may order the parties to prepare issues which may be
settled by the Court (or, on consent, by the Master – O. 33 rule 1 RSC).

If, after issuing a summons, the parties differ on questions of facts,
they may agree to proceed directly to trial without further pleadings,
stating the questions for trial in the form of Appendix C Form 17 RSC.

Most interlocutory applications are brought at this stage because the
issues between the parties will not normally have become clear until the
close of pleadings.

CASE CONFERENCES

In a personal injury action in which liability is admitted, in order to cut costs and reduce the Court waiting list, the President of the High Court has proposed that preliminary hearings should be held by way of case conference.

The plaintiff, by letter to the Chief Registrar, may request a case conference before a judge of personal injuries actions. The case is then listed so that both sides may explore the possibility of an early settlement or a reduction in the number of issues to be decided. If the defendant objects, the judge will consider his objections.

Case conferences are held in chambers at 2pm on Mondays, attended by the parties' solicitors and Counsel. One week before the conference, the parties are required to complete a checklist (set out below).

At the conference, inquiries may be made in relation to matters including whether:

1   there has been compliance with any rules made under s.45 of the Courts and Court Officers Act 1995 relating to preliminary preparation of documents,
2   the parties are prepared to exchange medical and expert witness reports (or have already done so) or
3   the parties have exchanged witness statements or are prepared to do so.

The parties may be required to:

1   state concisely the nature of the case or defence so as to identify the remaining issues,
2   provide an exact statement of special damages claimed or admitted and
3   identify the areas on which they do not agree.

If both sides agree, the judge at the conference may help settle the action. If it is not settled, that particular judge will not preside at the hearing of the action. The conference judge may direct that appropriate steps be taken to refer specific issues for hearing in Court. After the conference, the case will be listed for a suitable early hearing date.

The check list to be prepared before the conference has the heading of the action:

THE HIGH COURT

Number 2001 P 4321

Between/

KENNETH MURPHY

Plaintiff

and

CATHERINE O'BRIEN

Defendant

PRE-TRIAL CHECK LIST

1. PLEADINGS
(a) Do you intend to make any amendment to your pleadings?
(a) If so, when?

2. PRE-TRIAL PROCEDURES
(a) Have all the orders which have been made to date in this case been complied with?
(b) If not, specify the orders which have not been complied with.
(c) What steps do you propose to take in relation to the outstanding orders?
(d) Do you propose to make any further applications to Court before the hearing?
(e) If so, what applications do you intend to make?
(f) When do you propose to make such applications?
(g) Have you given all the particulars of personal injury suffered by the plaintiff, with particulars of the consequences of these injuries, to enable the case to proceed without interruption or delay?
(h) If not, what particulars remain outstanding?
(i) When do you propose to give these particulars?
(j) Have you given all particulars of special damage and loss, to enable the case to proceed without delay?
(k) If not, state what particulars you propose to give.
(l) When do you propose to give these particulars to the defendant?
(m) Why have they not been given to date?
(n) Have you consider obtaining leave to deliver interrogatories?
(o) If so, have you decided not to do so?

3.   COURT FILE

Have you confirmed that the court file is now complete, and that there are no notices for particulars, replies to notices for particulars or other documents which should be on the file but remain unfiled?

4.   LENGTH OF TRIAL

What are the estimates for the minimum and maximum lengths of trial?

5.   RESOLUTION OF THE ISSUES BY NEGOTIATION
(a) Have you considered attempting to resolve this case by negotiation?
(b) Have negotiations taken place?
(c) If not, state why not.

6.   EXCHANGE OF EVIDENCE
(a) Have both sides exchanged medical reports?
(b) If not, are you prepared to do so?

7.   SPECIAL DAMAGES
(a) Have you calculated the special damages?
(b) Have you calculated the social welfare payments to be deducted from any award?

8.   SETTLEMENT
(a) Do you wish the judge presiding at the case conference to assist in the settlement of the action?

The checklist must be completed by the solicitor for each party and lodged with the Court file at least seven days before the case conference. A copy of the list is to be sent to each of the parties to the action. Parties to personal injuries actions should also be aware of the requirements of SI 391 of 1998 in relation to the disclosure and admission of reports and statements (see page 35).

If a plaintiff or defendant wishes to withdraw an action under O. 26 rule 2, his solicitor should write to the chief registrar of the High Court, quoting the record number and list number and enclosing a letter of consent from the solicitor for the other side. This does not apply to actions involving wardship, minors or fatal injuries. In actions where money has been lodged, an order of the Court will be necessary, except where the money is being accepted in satisfaction of a claim where the claimants are of full legal capacity.

5. Affidavits

An **affidavit** is a written sworn statement, drawn up in the first person and generally confined to the facts about which the deponent (the person swearing the document) has personal knowledge (O. 40 rule 4 RSC). It must be sworn before a person entitled to witness it, such as a Commissioner for Oaths or practising solicitor. Its purpose is to save time and expense, by avoiding evidence having to be given under oath in court. O. 39 rule 1 RSC says that "the Court may, at any time for sufficient reason, order that any particular fact or facts may be proved by affidavit, or that the affidavit of any witness may be read at the hearing or trial, on such conditions as the Court may think reasonable."

In *Phonographic Performance (Ireland)* v. *Cody* [1998] 4 IR 504, Keane J said evidence could be admitted on affidavit, instead of viva voce, where:

1 the affidavit did not relate to issues which were significantly in dispute,
2 the deponent was *bona fide* not required for cross-examination,
3 the difficulty or expense of producing the deponent caused a serious risk of injustice and
4 the application was made before the trial began.

But the Supreme Court said that, where one side *bona fide* required the other for cross-examination, the High Court had no discretion to order that the evidence be given on affidavit instead.

The language of the **affidavit** may follow the personal style of the person swearing it, but it should preferably be limited to one fact per numbered paragraph (O. 40 rule 8 RSC). Dates, sums and figures should be expressed in figures, rather than words. If an affidavit is used in an application, a copy must be produced for the Court. An unattested photocopy of an original **affidavit** which has been filed may be used, provided that the solicitor who filed the original attests that it is a true copy and gives the date of filing.

In most applications, the person who should swear the **affidavit** will be the party applying for relief, because he will have personal knowledge of the facts. On interlocutory motions, a statement of belief – with the grounds for such belief – may be included in the affidavit. But if hearsay is unnecessarily included, the costs of the affidavit will not be allowed (O. 40 rule 4 RSC).

Statements made in an affidavit are absolutely privileged and may not form the basis for an action for libel or slander. In *Looney* v. *Bank of Ireland* [1996] 1 IR 157, Murphy J said it would be impossible and impractical to confine the evidence of witnesses to matters directly in issue, but if a witness made a wholly irrelevant and unwarranted attack on the good name of another citizen, such an abuse of the legal process would constitute contempt of Court.

An **affidavit** may use the phrases "I say that ... " (meaning the deponent has personal knowledge of the fact), "I say and believe that ... " (meaning he has reason to believe a fact from his or another's knowledge) or "I am informed and believe that ... " (meaning that he has been told a fact by a third party, but has not been able to verify it).

Solicitors should only swear **affidavits** on behalf of a plaintiff in exceptional circumstances, as a solicitor's **affidavit** would normally be hearsay and inadmissible (O. 40 rule 4 RSC). One exception is an application for substituted service, where the solicitor or summons server is likely to be the deponent. But in an application for **service out of the jurisdiction**, the deponent would be the plaintiff.

In a case of *compelling urgency*, where the plaintiff may not be physically available (such as in a *habeas corpus* application), a solicitor could swear the **affidavit**, but he should include an explanation of his reasons for doing so. Affidavits grounding interlocutory applications may also be sworn by someone without firsthand knowledge, but giving the grounds for belief.

In *Banco Ambrosiano Spa* v. *Ansbacher and Co.*, High Court, 19 July 1985, Murphy J refused an application for security for costs, grounded on an affidavit sworn by the defendant's solicitor. The judge said the affidavit was "hearsay upon hearsay" and that it was well settled law in this jurisdiction that, *prima facie*, such an affidavit should be sworn by the defendant himself. He cited the judgment of O'Dalaigh CJ in *Power* v. *Irish Civil Service Building Society* [1968] IR 158 in relation to the requirements for a satisfactory affidavit within the meaning of O. 29 rule 3 RSC.

If the application is for an infant settlement, the affidavit should be sworn by the next friend. If a defendant is applying to join a third party, the defendant himself should swear the document. Where a company is involved, the secretary should be the deponent. One deponent may swear an **affidavit** on behalf of a number of plaintiffs.

An **affidavit** has the title of the action, followed by *Affidavit of (name of deponent)*. If there is more than one plaintiff or defendant, it is acceptable to give the full name of the first plaintiff or defendant and say that there are other plaintiffs or defendants. The **affidavit** then sets out the deponent's name, age (or the fact that he is over 18), address and occupation (O. 40 rule 9 RSC).

> *I, Philip Murphy, aged eighteen years and upwards, company*
> *secretary, of 1 Ballinteer Rise in the City of Dublin, MAKE*
> *OATH and say as follows:*

The first numbered paragraph will give the relationship of the deponent
to the action, and his means of knowledge:

> 1.   *I am the secretary of the plaintiff company, and I make this*
>   *affidavit on its behalf and with its authority and consent from*
>   *an examination of the files, books and records of the plaintiff*
>   *company and from facts within my knowledge, save where*
>   *otherwise appears and where so appearing, I believe those*
>   *facts to be true.*

A document exhibited in an affidavit should be marked with an
identifying letter and signed by the deponent before the swearing of the
affidavit (O. 40 rule 27 RSC). The wording used is:

> *I beg to refer to (exhibit), upon which marked with the letter 'A' I*
> *have signed my name prior to the swearing hereof.*

The deponent's signature on the exhibit is witnessed by the Commissioner
for Oaths or practising solicitor before whom the affidavit is sworn. (This
cannot be the solicitor for the deponent or his partner – O. 40 rule 17
RSC.) If an affidavit is taken abroad, it may be witnessed by an Irish
diplomatic or consular official or notary public (O. 40 rule 7 RSC).

Although s.30 of the Criminal Evidence Act 1992 allows the use of
photocopies in certain criminal cases, the *best evidence rule* requires that
originals of documents should be produced in civil cases. Exhibiting a
document in an **affidavit** has the same effect as proving the document in
Court. (Proving involves a witness identifying a document which is
handed to the Court and noted as an exhibit by the registrar.)

Affidavits must normally be filed in the Central Office, Wards of
Court Office, Probate Office or Examiner's Office (O. 40 rule 2 RSC).
Once a document is filed in a Court of record, it need not actually be
produced in Court. Other official documents, such as foreign Court
documents, Land Registry documents and birth certificates are *not*
documents of record and must be proved. Examples of Court documents
which prove themselves would include **notices of motion**, judgments,
grants of probate and **affidavits**. Such documents are referred to in the
affidavit "*when produced*".

Original documents which should not be marked (such as wills) may be placed in an envelope and sealed, and an identifying letter marked on the sealed envelope. The affidavit should say:

> *I beg to refer to the said original (document) which I have placed*
> *in an envelope and sealed and upon which envelope marked with*
> *the letter 'B' I have signed my name prior to the swearing hereof.*

If several inter-related documents are being exhibited, the wording is:

> *I beg to refer to the medical reports of Dr (name), dated ___ and*
> *___, upon which, pinned together and marked with the letter 'C',* ·
> *I have signed my name prior to the swearing hereof.*

The *jurat* (or oath) appears on the right hand side at the end of the **affidavit,** so that the deponent may sign to the left of it. It says: "Sworn by the said (name of deponent) on (date) at (place) before me, a Commissioner for Oaths/practising solicitor, and I know the deponent."

Any corrections or additions must be initialled by the Commissioner or solicitor (O. 40 rule 13 RSC), but faulty affidavits may be received by the Court under O. 40 rule 15 RSC. Where an affidavit is sworn by someone who is blind or illiterate, the Commissioner or solicitor must certify that the affidavit has been read over to the deponent and that he seems to understand it. (O. 40 rule 14 RSC)

Every **affidavit** ends with a **filing clause** (O. 40 rule 11 RSC), which says: "Filed on the (date) by (name and title – for example, *plaintiff in person or solicitor for the respondent*)

A checklist in the Central Office warns that affidavits won't be accepted unless they conform with O. 40 of the RSC, in particular:

* rule 6: jurat time and place
* rule 8: numbered paragraphs
* rule 9: description and residence
* rule 11: filing clause
* rule 13: alterations
* rule 14: "and I know the deponent" and
* rule 16: the use of certified or attested copies

6.   Service

Order 9 of the **Rules of the Superior Courts** requires that all *originating* summonses be served personally on the defendant where "reasonably practicable". One exception is where the defendant is a limited company incorporated under the Companies Acts 1963–1990. Section 379 of the 1963 Act says the summons may be left or sent by ordinary prepaid post to the registered office of the company. If the company has not informed the Registrar of Companies of its registered address, the summons may be registered at the Companies Office. Any letter left at (or sent to) the registered office of a company is deemed to have been served, even if the company has since moved. (s.379(2) Companies Act 1963).

Special rules apply (O. 9 RSC) to service in the case of

- husbands and wives who are joint defendants,
- children,
- lunatics,
- corporations,
- the inhabitants of a county district and
- the recovery of land.

Different rules also apply to service on partners in a firm (O. 14 rules 3–7)

Personal service involves *delivering a copy of the summons to the defendant, and showing him the original sealed copy or duplicate original*. It is not sufficient just to hand the defendant an envelope containing the summons, where he is unaware of its contents or that an action has been taken against him.

In the case of *Petronelli v. Collins* [1996] High Court, 19 July 1996, the boxer Stephen Collins claimed he had been approached in a pub by an unknown woman who said she wanted to give him something, then attempted to hand him an envelope, which he did not accept. He said he was not shown any document. The woman – a private investigator – claimed she had handed a copy summons to Mr Collins with a yellow sticker on it. She had asked him for his autograph on the sticker, then handed the copy to Mr Collins, showed him the original summons and told him "Mr Collins, you are served." Unfortunately for the boxer, the investigator was able to produce the sticker signed "Joan, with best wishes,

Stephen Collins"! Costello P ruled that the defendant had been properly served.

After a summons has been served, details of the day and date of service should be endorsed on the original within three days. Any **affidavit of service** sworn by the summons server should mention the date of the endorsement (O. 9 rule 12 RSC). The affidavit should give the title of the action and say (O. 40 rule 9 RSC):

> *I (name and description) of (address), aged 18 years and upwards, MAKE OATH and say:*
>
> *1. THAT I did on (date) at (address) personally serve the above-named defendant by delivering unto and leaving with him/her a true copy of the summons in this action issued under the Seal of the High Court and dated (date) and marked (record number), upon which summons and copy the required memorandum and endorsements were duly subscribed and made,*
> *2. THAT at the time of such service I was acquainted with the appearance of the said defendant, to whom I showed the original of the said copy,*
> *3. AND I further say that I did afterwards on (date) indorse on the said summons the day of the week and month of such service.*
>
> *Sworn before me etc.*

If the defendant's solicitor undertakes in writing to accept the summons and enter an appearance, proof of service is not required (O. 9 rule 1 RSC).

Where papers are served after 5pm on a weekday, the date of service is reckoned to be the following day. Where papers are served after 1pm on a Saturday, the date of service is reckoned to be the following Monday.

If personal service on a defendant within the jurisdiction has not been possible, despite "due and reasonable diligence", the summons may be served (O. 9 rule 2 RSC) without any special Court order by delivering a copy to the defendant's

- home, office, shop or place of business,
- spouse,
- child (over 16),
- parent,
- sibling,
- partner or
- employee.

If the defendant's attention has been drawn to the proceedings, even though it has not been possible to serve the summons, the Court may not require any further attempts at service (O. 9 rule 15 RSC).

SUBSTITUTED SERVICE

If prompt, personal service still proves impractical (where, for example, the summons server is threatened or the defendant leaves the jurisdiction to avoid service), an application may be made for **substituted service**. The Court must first be satisfied that there has been a *bona fide* attempt to serve the document. Several attempts should have been made at various times when the defendant might reasonably be expected to be available – although it's not specifically necessary to make three attempts.

An application for an order of **substituted service** (O. 10 rule 2 RSC) is made *ex parte* – that is, where nobody is on notice – in the Common Law *ex parte* list.

The Court will require the original sealed copy of the **plenary summons** and a **grounding affidavit** sworn by the summons server, setting out:

1   the defendant's home or business **address**,
2   details of the **"reasonably diligent" attempts** to serve the summons,
3   the deponent's belief that the defendant is **evading service** and
4   suggestions for **alternative means of service**.

Alternative means of service might include registered or ordinary post, service on a close relative of the defendant, fixing the document to the defendant's shop or factory, or advertising the summons in a journal likely to be read by the defendant.

The judge should be asked to fix a time for entry of appearance (usually eight days, but if the defendant is outside the jurisdiction, possibly longer). *A copy of the judge's order* should be served with the summons (O. 10 rule 3 RSC).

The **affidavit of service** and particulars of service endorsed on the summons should specify that the judge's requirements have been complied with, in case of a subsequent application for judgment in default of appearance or defence.

SERVICE OUT OF THE JURISDICTION

Until 1988, if the defendant was resident outside the jurisdiction of the Republic of Ireland, no summons could be issued without leave of the Court (O. 5 rule 14). But now, in certain circumstances, a summons may be served abroad without a prior Court application.

The Jurisdiction of Courts and Enforcement of Judgments (European Communities) Acts 1988, 1993 and 1998 gave legislative effect to Article 24 of the 1968 Brussels Convention. The Convention aimed to provide a machinery to enforce judgments of any Court of a contracting state in the other contracting states.

The dispute must be of a civil or commercial nature within the nature of the convention. Actions which are specifically *excluded* include:

- Revenue and Customs matters,
- matrimonial property rights (except maintenance payments),
- wills,
- succession rights,
- bankruptcy,
- winding-up,
- social security and
- arbitration.

Since 31 May 2001, the service of judicial and extrajudicial documents in civil or commercial matters has been governed by EC Regulation 1348/2000. Under the Regulation, county registrars are the transmitting and receiving agencies for all documents to be served within the EU (excluding Denmark). The text of the document is available online at http://europa.eu.int/eurlex/en/lif/dat/2000/en_300R1348.html

In *Short* v. *Ireland* [1997] 1 ILRM 161, the Supreme Court said that the question to be asked when deciding whether to allow service outside the jurisdiction under O. 11 rule 1(h) was: if the person were inside the jurisdiction, would he be a proper person to be joined as a defendant?

A summons to be served out of the jurisdiction may now be issued without leave of the High Court under the terms of Order 11A if

(a) the Court has power to hear and determine the claim under the Jurisdiction of Courts and Enforcement of Judgments Act 1998,
(b) no proceedings involving the same cause of action are pending in any other contracting State and
(c) *either*
    (i) the defendant is domiciled in a contracting State

or

(ii) the Court has exclusive jurisdiction (under Article 16 of the 1968 Brussels Convention) to decide the original proceedings

or

(iii) the defendant has agreed in writing to the Court having jurisdiction (under Article 17).

The "agreement in writing" may amount to no more than the terms and conditions of sale printed on an invoice, as in the case of *Clare Taverns t/a Durty Nelly's* v. *Charles Gill t/a Universal Business Systems*, [1999] IEHC 40. In that case, McGuinness J – citing the English decision in *Hough* v. *P & O Containers Ltd* [1998] 2 All ER 978 – ruled that the terms of Article 17 of the Convention were mandatory and had the effect of excluding the "merely permissive" terms of Article 6(2).

In the case of *Société Lacoste SA* v. *Kelly Group Ltd* [1999] 3 IR 534, O'Sullivan J said the Convention only required that there be an agreement in writing or evidenced in writing to confer jurisdiction. The fact that a defendant might not be aware of the terms of the agreement did not mean that such an agreement did not bind the parties.

The summons and statement of claim must specify the provisions of the 1968 Convention under which the Court has jurisdiction (O. 19 rule 3A RSC). The endorsement of claim and statement of claim should also be endorsed with the formula:

The Court has power under the Jurisdiction of Courts and Enforcement of Judgments Act 1998 and Articles (number) of the Brussels Convention 1968 to hear and determine the claim, and no proceedings involving the same cause of action are pending in another contracting State.

In bygone days, it would have been regarded as an infringement of sovereignty to serve the writ of one country on the citizen of another country, so *notice* of the writ is served on anyone who is not an Irish citizen. The notice should say:

> *To (name of defendant): TAKE NOTICE that (name of plaintiff) has commenced an action against you (name of defendant) in the High Court in Ireland, by writ of that Court, dated (date), which writ is indorsed as follows (copy of all indorsements). You are required within X days after the receipt of this notice, excluding the day of such receipt, to defend the said action by causing an appearance to the said action to be entered for you in the said Court. In default of your so doing, the said (name of plaintiff) may proceed*

> *therein and judgment may be given in your absence. You may*
> *appear to the said writ by entering an appearance personally or by*
> *your solicitor at the Central Office, Four Courts, Dublin.*

The countries covered by the Convention include Ireland, the UK, Denmark, France, Germany, Greece, Italy, Luxembourg, the Netherlands, Portugal and Spain. The defendant has five weeks from the service of the summons (or six weeks where the summons is served in a non-European territory) in which to enter an appearance (O. 11A rule 3 RSC).

Where the cause of action is not within the Brussels Convention, or where one of the defendants is not resident in a contracting State, the Court may grant leave for service out of the jurisdiction where it is satisfied that the defendant is domiciled in this State or the subject matter of the proceedings makes him amenable to the judgment of the Court or the parties have contractually agreed to submit themselves to the Court's jurisdiction (O. 11 rule 3 RSC). An application must be made to the Court for liberty to

1 **issue** and
2 **serve** the summons (or notice of the summons) on the party outside the jurisdiction.

O. 11 rule 1 of the **Rules of the Superior Courts** sets out the limits in which service out of the jurisdiction will be considered. If the action does not come under one of the 17 paragraphs in the order, the Court will not grant leave. The affidavit *must* refer to the sub-head of the rule under which the application is made. In *United Meat Packers* v. *Nordstern Allgemeine* [1996] 2 ILRM 260, Carroll J set aside service of a notice of summons because the original application was wrongly granted under O. 11 rule 1(e)(ii), instead of O. 11 rule 1(e)(iii), but the Supreme Court reversed that finding on appeal (*United Meat Packers* v. *Nordstern Allgemeine* [1997] 2 ILRM 553). The Court said that, once the High Court had established that it had jurisdiction under O. 11 rule 1(e), it should have exercised its discretion to amend the pleadings in favour of the plaintiff.

In *Caudron* v. *Air Zaire* [1986] ILRM 10, the plaintiffs, who had obtained judgment in the sum of 114 million Belgian francs in the Belgian Courts, sought liberty to issue a summons outside the jurisdiction for breach of contract. The plaintiffs were former employees of the first-named defendants. Neither the plaintiffs nor the first-named defendant had any substantial connection with this jurisdiction.

The action was brought in the Irish High Court because a Boeing 737 aircraft belonging to the first-named defendants was being held at Dublin airport by Aer Lingus, the second-named defendants, as security against money owing by Air Zaire. The plaintiffs wanted to prevent removal of the aircraft from the jurisdiction, so that judgment could be executed on it.

In the High Court, Barr J allowed service outside the jurisdiction by the plaintiffs, since paragraph (g) of O. 11 rule 1 referred to the grant of *any* injunction, without qualification, and the plaintiffs were seeking a Mareva injunction. But in the Supreme Court, Finlay CJ said that, if the injunction referred to in O. 11 provided the only connection with the State, it must be an injunction issuing at the end of a substantive action. A Mareva injunction was not a substantive relief, but ancillary to the main relief sought, and did not therefore confer a right to serve outside the jurisdiction. (That restriction was removed by s.13 of the Jurisdiction of Courts and Enforcement of Judgments Act 1998, as reflected in Order 42A of the RSC.)

In *Short* v. *Ireland, the AG and British Nuclear Fuels plc* [1996] 2 IR 210, O'Hanlon J said the titles of the affidavits were not in accordance with the requirements of O. 11 rule 6, there was no formal statement in the affidavits that the deponent believed the plaintiffs had a good cause of action and the order failed to specify the paragraph of O. 11 rule 1 under which it was made. O'Hanlon J said that he would overlook those breaches of the procedural requirements, but notice of the summons (rather than the summons itself) should have been served on the defendant, so he set aside the service of the summons. The High Court decision was upheld by the Supreme Court on appeal.

Similarly, in *O'Connor* v. *Commercial General and Marine Ltd* [1996] 2 ILRM 291 Morris J set aside service of a plenary summons because the summons itself, rather than notice of the summons, had been served on a Belgian national.

In *Schmidt* v. *Home Secretary* [1995] 1 ILRM 301, Geoghegan J said proceedings could not be served out of the jurisdiction on British police officers because they were officers of the Crown and had sovereign immunity. He said breaches of constitutional rights and actionable breaches of community law which gave rise to a claim for damages were "matters relating to tort" within the meaning of article 5 of the Brussels Convention and there was therefore no power to grant leave for service under O. 11 rule 1.

As the summons has not been issued when the application for service out of the jurisdiction is made, the application is ex parte and the affidavit should be headed:

> *In the matter of an intended action between (plaintiff) and (defendant) and In the matter of the Courts of Justice Acts 1924 to 1961 and the Courts (Supplemental Provisions) Acts 1961 to 1981.*

The affidavit (O. 11 rule 5 RSC) should refer to the *intended plaintiff* and *intended defendant*. The affidavit, sworn by the plaintiff or company secretary, sets out in full the relief sought and includes:

1   the fact that the plaintiff has a **good cause of action**, exhibiting any document supporting the claim (such as a contract),
2   how the cause of action comes within **O. 11 rule 1**,
3   the **defendant's address,**
4   whether the defendant is an **Irish citizen,**
5   the **amount** claimed,
6   why Ireland is the *forum conveniens* for the action (for example, because the witnesses are in Ireland) and
7   a prayer for **liberty to issue and serve** the summons(or notice) outside the jurisdiction, referring to the relevant sub-paragraphs of rule 1.

If the application is by **motion on notice**, the prayer would seek an order in the terms of the **notice of motion**.

The Court will fix a time for entry of appearance, depending on where the defendant lives (O. 11 rule 7 RSC). The plaintiff must ensure personal service on the defendant or apply to the Court for substituted service. A copy of the Court order must be served with the summons (O. 11 rule 10 RSC).

In the case of service of documents under the 1965 Hague Convention on the Service Abroad of Judicial and Extrajudicial Documents in Civil or Commercial Matters, an application should be made to the Master of the High Court.

The solicitor should lodge with the Master:

1   a **request for service** of the document (in the form specified by the annex to the Convention), with a **copy** of the request,
2   two **copies of the document,**
3   an **extra copy** of the document for each person to be served,
4   a **translation** of the document into the official language of the State addressed and
5   an **undertaking** to pay the costs of service.

Once the Master is satisfied that the person who submitted the request is a "competent judicial officer", that the document needs to be served in the State addressed and that the request complies with the Convention, he returns the request to the solicitor with a certificate for direct transmission to the Central Authority of the other State, the address of which is available from the Central Office.

In 2001, the Convention had been ratified by Antigua, Barbados, Belgium, Botswana, Canada, China, Cyprus, Czech Republic, Denmark, Egypt, Finland, France, Germany, Greece, Israel, Italy, Japan, Luxembourg, Malawi, the Netherlands, Norway, Pakistan, Portugal, St Helena, Slovakia, Seychelles, Spain, Sweden, Switzerland, Turkey, United Arab Republic, the UK and the USA.

DEEMING SERVICE GOOD

Occasionally there may be formal defects in the service of a summons – for example, the original of the summons may not have been shown to the defendant, it may have been served on a Sunday or it may have been served on the wrong person, although it may be possible to prove that the defendant still knew about the proceedings.

In such cases, the Court may **deem service good**. For example, in *Barnaby (London) Ltd* v. *Mullen* [1996] 2 ILRM 24, where the defendant claimed he did not live at the family home, Kinlen J said that service of an order of the Master on the defendant's wife and solicitor was sufficient.

In *Uwaydah* v. *Nolan*, High Court, 21 February 1997, a summons was served on the defendant's wife after several fruitless attempts to serve the defendant personally. The defendant claimed he was permanently resident outside the jurisdiction, and was not in Ireland on the date of the alleged service. But Barron J said that, although service cannot generally be effected if a defendant is not in the jurisdiction, an exception may be made where the defendant has left the country to avoid service. He deemed service good.

In *Gabrel* v. *Governor of Mountjoy Prison*, Supreme Court, 8 February 2001, documents concerning a deportation order were served on the applicant by way of service on the Refugee Legal Service. The Supreme Court held that there was no power under the Immigration Act 1999 to deem the service good.

In *Fox* v. *Taher*, High Court, 24 January 1996, a summons had been served on a solicitor whose firm had originally agreed to accept service on behalf of the defendant, but who subsequently refused to accept service or enter an appearance. Costello P said the object of effecting service was to bring home to the defendants the nature of the proceedings and the documents relating to the claim against them. In this case the solicitors were in daily, if not hourly, contact with the defendant. The judge refused to set aside an order deeming service good.

An application to have service deemed good may be made *ex parte*, or it may form part of the relief sought in a later application (such as a

motion for judgment in default of appearance). An **affidavit of service** should be sworn, explaining precisely how service was effected and swearing that the defendant has notice of the proceedings. The first order sought in the **notice of motion** grounding the application would be for the Court to deem service good.

Defective service may also be cured if the defendant enters an appearance or defence, or if he turns up in court (*DPP* v. *Hennessy* [1990] 8 ILTSJ 102).

7. Interlocutory Applications

Once the pleadings are closed, various intermediate applications may be made by motion to the Court, depending on the facts and issues. There may be a need to preserve the *status quo* until the hearing of the action. There may be some inadequacy in the pleadings which needs to be rectified. Further information may be required before bringing the case to trial.

NOTICE OF MOTION

A **notice of motion** is used in interlocutory applications on notice, for example to apply for **discovery**, to join a **third party**, to deliver **interrogatories** or to seek liberty to **enter judgment**. Usually the notice party will be the other party to the action, but occasionally it may be a third party. The **motion on notice** (as distinct from an *ex parte* motion, where there is no notice party) is the *application*, while the document itself *is* the **notice of motion**.

The notice sets out the date, time and place at which the motion will be moved, as well as the name of the solicitor on behalf of the party making the application:

THE HIGH COURT

Record number: 2001 / 4321 P

Between/

KENNETH MURPHY

Plaintiff

and

BRENDAN O'BRIEN

Defendant

DRAFT NOTICE OF MOTION

*TAKE NOTICE that on the   day of   200 at 10.30
a.m. or at the first opportunity thereafter* (or, if the motion is for
the sitting of the Court, *at the sitting of the Court) Counsel on
behalf of the plaintiff will apply to this Honourable Court,
(*Circuit Court motion includes *sitting at court number   )
Four Courts, Inns Quay, in the City of Dublin for an order
pursuant to O. 31 rule 12:-*

1. *Directing the defendants and each of them to make discovery
   on oath of all documents notes memoranda plans work records
   and any other documents relating to the works carried on
   at_____within a 300 metre radius of the place of the
   accident, the subject matter of these proceedings, within five
   years previous to the date of the said accident on or about the
   ____day of_____ 200_*
1. *Further or other order*
2. *Costs*

*WHICH MOTION will be grounded upon the pleadings already
had herein, the nature of the case and reasons to be offered.*

*Dated the____day of_____200_*

Signed_____

Name and address of solicitor for the applicant

To: *The Chief Registrar of the High Court
             Inns Quay,
             Dublin 7*
Also to: *Solicitors for each notice party (*or *The notice party,*
             if not represented)
             Addresses

Motions in Common Law actions are brought in the Common Law
motions list. If the motion is for equitable relief, it is brought in Chancery
1 or Chancery 2 and, because of the discretionary nature of equitable
relief, a **grounding affidavit** must be filed setting out why the plaintiff
claims to be entitled to the relief.

CO-DEFENDANTS AND THIRD PARTIES

Any number of plaintiffs may bring an action, as long as the claim arises out of the same transaction or there is a common question of law. If, after proceedings have already started, a *plaintiff* believes he may be entitled to redress from someone other than the existing defendant, he may join one or more other *defendants*, known as **co-defendants**, to the proceedings using O. 15 of the **Rules of the Superior Courts**. A *defendant* who wishes to join a **third party** should use O. 16. Where an action has begun in the name of the wrong plaintiff, the Court may correct the mistake under O. 15 rule 2 RSC. (O. 15 rule 13 of the Rules says that no matter shall be defeated merely by the misjoinder or non-joinder of parties.)

With an Order 15 application by a plaintiff, there is a connection between the plaintiff and the new co-defendant. With the Order 16 procedure, there is no such link between the plaintiff and the third party, and there is a *new cause of action* between the defendant and the third party. If the Court eventually decides that the third party was entirely liable, the plaintiff can only succeed against him if he has joined him as a co-defendant.

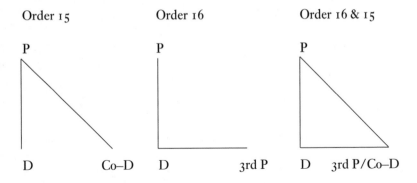

| Order 15 | Order 16 | Order 16 & 15 |

P   P   P

D   Co–D   D   3rd P   D   3rd P/Co–D

In *Gaspari* v. *Iarnrod Eireann*, Supreme Court, 15 December 1993, a train carrying pilgrims to Knock collided with a herd of cattle on the line. The plaintiff, who was a passenger on the train, sued Iarnrod Eireann alone, on the basis that they owed him a duty as a fare-paying passenger, both contractually and at Common Law, to take him safely to his destination. Just as the three year statutory limit was about to expire, Iarnrod Eireann brought a motion under O. 16 to join as third parties Michael Diskin and his son Patrick, respectively the owner of the land and the owner of the cattle, whom they believed would be wholly or partially liable.

If the plaintiff had allowed the two men to be joined as third parties, and the Court subsequently found that either or both of them were exclusively liable, the plaintiff could not recover his costs and could not sue either of the two men, because the action would be out of time. The plaintiff therefore decided to join the father and the son as co-defendants.

The High Court found that the father, who owned the land, had rented it to his son who kept his own cattle on the land. The father had not been responsible for the cattle being moved at the time of the accident, and was therefore not liable. The Court decided that Iarnrod Eireann was 30% liable and Patrick Diskin was 70% liable.

Because of the doctrine of joint and several liability, the railway company realised it could find itself paying all the damages, so it appealed to the Supreme Court. Iarnrod Eireann argued that, because the landowner owned the land, and it might be impossible to keep track of changes in ownership or occupation of the land adjoining the railway, he should be vicariously liable for the acts of negligence of anyone in occupation of the land. The Supreme Court said that this would require radical judicial intervention, and rejected the appeal.

Joinder of co-defendant (O. 15)

An application to add, strike out or substitute a plaintiff or defendant may be made at any time before trial by way of notice of motion. If the trial has already started, the application may be made directly to the Court. Where a large number of people have the same interest in a matter, one of them may sue or be sued as a representative of the others, and all will be bound by the judgment (O. 15 rule 9 RSC)

A **third party** joined under Order 16 RSC may have a duty of care to the defendant, but not to the plaintiff. If the plaintiff *wrongly* applies under O. 15 to join a third party as co-defendant, he will be liable for the third party's costs.

An application to join a co-defendant is brought by **motion on notice** in the Master's Court (O. 63 rule 1(12) RSC). The person on notice is the *existing* defendant, *not* the proposed co-defendant. The motion is grounded on an **affidavit** referring to the existing pleadings and explaining why the proposed co-defendant is liable to the plaintiff. The affidavit should also explain why the proposed co-defendant was not originally sued.

The Court will decide whether or not a party should be joined as co-defendant. The case of *Tromso Sparebank* v. *James Beirne*, Supreme Court, 15 December 1989 related to a claim for £8.8 million on two promissory notes allegedly endorsed by the manager of the Northern Bank in Carrick-on-Shannon. A manager in the London head office of the Midland Bank, which then owned the Northern Bank, confirmed the manager's signature. Midland later sold Northern Bank to the National Australia Bank. Midland was joined as a **co-defendant** to the proceedings, but claimed that the cause of action against it was an entirely separate and new cause of action which turned on different facts.

In the Supreme Court, McCarthy J disagreed. He said that if Midland had been in this jurisdiction, it would have been joined in the action without leave. That gave the Court ample jurisdiction within O. 11 rule 1(h). He said the making of an order joining Midland was, *prima facie*, a matter for the trial judge.

In *Allied Irish Coal Supplies Ltd* v. *Powell Duffryn International Fuels Ltd* [1998] 2 IR 519, the Supreme Court said that an existing defendant had a right to be heard about whether a new defendant should be joined, as it might well cause prejudice such as delay or unnecessary additional costs.

If the co-defendant is outside the jurisdiction, the application should contain the necessary proofs for an order for **service out of the jurisdiction**.

If the Court grants the O. 15 application, the plaintiff will have to file, take out and serve an **amended plenary summons** and **amended statement of claim** (O. 15 rule 15 RSC), and the existing defendant may have to file an **amended defence**. If the co-defendant fails to enter an **appearance** or **defence**, the plaintiff may seek a **motion for judgment in default**. All the parties to the action may make any of the usual interlocutory applications.

Joinder of third party (O. 16)

Where a defendant claims relief from another defendant in an action, he may serve notice of that claim without seeking permission and no appearance is necessary (O. 16 rule 12 RSC). Where a defendant claims that he is entitled to a contribution or indemnity from someone who is not already a party to the action, or that he is entitled to the same relief as the plaintiff, he may apply to join a third party within 28 days of delivery of the defence (O. 16 rule 1(3) RSC). Joinder of a third party is done by **motion on notice** to the plaintiff, *not* to the third party. This gives the plaintiff the opportunity to join the third party as co-defendant under O. 15. Although the Rules allow the motion to be brought *by consent* in the Master's Court, it will usually be brought in the Common Law motion list, within 28 days of the delivery of the **defence** or **reply**.

Section 27(1) of the Civil Liability Act 1961 says the notice must be served "as soon as is reasonably possible". In the case of *SFL Engineering Ltd* v. *Smyth Cladding Systems Ltd*, High Court, 9 May 1997, Kelly J said that the obligation to serve the notice as soon as reasonably possible was "mandatory in nature, and a failure to comply with that temporal obligation may lead to the application for liberty to issue and serve the third party notice being refused or, if granted, being set aside on the application of the newly-joined third party."

In *Connolly* v. *Casey*, High Court, 12 June 1998, Kelly J ruled that a defendant's failure to serve a third party notice as soon as reasonably possible did not bar him completely from recovering an indemnity or contribution, but such a claim would be subject to the discretion of the Court.

The **affidavit** grounding the **notice of motion** refers to the nature and grounds of the plaintiff's proceedings and to the **defence**, which would claim that the third party was wholly or partly responsible for the plaintiff's injury.

The **affidavit** must set out the facts which give rise to the third party's liability to indemnify the defendant. In *Johnston [a minor]* v. *Fitzpatrick* [1992] ILRM 269, a 10-year-old plaintiff had been injured when he ran into the road in front of a car. The defendant sought liberty to issue and serve a third party notice on the infant plaintiff's parents, claiming they had been negligent. But the Supreme Court said the boy was too old to support the allegation that the parents had contributed to his dash across the road. The Court said a third party notice could not be served unless the facts suggested that the proposed third party had contributed to the accident.

A third party outside the jurisdiction may not be joined

If a third party disputes the right of a defendant to join him in an action, he may enter an appearance to the third party notice without prejudicing his position. But in *Grogan* v. *Ferrum Trading Company*, High Court, 13 February 1996, Morris J said that, once a third party notice had been served, an appearance entered, a statement of claim sought and delivered and a defence to the third party statement of claim delivered, the parties would be entitled to assume that the procedure met with the approval of the third party. He said the delivery of the defence precluded the third party from applying to set aside the notice.

If the plaintiff consents to the joinder of the third party, he does not need to attend the hearing, but should simply consent in writing to the defendant. If he does attend Court, he will *not* be entitled to costs, except by special direction of the Court (O. 16 rule 1(2) RSC). If the plaintiff wishes to join the third party as a co-defendant, he should attend the hearing.

That right was challenged in the case of *Dowling* v. *Armour Pharmaceutical Co.* [1996] 2 ILRM 417. The defendant applied to join a company as third party but, at the hearing of the motion, the plaintiff applied to have the company joined as a co-defendant. The defendant claimed that O. 16 rule 1(2) merely dealt with the matter of costs and did not give the plaintiff the right to join a third party at the hearing.

But Morris J said the plaintiff had attended the motion in the expectation that the Court would deal with the application to join the company as a co-defendant, and it would be wrong to deny the plaintiffs their order on formal grounds. In any case, he said, under O. 15 rule 13 of the Rules, the Court could join a co-defendant at any stage of the proceedings.

Where a third party is joined by a defendant, the order will give liberty to serve the notice on the third party in the form of the draft exhibited in the affidavit grounding the application, based on the RSC Appendix C Form 1 (for a claim for relief) or Form 2 (for determination of an issue). This notice must be served within 28 days, with a copy of the originating summons and any pleadings to date.

The order will also fix the time for entry of appearance by the third party (normally within eight days of service), delivery of a **third party statement of claim** by the defendant to the third party (usually within 21 days of the third party's entry of appearance) and delivery of the third party's defence (normally within 28 days of delivery of the **statement of claim**). The order may direct that the issue between the third party and the defendant be tried at the hearing of the action between the plaintiff and the defendant – or whenever the trial judge directs.

Usually the issues between the plaintiff and the defendant, and between the defendant and the third party, will be tried at the same time. If the defendant and the plaintiff settle their action, the issue between the defendant and the third party may still proceed, as it is an entirely separate action.

If the third party fails to enter an appearance or defaults in his pleadings, he is bound by any judgment in the matter and is deemed to admit liability (O. 16 rule 5 RSC). A **motion for judgment in default of appearance** may then be brought by the defendant on notice to the third party. The third party will be unrepresented, so it will be a **motion for the sitting of the Court**, brought in the Common Law motion list under *Motions for judgment*.

The necessary proofs are the:

1   **order giving liberty** to join a third party,
2   **original third party notice**, issued from the Central Office and served,
3   **affidavit of service** of third party notice,

4   **certificate of no appearance** of third party,
5   **third party statement of claim**, filed in lieu of delivery,
6   **notice of motion** addressed to the third party and
7   **affidavit of service** of notice of motion on the third party.

The **third party** may seek further time to enter an appearance but, if he does not appear, the defendant will be granted judgment, amounting to a full indemnity against the third party in favour of the defendant.

If the **third party** fails to enter a defence, the defendant may bring a **motion for judgment in default of defence**. He will need the:

1   **order giving liberty** to join a third party,
2   **original third party notice**, issued from the Central Office and served,
3   **notice of entry of appearance** by the third party,
4   **third party statement of claim** with certificate endorsed that no defence has been delivered,
5   **affidavit of delivery** of third party statement of claim (if any),
6   **notice of motion** and
7   **affidavit of service** of notice of motion on third party.

The **third party** will probably be represented, so the motion will not be for the sitting of the Court. If he looks for an extension of time to put in a **defence**, it will be granted, with costs to the defendant. If the **third party** does *not* appear, judgment will be granted, giving a full indemnity to the defendant.

All the usual interlocutory orders (such as discovery and interrogatories) are also available against a **third party**.

If the Court finds that a defendant is only partly to blame for an accident, and a non-party (or **third party**) who wasn't sued is also partly liable, the plaintiff will be deemed to be contributorily negligent to that extent. The plaintiff should only decide *not* to sue a **third party** where the third party owes him no duty of care or contractual duty, or if he is not in breach of such a duty.

DISCOVERY

The purpose of discovery in civil cases (O. 31 RSC) is to enable one party to obtain information from the other side (or from anyone else – O. 31 rule 29 RSC) about *relevant* documents in his possession, custody or power before the hearing of the action. (Kinlen J pointed out in *Quinlivan* v.

Conroy [1999] 1 IR 271 that O. 31 rule 12 RSC makes no use of the word "procurement".)

In *Johnson* v. *Church of Scientology* [2001] IESC 16, the Supreme Court allowed an appeal against a High Court discovery order on the basis that the documents ordered to be discovered were not in the possession, custody or power of the defendants and the defendants had no enforceable legal right to obtain them.

Denham J said "Documents which are in the possession, custody or power of a party must be discovered. A document is in the power of a party when that party has an enforceable legal right to obtain the document. To this rule there may be rare exceptions. However, these rare exceptions are examples of the judge, in his or her discretion in the circumstances of a particular case, making a determination on the facts." The High Court order was based on the premise that the documents were in the possession of the English Church of Scientology Corporation, as agents of the first-named defendant.

But Denham J said that, on the basis of the facts in the application, the first-named defendant was a separate corporate body which had acted independently and not as agent for the Dublin Mission.

In *Stafford* v. *Revenue Commissioners*, Supreme Court, 27 March 1996, O'Flaherty J said "the most singular thing about discovery is that the documents sought to be discovered have to be relevant to the matter in issue."

If discovery is sought against an agency established by statute and the agency claims that disclosure would be contrary to the public interest, the Court will examine the documents and decide whether they should be discovered. But in *Murphy* v. *Flood* [1999] 3 IR 97, the Supreme Court said that where a statutory tribunal demanded documents and there were no Court proceedings in being, the Court would not intervene. Any infringement of fair procedures or constitutional rights could be corrected by judicial review proceedings.

Discovery ensures that one side cannot unfairly take advantage of the other and may thus simplify the issues, saving on time and costs. "Documents" may include papers, financial records, bank statements and books, including confidential material, such as tax returns. In *Fields* v. *Woodland Products Ltd*, Supreme Court, 16 July 1999, the Court said that, while tax returns were normally confidential to the taxpayer and the Revenue, that situation would change if the parties came to litigation.

"Documents" also include photographs, X-rays, computer disks, tape recordings, video recordings, e-mails or other materials which provide information.

It's estimated that up to 30 percent of the data stored on computers is never reduced to printed form, so discovery of electronically-stored material is vital – especially as the electronic version of a document may contain information that does not appear in the printed version.

In the United States, electronic evidence – especially e-mail – is now routinely sought as part of discovery (*Seattle Audubon Society* v. *Lyons*, 871 F Supp 1291 (WD Wash 1994), but few lawyers have experience of collecting or analysing the data which may be discovered.

It is vital that all parties be put on notice that electronic documents – as well as paper – should be produced. "Documents" should be defined to include data compilations, e-mail and any other electronically-stored data.

One of the most fruitful sources of evidence may be routine backup tapes, disks or CDs created by most companies to protect data in case of a system error. Weekly or monthly backups may be stored by some companies for a matter of years.

Computer users may also have material which has been transferred onto floppy disks or other portable media – particularly information which they may not wish to store on a company computer.

Home computers may also be a valuable source of material for discovery, particularly in the case of employees who log on to a company network from home. Laptops may also be useful sources of evidence, as they may be shared by a number of users.

In the United States, Courts have shown themselves willing to impose sanctions when electronic records are altered or destroyed once a party is on notice that such records are relevant to pending or threatened litigation. (*Computer Assoc International* v. *Am Fundware*, 135 FRD 166 (D Colo 1990).

Many files which have been deleted may still be recovered from hard drives and floppy disks. In the US case of *Playboy Enterprises Inc* v. *Terri Welles* (60 F Supp 2d 1050), the Court ruled that deleted e-mails were subject to discovery and appointed a neutral expert to recover the deleted files.

Any electronic data which is obtained on discovery should be protected from corruption or erasure by "write protection" and virus checking.

Anyone collecting computer data for evidentiary purposes should use whatever method would yield "the most complete and accurate results". In *Gates Rubber Co.* v. *Bando Chemical Indus Ltd*, 167 FRD 90, 112 (D Colo 1996), the Court criticised the plaintiff for failing to make image copies and properly preserve undeleted files.

As a general rule, discovery may only be sought when the pleadings are closed. *Exceptionally*, early discovery may be sought (for example in judicial review cases, where an applicant may apply for discovery before proceedings are issued, or in a complicated financial case, where documents may be discovered before a statement of claim has been delivered).

NEW DISCOVERY RULES

The Rules of the Superior Courts formerly permitted a person to apply for discovery without filing an affidavit. But in *Brooks Thomas Ltd* v. *Impac Ltd,* Supreme Court, 29 July 1998, Lynch J suggested that, because of the prevailing tendency to seek discovery in almost every case, the Superior Courts Rules Committee might consider changing O. 31 rule 12 to require an affidavit in every case.

SI 233 of 1999 substantially altered the procedure for discovery. Except in urgent cases, a motion for discovery may now be brought only if voluntary discovery has failed.

The new O. 31 rule 12(4) says that the Court *shall not* make an order directing discovery unless:

1   the applicant has sent a letter to the other side requesting voluntary discovery,
2   a reasonable period has been allowed for such discovery and
3   the person requested has failed, refused or neglected to make discovery, or has ignored the request.

The letter must state that discovery is being sought under O. 31 rule 12(4) and must specify the precise categories of documents sought and the reasons for seeking each category. The letter should also explain that discovery must be made in the same way as if ordered by the Court and that, if discovery is not made, an application may be made to the Court for an order under O. 31 rule 21.

In *Swords* v. *Western Proteins Ltd* [2001] 1 ILRM 481, Morris P said that, if a party disputed his obligation to make discovery, this letter would be used be the court to discover precisely why the documents had been sought and the grounds for believing that they might help dispose of the case fairly or save costs.

If the parties agree a time for making discovery and the deadline is not met, an application may be made to the Court for a discovery order. Providing that all the requirements have been followed, the Court may, "if it is satisfied that it is proper to do so", make whatever order appears just in the circumstances.

An application for discovery must be made within 28 days of the action being set down or listed for trial – although that time may be extended by the Court or the parties where it appears "just and reasonable" to do so.

A **motion for discovery** may be general or specific. Wide-ranging discovery may be appropriate in a complex case with a variety of issues, but the party seeking discovery is usually required to specify the documents he believes exist.

In *Controller of Patents, Designs and Trademarks* v. *Ireland*, High Court, 18 February 1999, the Court held that documents in respect of which an order for *specific* discovery had been refused could not be discovered under a *general* order for discovery.

In *McBride* v. *Galway County Council* [1998] 1 IR 485, Laffoy J refused to make an order for third party discovery which was "onerous both in terms of scope and in terms of the period of time" for which discovery was sought.

The Court will not allow a "fishing expedition", effectively forcing one party to make the case for the other. In *Galvin* v. *Graham-Twomey* [1994] 2 ILRM 315, O Flaherty J said the purpose of the discovery procedure was to help in the progress of litigation. It was not to be invoked to enable a person to plead a cause of action which he would not otherwise be in a position to plead. "He must set forth with some particularity in his pleadings the details of his complaint. He cannot be permitted to launch his proceedings and then hope by discovery to be able to amend his pleadings and thereby make his case."

In *Dunnes Stores Ireland & Others* v. *George Maloney and the Minister for Enterprise, Trade and Employment* [1999] 1 ILRM, the Minister had refused to explain why she had appointed an "authorised officer" under the 1990 Companies Act. Laffoy J said that, without knowing the reason for the appointment of the authorised officer, she could not decide whether the Minister had a right under the Act to obtain discovery of the documents sought. "The inclusion of the categories which are of a general nature gives the demand as a whole the hallmark of a trawl," she said. "That being the case, the only reasonable inference is that the demand was excessive in content".

But in the case of *McDonnell* v. *Sunday Business Post, Damien Kiberd and Ted Harding* [2000] IEHC 19, O'Sullivan J said: "The fact that a discovery may be comprehensive and wide ranging does not, of course, mean that *ipso facto* it is an exploratory or fishing operation. I would consider a fishing or exploratory operation to be one where there was no stated objective or delimitation by reference to the pleadings."

Discovery may not be sought of documents which were prepared in contemplation of the proceedings. But in cases involving, for example, road traffic accidents, discovery may be sought of maintenance, repair or "spy-in-the-cab" records. In an industrial accident where there have been previous similar accidents, documents might be sought relating to the defendant's past safety record.

If the plaintiff has been a claimant in a previous personal injury action, the defendant may request details of the previous accidents. Records of previous claims are now kept by some organisations to deter fraudulent claimants. In personal injuries actions involving local authorities, the plaintiff should seek discovery of all documents and records relating to any work in the area at the time of the alleged injury. In cases involving breach of contract, discovery may reveal a note or memorandum in writing, for the purpose of the Statute of Frauds.

All the documents sought should exist and be relevant. In *McDonnell* v. *Sunday Business Post*, which related to a libel claim, O'Sullivan J said that any document which came into existence after the date of publication of the offending article would only be discoverable if a draft, earlier edition or working papers relating to it existed at the time of publication.

In *Irish Shell* v. *Dan Ryan Ltd and Esso Ireland*, High Court, 22 April 1986, which involved an alleged breach of a solus trading agreement by Dan Ryan, an order for discovery was made against Esso. Shell said the affidavit of discovery failed to comply with the Rules. Esso accepted that the affidavit had incorrectly claimed privilege for correspondence, and a number of other documents should have been discovered and properly identified.

Costello J cited the judgment of Kenny J in *Sterling Winthrop Group* v. *Farbenfabriken Bayer* [1967] IR 97, in which he analysed the requirements of discovery under O. 31 rule 12. He said a discovery affidavit "must not merely comprise those documents which would support or defeat any issue in the case, but (also those documents) which could reasonably be said to contain information which might either directly or indirectly enable a plaintiff who has sought discovery to advance his own case or damage the case of a defendant." Costello J said the documents sought by Shell did not relate to the matter in question and need not be discovered.

In *McKenna* v. *Best Travel* [1995] 1 IR 577, Morris J said only documents which would tend to support or defeat matters in issue between the parties were subject to discovery. And in *Deutsche Bank* v. *Murtagh* [1995] 1 ILRM 381 Costello P said the Court also had power to order discovery in relation to assets outside the jurisdiction.

The Court will not normally make a second order for discovery against a party who has already made full discovery. In *Bula* v. *Tara and others* (No. 5) [1994] 1 IR 487, the first 14 defendants filed an affidavit of discovery. More than two years later, the plaintiffs sought further and better discovery.

The application related to documents which had not been in existence at the time of the motion for discovery. The plaintiffs said anyone who had sworn an affidavit of discovery had a continuing duty to swear further affidavits if additional relevant material came into existence before the trial. But Murphy J said a respondent discharged his obligation by swearing an affidavit which was correct at the date it was sworn.

The Supreme Court agreed and said a Court would only rarely order discovery of documents created after the swearing of an affidavit of discovery. The Court would only use that jurisdiction where the applicant:

1   specified the document sought,
2   could not obtain the document from any other source and
3   could prove that the document had a significant and important relevance of a specified or identifiable kind.

Discovery would not be ordered where the new document had arisen from the proceedings and was therefore privileged.

If a person swears in an affidavit that the documents sought are not in his power or possession, the Court will not generally go behind that affidavit. In *Phelan* v. *Goodman*, Supreme Court, 24 January 2000, Murphy J said that general rule would be qualified if it turned out that the person making the affidavit had misunderstood the the issues in the action or had wrongly come to the view that the documents were not relevant.

Discovery is not an alternative to oral evidence. In *McGee* v. *O'Reilly* [1996] 2 IR 229, Keane J said: "In our system of civil litigation, the case is ultimately decided having regard to the oral evidence adduced at the trial. The machinery of pleadings and particulars, while of critical importance in ensuring that the parties know the case that is being advanced against them and that matters extraneous to the issues as thus defined will not be introduced at the trial, is not a substitute for the oral evidence and witnesses and their cross-examination before the trial judge."

MOTION FOR DISCOVERY

A **motion for discovery** is brought in the Master's Court, on notice to the party from whom discovery is sought. The **notice of motion** should set out the precise documents required (unless general discovery is sought).

The motion is grounded on affidavit (O. 31 rule 12 (1) RSC):

1   verifying that discovery is necessary to dispose fairly of the matter or to save costs and

2   giving reasons why discovery is necessary for each category of
     documents.

The proofs required for a **motion for discovery** are:

1   copy of the **letter** requesting voluntary discovery,
2   **notice of motion** setting out the precise categories of documents
     required,
3   **grounding affidavit**.
4   **affidavit of service** of the notice of motion and affidavit and
5   **pleadings** to date.

The **motion for discovery** will appear in the Master's list on Tuesday,
Thursday or Friday under *Motions on notice*. He will consider the
relevance and *necessity* for discovery to ensure a fair trial. He will not make
an order unless he is given the name of the person who is required to
make discovery. If the party making discovery is a body corporate or local
authority, the Master should be given the name of the proper officer
authorised to make discovery on its behalf.

The Master has no power to order discovery where a party has failed to
comply with the rules. In *Swords* v. *Western Proteins Ltd*, [2001] 1 ILRM 481,
the plaintiff's solicitor had failed in his original letter to specify the precise
categories of documents sought and to give reasons why he was seeking
discovery of each category. When the defendant failed to produce the
documents, the Master granted an order of discovery. But, in the High
Court, Morris P said that the plaintiff had failed to comply with O. 34, so the
court did not have jurisdiction to make an order for discovery.

The **order of discovery** will contain:

1   the **terms of discovery** required,
2   the name of the **person who is to swear the affidavit** and
3   the **time limit** within which discovery is to be made

The Master may be asked to grant an order for **non-party discovery** against
someone who is not a party to the action, such as a bank (O. 31 rule 29 RSC).
This procedure *always* requires a **grounding affidavit** to establish:

1   the **documents** in the possession of the non-party,
2   their **relevance** and
3   the **necessity** of discovery for a fair trial.

The **notice of motion** must be served on *all* parties, in case anyone wants to claim privilege in relation to any documents. An order against a non-party will normally only be made where the documents are not discoverable elsewhere. The party seeking discovery must pay the costs of the non-party.

Non-parties may seek an undertaking that documents such as bank records will only be used for the purposes of the proceedings. But, even without such an order, anyone who misuses discovered documents may be liable to be attached for contempt. In *Ambiorix* v. *Murphy* [1992] 1 IR 277, Finlay CJ said: "A party obtaining the production of documents by discovery in an action is prohibited by law from making any use – of any description – of such documents or the information contained in them, otherwise than for the purpose of the action. To go outside that prohibition is to commit contempt of Court."

And in *Countyglen plc* v. *Carway* [1995] 1 IR 208, Murphy J said: "Discovery is made solely for the purposes of the particular litigation in which the order is made and ... the use or abuse of the information obtained in discovery for any other purpose would be a clear contempt of the Court and punishable accordingly."

But in *Roussel* v. *Farchepro Ltd* [1999] 3 IR 567, Kelly J gave leave to the plaintiffs to use material which had been discovered for the Irish action in other proceedings in Spain. The judge said the Court had a discretion to lift or modify the implied undertaking given in respect of materials produced on discovery.

And in *Doyle* v. *Commissioner of An Garda Siochana* [1999] 1 IR 249, Lagffoy J said that the Court would not refuse an order for discovery where the material disclosed would be used in proceedings outside the State as long as the Court could effectively control the use of the material by editing the documents or requiring an undertaking that they would only be used for the purpose for which discovery was granted.

If a defendant fails to comply with an order for discovery, his defence may be struck out. In *Radiac Abrasives* v. *Prendergast*, High Court, 13 March 1996, Barron J said that a party which deliberately concealed documents in its discovery could not, when it was found out, merely be allowed to amend its discovery. The proper remedy would be to strike out the defence.

But in *Murphy* v. *Donohoe and Fiat*, Supreme Court, 13 February 1996, Barrington J said a defence would only be struck out in an extreme case. He said O. 31 rule 21 existed, not to punish defaulters, but to facilitate the administration of justice by securing compliance with discovery orders.

An **appeal against a discovery order** by the Master lies to the Common Law motion list (in Common Law actions), or to the Chancery 1 or 2 list (in chancery or equity matters). On appeal, the **motion for discovery** will be heard afresh. Thereafter any appeal would be heard by the Supreme Court.

In *Decospan NV* v. *Benhouse Ltd* [1995] 2 ILRM 620, the defendants had their defence and counterclaim struck out by the Master for failure to make discovery. The High Court reinstated the defence and counterclaim under O. 37 rule 10, on terms that £30,000 be lodged in court as a sign of the defendant's *bona fides*. The Supreme Court upheld the High Court judge's action.

A person making discovery must swear an **affidavit as to documents** which refers to the affidavit's two schedules. **Part one** of the **first schedule** lists all the documents in the *power, possession or procurement* of the person making discovery. **Part two** of the **first schedule** lists the documents which he has in his *power, possession or procurement*, but over which he claims *privilege*.

In the past, a standard paragraph was often incorporated in this schedule claiming privilege for a general group of documents. But the Supreme Court has ruled that a detailed list of the privileged documents must be set out, so the other party can challenge any specific claim to privilege.

Even where a person does not physically have certain documents, they may still be in his "power and possession". In *Quigley* v. *Burke* [1996] 1 ILRM 469, the Supreme Court said that an accountant preparing accounts for an appeal against a tax assessment was an agent of the taxpayer. The taxpayer therefore had a right to demand any papers drawn up by the accountant, so the papers were within the power and possession of the taxpayer.

The **second schedule** sets out the documents which were once – but are no longer – within the *power, possession or procurement* of the party making discovery. This schedule should indicate where the documents may now be found, so a non-party application may be brought, if necessary.

The precedent for an "**affidavit as to documents**" is in Appendix C, No. 10 of the Rules. All relevant documents should be put in the schedule and described *precisely*. If there are no relevant documents in a particular schedule, the paragraph should say "*None*".

The person seeking discovery may then use the form in Appendix C No. 11 RSC to require production of the documents for inspection and copying. When the respondent receives a notice to produce documents, he has three days in which to deliver a notice to inspect (O. 31 rule 17 RSC).

Anyone making discovery is required to be scrupulously honest. If relevant documents are not discovered, the party failing to make full disclosure will *not* be allowed to rely on the undiscovered document at the trial. Deliberate failure to make discovery may be treated as contempt of Court.

PRIVILEGE

The privilege claimed in part two of the first schedule of the **affidavit as to documents** may include lawyer/client privilege, privilege against self-incrimination, marital privilege, police informer privilege, State privilege (public interest immunity) or sacerdotal privilege. If privilege is claimed, the Court may inspect the document to decide whether the claim is valid (O. 31 rule 20(2) RSC). In *O'Brien* v. *Ireland* [1995] 1 IR 568, O'Hanlon J said the legislature had power to extend privilege to specified categories of documents, as long as the legislation was not unconstitutional.

Sacerdotal privilege normally relates to the seal of confession. It has not yet been extended to non-Christian religions. In *Johnson* v. *Church of Scientology* [2001] IESC 16, sacerdotal privilege over counselling notes was refused by the High Court.

In *PB* v. *AL* [1996] 1 ILRM 154, Costello P said s.8 of the Adoption Act 1976 allowed An Bord Uchtála to claim privilege over documents relating to the suitability of prospective adoptive parents. The judge said that, where the Oireachtas had established documentary privilege by statute (and in effect established public policy), this took precedence over the Common Law rules of privilege. (Such privilege is, for example, established by s. 9 of the Family Law (Divorce) Act 1996, which makes evidence of attempts at reconciliation between spouses inadmissible in Court.)

But in *Skeffington* v. *Rooney*, Supreme Court, 13 March 1997, the Court said that the Garda Siochana Complaints Act 1986, which prohibits disclosure of confidential information about a complaint, did not confer any statutory privilege against discovery.

Even if a party successfully claims privilege on a document, secondary evidence can still be admitted. In *Calcraft* v. *Guest* [1898] 1 QB 759, a *copy* of a privileged document about fishery rights on the River Frome in Dorset was obtained by solicitors for the defence. The Court of Appeal said secondary evidence was admissible. Even if the document had been improperly or illegally obtained, it could still be admissible (although the owner of the original could seek an injunction to prevent the use of the copy, if he did so before it was produced in evidence).

The Court said that, once a document was privileged, it was *always* privileged. So, where a document is prepared for one set of proceedings, it's privileged in later litigation, even if the first proceedings don't go ahead.

In *Blunt* v. *Park Lane Hotel* [1942] 2 KB 253, the plaintiff sued for defamation after a hotel manager suggested she was a woman of easy virtue. The hotel sought discovery, but the defence said adultery was treated as a quasi-criminal offence, so a person could not be required to incriminate herself. Goddard LJ said no-one was bound to answer any question if the answer would:

1   in the *opinion* of the judge, have a
2   *tendency* to expose him to
3   *any criminal charge, penalty or forfeiture* which the judge regarded as
4   *reasonably likely* to be preferred or sued for.

But privilege can't be pleaded to avoid exposure to risk in a *civil* action. In *S* v. *E* [1967] 1QB 371, the alleged father of an illegitimate child claimed privilege concerning his relationship with the child's mother. (There was no allegation of rape.) The Court said civil affiliation proceedings were not intended to punish but to compel payment of maintenance. In *Westinghouse Uranium* v. *Rio Tinto Zinc* [1978] AC 547, the Court ruled that exposure to EU penalties could give rise to the privilege against self-incrimination.

In *Burke* v. *Central Independent Television* [1994] 2 ILRM 161, Murphy J rejected the notion of journalistic privilege. He also rejected a claim for privilege on the grounds that discovery could endanger lives, but he ordered that the documents should be shown only to the plaintiffs' lawyers, not to the plaintiffs themselves. That decision was overturned by the Supreme Court, which said the right to life and bodily integrity took precedence over the plaintiffs' right to vindication of their good name.

In *Fusco* v. *O'Dea* [1994] 2 ILRM 389, Lynch J refused to order the British Government to make discovery of documents in an extradition case, on the grounds of diplomatic immunity. The decision was upheld by the Supreme Court.

In *Miley* v. *Flood* [2001] 1 ILRM 489, Kelly J said a solicitor was not entitled to invoke legal professional privilege to refuse to identify his client. That principle might, however, be diluted where such iden-tification would incriminate the client or where the client's identity was so bound up with the nature of the advice sought that identifying the client would also identify the advice.

Legal professional privilege is a major exception to the general lack of privilege attaching to communications between professionals and their clients. In *R* v. *Derby Magistrates' Courts, ex parte B* [1995] 4 AER 526, Lord Taylor said: "(A) man must be able to consult his lawyer in confidence, since otherwise he might hold back half the truth. The client must be sure that what he tells his lawyer in confidence will never be revealed without his consent. Legal professional privilege is thus ... a fundamental condition on which the administration of justice rests."

But not everything discussed between a lawyer and his client is privileged and in the case of *Irish Press plc* v. *Ingersoll (No. 2)* [1994] 1 IR

208, the Supreme Court ordered discovery of relevant attendance notes and other memoranda prepared by solicitors.

Legal professional privilege is the *client's* privilege over two types of *confidential* communication (whether *oral* or *written*):

1   between client and lawyer for the purpose of *obtaining or giving legal advice* (but not legal *assistance*) and
2   between client and lawyer, or *client and third party*, or *lawyer and third party*, the *dominant purpose* of which is the preparation of contemplated or pending litigation.

In the case of *McMullen* v. *Carty*, Supreme Court, 27 January 1998, the Court ruled that, where a client subsequently sues his solicitor or counsel for negligence, he puts in issue communications between himself and his legal advisers, and therefore impliedly waives the privilege of confidentiality.

The privilege attaches to the communication, so the *client* can refuse to allow the lawyer or third party to produce the documents. "Lawyer" includes, not just a practising lawyer, but also foreign and in-house lawyers.

In *AM & S Europe* v. *Commission* (155/79) [1982] ECR 1575, the European Court held that certain correspondence between a client and an independent EU-based lawyer was privileged, but correspondence with an in-house lawyer or lawyer outside the EU was not. But in *Hilti* v. *Commission* (T7/89) [1991] ECR II 1711, the Court held that privilege *did* attach to an internal memorandum prepared by an in-house lawyer, reporting what an independent lawyer had said.

In *Alfred Crompton Amusement Machines* v. *Commissioners of Customs and Excise* [1972] 2 QB 102, the Court said communications between the Commissioners and their permanent salaried legal advisers to obtain evidence for *arbitration* proceedings were privileged, but other documents assessing purchase tax were not. The Court said it would inspect documents in case of doubt.

In *Silver Hill Duckling* v. *Minister for Agriculture* [1987] ILRM 516, the plaintiffs claimed a sum in compensation for slaughter of their flock of ducks after an outbreak of poultry disease. The Department of Agriculture offered a much lower sum in settlement. The plaintiffs sought discovery of documents, which the defendants resisted. O'Hanlon J said that the difference between the plaintiff's claim and the defendant's offer was so great that the dispute could obviously only be settled by litigation – so Court action must have been contemplated. He ruled that legal professional privilege attached to documents advising the Ministry on the claim, but refused the claim of privilege for other documents, on the basis of public interest.

Legal professional privilege only attaches to *confidential* documents. In *Bord na gCon* v. *Murphy* [1970] IR 301, the defendant instructed his solicitor to write a letter (not in contemplation of litigation) to the Bord. The Court said it was not a confidential exchange between the client and the lawyer (although, as hearsay, it was inadmissible anyway).

But in *Buckley* v. *Incorporated Law Society* [1994] 2 IR 44, Costello J ordered discovery of confidential documents concerning the Law Society's investigation of previous complaints against a solicitor. He said the solicitor's replies to the Law Society did not form part of the advice given to his clients and, even though the investigations were confidential, the documents should be discovered.

And in *Kennedy* v. *Law Society of Ireland* [2000] 2 IR 104, Kearns J said that, where the Law Society was carrying out an authorised investigation of a solicitor, legal professional privilege was not a valid ground of objection to disclosure of relevant documents on condition that:

1   the disclosure of the documents was truly necessary to ascertain whether the solicitor had complied with the accounts rules and
2   the material would not be used for any purpose except the investigation and any consequent proceedings.

Legal professional privilege extends to documents brought into existence to instruct a lawyer, but *not* to documents or things which came into existence *before* the client asked for the legal advice, even if the document is later sent to the lawyer.

In *Buttes Gas and Oil Company* v. *Hammer* (No. 3) [1980] 3AER 475, the Court said that, where a solicitor was instructed by two clients, communications between him and one client wouldn't be privileged against the other client insofar as they concerned the subject in which they were jointly interested.

Where the communication has more than one purpose, litigation must be the *predominant* purpose. In *Waugh* v. *British Rail Board* [1980] AC 521 the plaintiff's husband was killed while working on the railways. On the day of the accident, a brief report was made to the railway inspectorate, after which a joint inquiry report was prepared with witness statements and also sent to the inspectorate. The inspectorate then sent its own report to the Department of the Environment. The heading of the joint inquiry report said it had to be sent to the Board's solicitor for him to advise the Board.

The plaintiff sought discovery of the inspectorate's report. The House of Lords said it was prepared for two purposes – litigation and to inform the

Board how the accident happened so it could avoid similar accidents. The House of Lords said both purposes were equal. The evidence was not only relevant but was the best evidence, so disclosure was ordered.

In *Smurfit Paribas Bank* v. *AAB Export Finance* [1990] ILRM 588, the Supreme Court said the public interest did not justify the extension of legal professional privilege to communications to obtain legal *assistance* on the drafting of Court documents.

Fraud or dishonesty may defeat a claim of privilege. In *Murphy* v. *Kirwan* [1994] 1 ILRM 293, the plaintiff sought an order of specific performance against the defendant for sale of shares in a company. The defendant asked the Court to dismiss the case for showing no cause of action or for abuse of process. The defendant's motion was dismissed, as there was a full defence that the plaintiff had tried to forestall the defendant's sale of property connected with the shares. At the end of the plaintiff's evidence, Costello J dismissed his claim.

The defendant then sought discovery of all the documents concerning legal advice given to the plaintiff before and during the plaintiff's proceedings for his counterclaim. The plaintiff objected, but Costello J ordered discovery because "those guilty of moral turpitude or dishonest conduct, even though not fraud, cannot hide behind legal professional privilege."

Communications between the plaintiff and his solicitor were relevant to the counterclaim as, if the plaintiff had stated the facts correctly and been advised not to proceed, or had misstated the facts, this would suggest an abuse of process.

The judgment was upheld on appeal but, three months later, in *Bula* v. *Crowley (No. 4)* [1994] 1 ILRM 495, the Supreme Court refused to order discovery of correspondence between the defendant and his lawyers. The plaintiff claimed he had suffered loss by the defendant's negligence, but the Court distinguished between negligence and the criminal behaviour in the **Murphy** case.

Section 45 of the Courts and Court Officers Act 1995 authorises the Rules Committee to make rules concerning disclosure by litigants in personal injuries action, even though such disclosure might affect legal professional privilege.

Generally communications between parties to *civil* proceedings are *not* privileged, but where both sides are negotiating in an attempt to reach a settlement, any document or statement made in negotiations is generally inadmissible as evidence. Any communication aimed at settlement should be marked with the words "without prejudice", but a letter initiating such discussions is privileged, even if not marked "without prejudice". Equally, a letter marked "without prejudice" may not be privileged.

In *Greencore Group plc* v. *Murphy* [1995] 3 IR 520, Keane J said: "It may well be that documents which *prima facie* are protected by the 'without prejudice' rubric may on inspection turn out not to be so protected ... Since the primary object of the rule is to ensure that a party is not embarrassed by having admissions made by him solely for the purpose of settlement negotiations subsequently used to his detriment in litigation, it is obvious that statements which relate solely to future conduct, and could not be regarded as admissions made as part of an offer of settlement, would not necessarily be protected from disclosure."

It's usual to include the words in the letter but a document which only *initiates* negotiations, even without an offer, is still privileged. If the correspondence does not fall into this category, the words "without prejudice" are meaningless. A "without prejudice" document isn't liable for discovery without the consent of the maker *and* the receiver.

But the Court may examine "without prejudice" documents to decide if an agreement has been reached (*Tomlin* v. *STC* [1969] 1 WLR 1378).

A letter marked "without prejudice as to costs" is inadmissible on liability, but may be admitted on costs to show the unreasonableness of the behaviour of the party who did not accept the offer, taking the final outcome of the case into consideration.

The Courts have refused privilege to documents between other professionals and their clients. But in *ER* v. *JR* [1981] ILRM 125, the Court said a minister of religion acting as a marriage counsellor came within the privilege. It said advice given by a minister of religion had an added dimension not given by lay people.

The power of the Court to order discovery was considered in *Ambiorix* v. *Minister for the Environment* [1992] IR 277. The plaintiff property companies had sought a declaration that a decision taken by the Minister for the Environment to declare a site in George's Quay a "designated area" was *ultra vires*, on the basis that it had been reached on a consideration of incorrect or insufficient material.

In the High Court, Lardner J ordered discovery of documents on which the decision was based. The defendants appealed on the basis that the documents were subject to Cabinet confidentiality and were absolutely privileged in the public interest. They said documents coming from civil servants not below the rank of assistant secretary, and intended for the Government, should not be examined by a judge unless he was dissatisfied with the accuracy of the documents' description. They asked the Supreme Court to reconsider *Murphy* v. *Dublin Corporation* [1972] IR 215 and to rule that some of the principles decided in that case were wrong.

The Supreme Court dismissed the appeal, and upheld the decision in *Murphy*, which it said was of fundamental constitutional origin. Finlay CJ said that, under the Constitution, it was up to the Courts to resolve any conflict about whether the public interest was better served by the production of documents or by their confidentiality. (These constitutional principles do not apply in Britain.)

The Chief Justice said a person's right to challenge Government decisions depended on his right to use Court procedures, including discovery. But the Supreme Court later decided that certain documents, such as those relating to discussions in Cabinet, will *always* be privileged (*Attorney General* v. *Hamilton No. 1* [1993] 2 IR 250). The Government subsequently announced it would limit that immunity by legislation.

In *Corbett* v. *DPP* [1999] 2 IR 179, O'Sullivan J said no generally applicable class of documents was exempted from production because of the rank or position in the public service of the person who created or intended to use the documents.

In *Incorporated Law Society* v. *Minister for Justice* [1987] ILRM 42, the plaintiffs wanted to inspect a letter sent by the Minister for Justice to the Minister for Industry Commerce and Energy, and the reply. Privilege was claimed in the second part of the first schedule to the affidavit of discovery. Murphy J read the letters and said there was nothing in them which had any special potential for damage in the proper administration of the public service. He said the injustice to the plaintiffs of denying them access to the letters was greater than the potential damage to the public service, and he ordered discovery.

In *O'Brien* v. *Ireland* [1995] 1 IR 568, O'Hanlon J ruled that documents relating to an inquiry into the death of a member of the Defence Forces in Lebanon were exempt from production on the basis of statutory privilege. He said the ultimate power of the Court to decide what documents should be discovered was not intended to interfere with the power of the legislature to grant privilege to certain categories of document.

But in *Walker* v. *Ireland* [1997] 1 ILRM 363 – concerning discovery of documents supplied by the UK Attorney General to the Irish Attorney General in the Fr Brendan Smyth extradition case – Geoghegan J ruled that there was no absolute privilege against disclosure in relation to confidential communications between sovereign states. In order to succeed in such a claim, the party claiming privilege would have to show that disclosure would give rise to some particular injury to the public interest.

And in *Haughey* v. *Mr Justice Moriarty* [1999] 3 IR 1, Geoghegan J said that an alleged public interest in the confidentiality of a document was not normally a ground for refusing discovery. If an order for discovery was made, the document must be listed in the ordinary way, but privilege could be claimed in respect of it. He added that there was no obligation on a judge to examine a document before deciding it was exempt from production; in many cases, the Court would uphold a claim to privilege merely on the basis of a description of a document's nature and contents.

The person swearing the affidavit of discovery must categorise and enumerate each document for which privilege is claimed. But in *Irish Haemophilia Society* v. *Judge Lindsay*, ITLR, 11 June 2001, Kelly J said to describe them in any greater detail would run the risk of diluting – or even destroying – the privilege asserted.

MOTION FOR FURTHER AND BETTER DISCOVERY

If discovery is thought to be inadequate, or if a claim of privilege is contested, a **motion for further and better discovery** may be brought in the Master's Court, on notice to the person failing to make full discovery or claiming privilege. It's based on a grounding affidavit which refers to the Master's order (or the agreement to make voluntary discovery) and to the need for discovery of further material.

In *Bula Limited (in receivership)* v. *Crowley* [1991] 1 IR, Finlay CJ said that: " ... before making any order for further discovery (a Court) should not, in particular, permit the opposing party to indulge in an exploratory or fishing operation."

The Court may, at any stage, order a party to state on affidavit whether he ever had a specific document and, if not, what happened to it (O. 31 rule 20(3) RSC).

The test for a **motion for further and better discovery** (as for any discovery motion) is the *relevance* of the documents to the issues. If the party from whom discovery is sought claims not to have the documents, he has to swear an affidavit saying so.

In *Irish Permanent* v. *Utrecht Consultants*, Supreme Court, 31 October 1996, Murphy J refused to set aside a High Court decision refusing additional discovery. Adopting the test in *Compagnie Financière du Pacifique* v. *Peruvian Guano Co.* [1882] 11 QBD 55, he said the proposed documents "would not advance the case of the defendants or damage that of the (plaintiff) or put the defendants on a train of inquiry which would have either consequence".

MOTION FOR ATTACHMENT AND COMMITTAL

A person who deliberately fails to comply with an order for discovery is in contempt of Court, and an application may be made for his **attachment and committal** to prison (O. 31 rule 21 RSC). Attachment involves the gardai bringing the person in contempt before the Court to explain his failure to comply with the Court order. If his explanation is not satisfactory, he may be committed to prison until he purges his contempt. Purging involves an apology and an undertaking to comply with the order of the Court.

Before bringing a **motion for attachment and committal**, a copy of the Court order *with a penal endorsement* must be served on the person or his solicitor (O. 41 rule 8 of the RSC). This endorsement says: "*If you, the within-named (name), neglect to obey this judgment or order by the time therein limited, you will be liable to process of execution, including imprisonment, for the purpose of compelling you to obey the same order or judgment.*" (A solicitor who fails to tell his client about an order for discovery is also liable for attachment.)

In the case of failure to make discovery, a defendant obviously can't produce the required document if he's in jail, but in the case of a third-party, attachment and committal may be the only practical remedy.

If the *plaintiff* fails to make proper discovery, the defendant may bring a **motion staying proceedings** until discovery is made, or a **motion for dismissal for want of prosecution**. If the *defendant* is at fault, the plaintiff may bring a **motion to strike out the defence** for failure to make discovery (O. 31 rule 21 RSC). These motions are grounded on an affidavit exhibiting the Master's order and stating that the notice party is in default. Unless there has been persistent refusal to make discovery, the defaulter may be allowed more time, but he will not be allowed to reopen the original **motion for discovery**.

If, after the Master directs that discovery be made within a particular period, it is still not made, he will not re-hear the matter, but will order that the defence be struck out or proceedings be stayed. If the defence is struck out, a **motion for judgment in default of defence** may be brought and the defendant will not be granted an extension of time to file a new defence.

INTERROGATORIES

Interrogatories, which are also dealt with under O. 31, are written questions, normally to the defendant, aimed at obtaining admissions to limit the opponent's case. They may be used in any case seeking damages or where the plaintiff alleges fraud or breach of trust. The purpose of interrogatories is to obtain information about issues in the action or to relieve the plaintiff of proof of matters which may be expensive to prove or about which the defendant has special or sole knowledge. **Interrogatories** are drafted as leading questions, allowing only a yes or no answer, and must relate only to relevant issues. The answers, which are made on oath, are binding at the hearing of the action.

In *Bula* v. *Tara Mines (No. 9)* [1995] 1 ILRM 401, the plaintiffs originally sought liberty to deliver interrogatories comprising 479 questions against four defendants. Lynch J said the basic purpose of **interrogatories** was to avoid injustice where one party had the knowledge and ability to disprove important facts which the other party did not have the knowledge or ability to prove at all or without undue difficulty. **Interrogatories** must relate to facts in issue (or facts reasonably relevant to establishing facts in issue). **Interrogatories** about evidence, opinions or matters of law were not permissible. A Court was not required to go through **interrogatories** which were prolix, oppressive or unnecessary to decide which were admissible. It could disallow them as a whole, even though some might be proper.

In *Mercantile Credit* v. *Heelan* [1994] 1 ILRM 406, the plaintiffs claimed they had been induced to make loans by the defendants' fraud and they required the third-named defendant, a solicitor, to answer interrogatories relating to 33 loans. He was asked to identify documents, confirm journal entries and give information about security for the loans and about his instructions. He refused and the plaintiffs brought a motion requiring him to answer.

Costello J refused the order. He said actions begun by plenary summons were heard on oral evidence and the use of affidavit evidence was an exception which must be justified by some special exigency in the interests of justice. **Interrogatories** seeking information must relate to issues raised in the pleadings and could not be used to prove the case of the inter-rogating party. Admissions should first be sought informally by letter or under O. 32 rules 1–9. If they were refused, an application could be made under O. 31. The Court would normally grant the order if the admissions were sought merely to prove formally documents identified in an affidavit of discovery and in the possession of the interrogated party. An order should be refused if it might prejudice a fair hearing of the issues.

The plaintiff may deliver one set of **interrogatories** at any time after delivering his statement of claim, or a defendant may do so when delivering his defence, without seeking a Court order. The list of **interrogatories** – in the form of Appendix C Form 8 RSC – should be delivered to the person who is to answer them, with a notice stating that they must be answered under oath, and saying that, unless an answer is received within a specified period, an application will be made to Court to obtain **liberty to deliver interrogatories**. If the person receiving the interrogatories considers the questions unsuitable, he may ask the Master to decide on the questions to be asked.

If the defendant refuses to answer the **interrogatories**, the plaintiff may bring a **motion on notice** in the Master's Court (O. 63 rule 1(6) RSC), setting out the nature of the proceedings and the **defence** filed. The application may be grounded on an affidavit in a complicated case. The motion will:

1   explain why the **interrogatories** are necessary,
2   exhibit the **letter and the notice** requesting a response, and
3   seek permission to **deliver the interrogatories**.

The defendant may serve a **replying affidavit** within seven days giving reasons why the **interrogatories** should not be answered. He may claim they do not relate to any cause, they would be too expensive to answer, or that they are too wordy, irrelevant, scandalous or not *bona fide* (O. 31 rule 6 RSC).

The Master will examine each **interrogatory** and decide which (if any) to allow, taking into account any offer to deliver particulars, make admissions or produce documents (O. 31 rule 2 RSC). If he makes an order granting **liberty to deliver interrogatories**, he fixes a time for reply (normally 10 days). The name of the person to answer them is stated in the order (as in an order for discovery). The interrogatories should be answered in the form of Appendix C Form 9 RSC. If the respondent fails to comply with the order, a motion may be brought for an order compelling adequate answer (O. 31 rule 11 RSC).

In *Quilligan v. Sugrue*, High Court, 13 February 1984, the plaintiff claimed damages for injuries which he claimed resulted from being dragged along the road by the defendant's truck. The plaintiff said he could not remember what happened and the Master ordered the defendant to answer **interrogatories** about the details of the incident. On appeal, Hamilton J said the accident had been witnessed by three people and investigated by the gardai, so **interrogatories** were not necessary under O. 31 rule 2 "for the purpose of disposing fairly of the cause or matter". He allowed the appeal and restricted the interrogatory to one question: was the defendant driving his truck on a certain date in a certain place?

LODGMENTS

In jury and admiralty actions, a defendant may lodge money in Court in satisfaction of the plaintiff's claim at any time after entering an appearance and before the matter is set down for trial (O. 22 RSC). A *plaintiff* may also lodge money in respect of a **counterclaim**.

Substantial amounts of money are held by the Courts as lodgments. In 2001, the Courts Service reported that the Courts were managing lodgments totalling £45 million. As an alternative to lodging money in Court, certain parties may make an **offer of tender of payment**. They include a government minister, the Attorney General, a party indemnified by the State, an authorised insurance company and the Motor Insurers' Bureau.

In actions for libel, slander or title to land, money may not generally be paid into Court without admission of liability (O. 22 rule 1(3) RSC). But in *Norbrook Laboratories Ltd* v. *SmithKline Beecham (Ireland) Ltd* [1999] 2 IR 192, Kelly J ruled that a defendant in defamation proceedings could make a lodgment with an admission of liability relating to a specified part of a plaintiff's claim.

A lodgment may be topped up once at least *three* months before the action is first listed for hearing and on notice to the plaintiff, who may accept the payment within 14 days by giving notice to the defendant in the form of Appendix C Form No. 6 RSC. Thereafter, a lodgment may be made by permission of the Court and on notice to the plaintiff. A plaintiff may similarly lodge money in satisfaction of a counterclaim.

In *Donohoe* v. *Dillon* [1988] ILRM 654, Rita Donohoe claimed damages from a taxi driver who knocked her down outside Dublin Airport. The defence was delivered with a £5 lodgment. The lodgment was increased to £13,001 seven months later, four weeks after the case was first listed in the Legal Diary. The case was eventually listed for trial eight months after the second lodgment and the jury awarded £89,651 damages, but found the plaintiff 90% liable, giving a final award of £8,965.10, which was below the final lodgment. Lynch J said the case was "first listed for hearing" within the meaning of O. 22 rule 1(2) when it was included in a list of cases to be heard on a specified day and date, even though the chances of it actually beginning on that date might be remote. That date was five days before the hearing began, so the issue of costs was governed by O. 22 rule 6.

If there are several causes of action, the lodgment notice must specify the action(s) to which payment relates. The notice, which becomes part of the pleadings, must specify whether liability is admitted or denied (O. 22 rule 1(5) and 1(6) RSC).

In a personal injuries case (and other limited non-jury actions set out in s.1(1) of the Courts Act 1988), the defendant may lodge a sum, on notice to the plaintiff, at the time of delivery of the **defence** or within *four* months of the date of the **notice of trial**. No mention of the lodgment should be made in the **defence**. The lodgment may only be topped up by permission of the Court – unless the plaintiff serves the defendant with further particulars after the four month period, in which case the defendant may top up the lodgment within 21 days of receipt of those particulars, without leave of the Court but on notice to the plaintiff.

The defendant may also top up the lodgment without leave if more than 18 months has expired since the notice of trial. The lodgment must be on notice to the plaintiff and within 21 days of the expiry of the 18-month period. If the plaintiff does not accept the money, the lodgment does not take effect until two months after the money was paid into Court (O. 22 rule 1(10) RSC).

In *Rhatigan* v. *Gill*, High Court, 16 December 1998, the defendant claimed he did not have enough information to allow him to lodge a realistic amount in Court. He applied to increase the lodgment after unsuccessful negotiations, but the Court ruled that it would be unfair to allow an increase in the lodgment.

If the matter goes to trial and the plaintiff fails to beat the lodgment in damages, the excess is repaid to the defendant and the balance retained in Court to pay costs. The plaintiff is entitled to the costs of the action until the date of the lodgment, but will be liable for the defendant's costs thereafter (O. 22 rule 6 RSC).

Before the abolition of jury trials in High Court personal injuries cases, the **defence** revealed that a lodgment had been made (though not the amount). The judge therefore knew that there had been a lodgment, but the jury was not told. (In the Circuit Court, where a judge has to decide liability *and* quantum, the **defence** would *not* refer to the lodgment.) Since the abolition of juries in High Court personal injury cases, the **defence** no longer refers to the lodgment, so the judge remains unaware of it but a judge may ask "for good or sufficient reason" whether a lodgment was made (O. 22 rule 1(8) RSC).

In *King* v. *La Lavia*, Supreme Court, 16 December 1997, the Court had decided that the plaintiffs were entitled to be rewarded by the Commissioners for Public Works for their discovery of three Spanish Armada wrecks. Counsel for the Commissioners refused to disclose to the Court the amount of the lodgment they had made, so the Court refused to take the lodgment into account when awarding the full costs of the action to the plaintiffs.

If a client decides *not* to accept a lodgment, he should confirm his refusal in writing (and the instructing solicitor should keep a record of any such refusal at settlement negotiations). Where a notice of acceptance of money lodged is served in an action which has been set down for hearing (O. 22 rule 4 RSC), a Court order for payment out is not required. But before applying to the accountant, the chief registrar should be informed in writing that the action has been settled.

In cases involving infants (or death where there are infant dependants of the deceased) or persons of unsound mind, the Court must rule on any lodgment or settlement offer (O. 22 rule 10 RSC).

The procedure for ruling on a **lodgment**, which is governed by s. 63 of the Civil Liability Act 1961, is different from a ruling on a **settlement**. If the *Court* decides to refuse the lodgment after a s.63 application, the infant plaintiff or dependant will not be penalised in costs.

S.63 applications are brought *ex parte*, grounded on an affidavit sworn by the next friend of the infant or, in a fatal case, by the plaintiff bringing the action on behalf of the statutory dependants of the deceased (as set out in the Civil Liability Act 1961).

The affidavit states the name, age, address and occupation of the deponent and refers to:

1   the **pleadings to date** when produced
2   brief **details of the claim,**
3   the defendant's **lodgment** and **notice of lodgment**, when produced,
4   the **infant's birth certificate** and the **consent of the next friend** to act (or, in fatal injuries cases, the death, marriage and birth certificates of any statutory dependants) and
5   **Counsel's opinion** on liability and quantum.

If the deceased was unmarried and the claimants are his parents or siblings, the marriage and birth certificates should be exhibited, using the long form of the birth certificates. The originals of birth/death certificates or waivers must be exhibited; copies will not be accepted. In a fatal case, an actuarial report concerning loss of dependency and apportionment among the dependants should be exhibited, although the judge is not bound to accept the figures. Counsel's original opinion must be lodged with the papers, but not exhibited, following a direction by Kinlen J on 11 April 1994.

In the case of an infant or fatal *settlement offer*, the affidavit follows the same form as the s.63 affidavit, except that the affidavit refers to the *settlement offer*, not to a *lodgment*. A settlement cannot be ruled unless the defendant has entered an appearance, as these are consent applications.

In a fatal injuries case, the Court *may* be required to approve the amounts (in the case of infant dependants), but it *must* always apportion the damages among the statutory dependants. Money paid into Court in a fatal injuries case cannot be paid out without an order of the Court (O. 22 rule 13 RSC).

Damages for pain and suffering are not recoverable in a fatal injuries case; the only damages recoverable are for mental distress and loss of dependency. The £7,500 limit for damages for injury or mental distress caused by the death of a close relative, spouse or long-term partner as a result of a wrongful act was increased to £20,000 by the Civil Liability (Amendment) Act 1996. The Court now takes into account whether the claimant had a right to be financially maintained by the deceased person. Divorced spouses may also claim damages, but not for mental distress.

The Court should apportion the two amounts *separately* among the dependants. If any members of the family waive their entitlement, the waivers should be exhibited in the affidavit. Only a person of full age and sound mind, memory and understanding may waive his entitlement.

Lodgment and settlement applications are listed as *Ex parte applications in which papers have been lodged* because the papers are lodged in Court in advance. The application appears in the Monday list and the other side is notified so that they can consent to judgment in the amount of the settlement or lodgment.

After the defendant's representative – usually a solicitor – has consented to judgment in the agreed sum, he leaves court so that Counsel for the plaintiff can draw the judge's attention to all aspects – including the weaknesses – of the plaintiff's case.

If the time for acceptance of a lodgment (14 days) has passed before the matter comes to Court, the defendant's solicitor will need to give formal consent to late acceptance of the lodgment.

8. Injunctions

An injunction is a Court order directing a party to do – or to refrain from doing – a particular act. It is enforceable by committal to prison for contempt of Court. Injunctions are an equitable relief and so the laws of equity apply. Equitable remedies:

1   are **discretionary**,
2   are granted where a Common Law remedy (such as damages) would be **inadequate** or is **unavailable** and.
3   act *in personam* rather than *in rem*.

Equitable relief will not normally be granted if

- there has been delay (*laches*) or acquiescence by the plaintiff,
- the Court would have to supervise the injunction,
- the action relates to a contract for personal service,
- the order would be futile or
- the plaintiff does not come with "clean hands".

As soon as proceedings have been issued, an **interim injunction** may be sought *ex parte* to protect the plaintiff's legal rights by restraining a threatened action. The judge may decide that the matter may more conveniently be dealt with by an early trial, rather than an injunction (O. 50 rule 2 RSC).

The Court has wide powers to order (O. 50 RSC):

- the **preservation or interim custody** of the subject matter of the action,
- the **sale** of perishable goods,
- the **detention, preservation or inspection** of property,
- **samples** to be taken or **observations** made for the purpose of gathering information or
- **inspection** of any object.

The Supreme Court, in the case of *Attorney General* v. *Lee* [2001] 1 ILRM 553, ruled that the courts had an inherent jurisdiction to grant an injunction or other remedy to enforce the law where other remedies were inadequate and it was just and convenient to do so.

An **interim injunction** is normally granted for only a few days, to maintain the *status quo* until the defendant has an opportunity to give his side of the story.

An **interlocutory injunction** may also be sought, by **motion on notice** to the defendant, to restrain *or compel* an act pending the trial of the action.

A permanent injunction may be granted at the end of the case if the plaintiff establishes that his legal right has been infringed and damages are not an adequate remedy.

Because an application for an interim injunction is, of necessity, *ex parte* (O. 50 rule 7 RSC), the summons is issued in the Central Office *but not served*. The facts are set out in an **affidavit**, and a **notice of motion** is prepared for the interlocutory application. The affidavit is filed in the Central Office before the application is made in Court.

There is a requirement of **uberrimae fidei** (utmost good faith), so Counsel must reveal *all* the facts, even those which may damage his own case. The Court must be told about any relevant prior history, including all correspondence and undertakings (although previous breaches of undertakings may indicate that the defendant is unreliable).

The Court will require the:

1   sealed **original summons,**
2   certified **copy of the affidavit,**
3   **original exhibits** referred to in the affidavit and
4   **draft notice of motion,** ready for issue.

Counsel should inform the registrar in Chancery Court 1 or 2 that he plans to make an *ex parte* application – normally when the Court sits or rises (at 11am, 1pm, 2pm or 4pm).

Counsel opens the summons to the Court, refers to the substantive claim, gives a brief history of the facts and opens the affidavit and any law. The relevant law is the test in *Campus Oil* v. *Minister for Industry* [1983] IR 82, which says the Court must consider:

1   whether there is a **fair question to be tried** (not the *Cyanamid* test of a *prima facie* case and likelihood of success),
2   the **balance of convenience** (or possible prejudice to the plaintiff or defendant) and
3   whether **damages** would be an **adequate remedy.**

The affidavit includes:

1   the **facts** leading to the application, exhibiting any relevant documents,
2   the substantive facts, including how the **balance of convenience** favours the plaintiff,
3   why damages would be an **inadequate remedy**,
4   a reference to the **draft notice of motion** for interlocutory relief and
5   the plaintiff's **undertaking as to damages**.

The affidavit should not specify the potential financial damage to the plaintiff, as the Court may refuse an injunction if the defendant appears capable of paying the specified figure. In *Ryanair Ltd* v. *Aer Rianta cpt*, ITLR, 19 March 2001, the plaintiff's affidavit quantified the financial damage which might be suffered. Kelly J said that damages would provide a complete remedy and the defendant was capable of paying the sum specified, so he refused the injunction.

The **notice of motion** should list the reliefs which the plaintiff will seek at the *interlocutory* stage, even though they might not all be required at the interim stage.

In *Premier Dairies* v. *Doyle* [1996] 1 ILRM 363, the Supreme Court said that the role of the Court in an application for an interlocutory injunction was to adjudicate in as concise a manner as possible on the facts before the Court, and resist any temptation to give even tentative conclusions on the matters in contention in the main litigation.

The Court may order that the defendant be informed of the injunction by phone or fax, confirmed by letter. The Court registrar should be asked to initial the draft notice of motion, as the Central Office won't normally issue it without four clear days' notice. (This is required whether seeking interim relief or short service.)

The defendant should be personally served with the summons, notice of motion, affidavit, letter confirming the injunction and, if possible, a copy of the order with the penal endorsement. The summons must be endorsed with the particulars of service within three days.

Where a dispute is ongoing and there's not likely to be any infringement before the next motion day – or where there's been delay in seeking the injunction – Counsel might seek liberty to **issue short notice of motion**, instead of an interim injunction. The motion would then be returnable for the next motion day (without the normal four days' notice).

The application for the **interlocutory injunction** is made on the return date. Since the defendant will not have a solicitor on record, the motion will be for the sitting of the Court. The motion, which will be heard in Chancery 1 or 2, is *not* listed separately, so the registrar should be informed that it is a motion for the sitting of the Court.

If the defendant does not appear at first or second calling, the case will take its place in the list. The interlocutory application is similar to the interim application except that, where the application is for a mandatory injunction, an applicant must show more than a mere arguable case (*per* Lynch J in *ICC Bank* v. *Verling* [1995] 1ILR 123).

In *Ó Murchú t/a Talknology* v. *Eircell Ltd* [2001] IESC 8, Geoghegan J said the Court should be very slow to grant mandatory interlocutory injunctions. He gave the example: "If a plaintiff is looking for a mandatory injunction requiring a wall to be knocked down, he may in fact be attempting to obtain at an interlocutory stage what effectively is his final relief. Once the wall is gone it may not be practicable to rebuild it."

If the defendant is not represented, the Court should be asked for liberty to notify him of the interlocutory order by phone, fax or letter. The order with the penal endorsement should be served on the defendant as soon as possible.

If the defendant seeks time to put in a replying affidavit, the *status quo* may be preserved by continuing the interim injunction in the meantime or by an undertaking from the defendant. Alternatively, the defendant may consent to the granting of the interlocutory injunction, in which case the Court may make a consent order and reserve the costs to the trial. But, even if the defendant does give an undertaking, the solicitor should still serve the defendant with a copy of the Court order with the penal endorsement, so that if he breaks his undertaking, he can be attached and committed for contempt.

If the defendant is contesting the plaintiff's right to seek an interlocutory injunction, he will have to file a replying affidavit. If the application is adjourned by consent, the Court should be asked to fix a time limit for the filing of the defendant's affidavit, so the plaintiff has an opportunity to consider the defendant's affidavit and file a replying affidavit before the adjourned date.

A permanent injunction is a *substantive* relief, whereas interim and interlocutory injunctions are *ancillary* to the substantial relief sought. Permanent injunctions, which are often sought in cases such as trespass or nuisance, are only granted after full plenary hearings, so the defendant will be represented. But the Court's final order with the penal endorsement *must* be personally served on the defendant to ensure that it can be quickly enforced if he fails to obey it.

MAREVA INJUNCTIONS

A Mareva injunction (named after *Mareva Compania Naviera SA* v. *International Bulkcarriers SA* [1980] 1AER 213) is a freezing order, designed to prevent the removal or dissipation of assets to defeat enforcement of the successful party's judgment. The injunction may also be used to preserve the assets of a party ordered to pay costs.

The Supreme Court has laid down a dual test for the granting of a Mareva:

1   does the plaintiff have an arguable case which establishes the like-lihood of success (unlike the *Campus Oil* test) and
2   is the defendant likely to dispose of his assets deliberately to prevent a plaintiff recovering damages, and not just in the ordinary course of business?

The plaintiff must satisfy the Court that the defendant has assets in the jurisdiction and will remove them or dispose of them in some way. The Court must also be satisfied that, if the defendant disposes of his assets, the plaintiff will be unable to execute judgment against him.

The balance of convenience must be in favour of granting the injunction. If the defendant were to admit that he was about to leave the jurisdiction and refused to give an undertaking to the Court about a possible judgment, the balance of convenience would clearly lie with the plaintiff. But if a defendant swore a replying affidavit, explaining the potentially damaging effect on his business if his assets were frozen, the balance of convenience might swing the other way.

A Mareva injunction only runs until final judgment is granted, so it is important to continue the injunction until judgment has been executed.

Like any other injunction, a Mareva order operates against a specific defendant (*in personam*) and not against certain assets (*in rem*). It restrains the defendant *personally* from dealing with the frozen assets until the matter is finally decided, but it does *not* give any proprietary interest in the assets, which may subsequently be used to pay off other creditors.

Before 1988, a plaintiff who applied for a Mareva order only had to show that he had a cause of action within the jurisdiction. But in the case of *Caudron* v. *Air Zaire* [1986] ILRM 10, the Supreme Court held that the plaintiffs were not entitled to a Mareva injunction restraining the defendants from removing assets from Ireland, because a Mareva injunction is an *ancillary* remedy, not a substantive one. (This followed the judgment of Lord Diplock in *Siskina* v. *Distos Compania Naviera SA* [1977] 2AER 803.)

Since 1988, it has been possible to obtain a Mareva injunction against a defendant outside the jurisdiction. Section 13 of the Jurisdiction of Courts and Enforcement of Judgments Act 1998 provides:

On application pursuant to Article 24 of the 1968 Convention, the High Court may grant any provisional, including protective, measures of any kind that the Court has power to grant in proceedings that, apart from this Act, are within its jurisdiction, if–

(a) proceedings have been or are to be commenced in a Contracting State other than the State, and

(b) the subject matter of the proceedings is within the scope of the 1968 Convention as determined by Article 1.

S.13 provides that, where such an application is made to the High Court, it may refuse to grant the measures sought, if, in its opinion, the fact that it has no jurisdiction (apart from this section) in relation to the subject matter of the proceedings, makes it inexpedient to grant such measures.

The fact that the litigants have no connection with this jurisdiction (other than the defendant having assets here) would not mean that it would be inexpedient for the High Court to grant relief. In the case of *X* v. *Y* [1989] 3 WLR 910, a French bank began proceedings in France against a Saudi Arabian businessman. The French bank then began proceedings in the English courts under the English Civil Jurisdiction and Judgment Act, 1982.

The defendant argued that, as his only connection with the English jurisdiction was the presence of assets, it was inexpedient for the High Court to grant protective measures. The Court was, however, influenced by the fact that if the plaintiff succeeded in the French courts, he would not be able to execute the judgment in Saudi Arabia.

And in the case of *Deutsche Bank* v. *Murtagh* [1995] 1 ILRM 381 Costello P said that, if a defendant was ordinarily resident in the State and also a national of a contracting State, the Court has jurisdiction under the Convention and the 1988 Act. The Mareva injunction could also be used to freeze assets outside the jurisdiction, where such an order was warranted by the facts (a decision already reached by the English Court of Appeal in *Babanaft International* v. *Bassatne* [1990] Ch13).

A worldwide injunction may be granted where necessary. In *Bennett Enterprises Inc* v. *Lipton* [1999] 2 IR 221, O'Sullivan J said that the fewer assets the defendant had within the jurisdiction, the greater the necessity for taking protective measures in relation to assets abroad.

In *Countyglen* v. *Carway* [1995] 1 IR 208, Murphy J said that a party seeking a Mareva injunction must show that there was a substantial question to be tried, but did not have to prove as a matter of probability that his claim would succeed. He said the Court would not grant a Mareva injunction merely to preserve a defendant's assets in case the applicant's case succeeded. He ruled that the Court had power to make an order of discovery relating to such assets, ancillary to the Mareva injunction.

Application for a Mareva injunction

The initial application is always made *ex parte*, to avoid giving the defendant an opportunity to dispose of his assets before the hearing. It is grounded on a **plenary summons** and **affidavit**, but the order sought should also be drafted so that, if the Court grants the relief, the order can be drawn up quickly.

The requirements for an affidavit in support of applications for Mareva injunctions were confirmed by the Supreme Court in the case of *O'Mahony* v. *Horgan* [1995] 2 IR 411.

The most important consideration is that there must be full and frank disclosure of *all* material matters in the plaintiff's knowledge. He must exhibit full particulars of the claim, including the grounds and amount sought. Any documents helping to prove the claim should be exhibited. Because of the requirement for full and frank disclosure, any arguments the plaintiff might expect from the defendant should also be set out in the grounding affidavit.

The affidavit should also set out the grounds for believing that the defendant has assets within the jurisdiction. For example, if the plaintiff wishes to freeze a bank account, he should set out details of the branch and, if possible, the account number.

The affidavit should also refer to the grounds for believing that the defendant is about to remove or dissipate his assets. For example, if property is up for sale, a newspaper advertisement or brochure from the estate agent might be exhibited. The Court should be given the names of any third parties who should be served with a copy of the order (such as the auctioneer or bank).

The affidavit should include undertakings to indemnify the defendant against any consequential loss, to pay reasonable third party costs and to serve the defendant with the documents and the Court order.

Counsel acting for a small company should exhibit, in the grounding affidavit, a set of accounts, showing the company's assets. The Court may also require a plaintiff to enter a bond or some other form of security. But the case of *Allen* v. *Jambo Holdings Limited* [1980] 1WLR 1252 – a personal injuries action – established that Mareva injunctions may be granted even where a plaintiff is of limited means and where her undertaking in damages was only of restricted value.

Duty of disclosure

A Mareva injunction may be discharged if material facts are not disclosed by the plaintiff. The Court will decide what facts are material – not the plaintiff or his legal advisors. The duty of disclosure applies not only to facts known to the plaintiff, but also to those he would have known if he had made proper enquiries. The extent of such enquiries depends on the:

- nature of the case,
- likely effect of the order on the defendant,
- degree of *legitimate* urgency and
- time available.

If relevant facts are deliberately not disclosed, the Court may discharge the order immediately, without examining the merits of the case. But in the case of innocent non-disclosure, the Court has a discretion whether to continue the order or to grant a new order on specified terms. If there is a material change in circumstances after the grant of an *ex parte* order, the plaintiff must inform the Court. He must also persist with his substantive action.

If the plaintiff succeeds in freezing money in a bank account, he must immediately notify the bank. Where the injunction clearly identifies the account, the bank is likely to comply with the Court order. But if the plaintiff does not know the account details, he must undertake to pay the bank's reasonable costs in tracing the account.

It is not essential for the plaintiff precisely to locate the assets of the defendant, just to satisfy the Court they do exist. He can then bring a motion for discovery to find their exact location.

The risk of removal is obviously greater if the defendant or assets are outside the jurisdiction, but the mere fact that a defendant is a foreign resident is not enough to justify a Mareva; the plaintiff has to establish, to the satisfaction of the Court, that the defendant is about to dissipate his assets with the intention of frustrating a future Court order.

Evidence from the defendant's business may establish whether assets are likely to be removed or dissipated. In *Third Chandris Shipping Corp* v. *Unimarine SA* [1979] QB 645, the Court said it could infer that a defendant had assets within the jurisdiction from the existence of a bank account – even if it were overdrawn. In that case, the defendant was a Panamanian company without any property in the country and had failed to make any financial returns. The size, origins and domicile of the business were all taken into account, as well as the length of time the business had existed as a going concern and the location of the assets. The Court said that it would take into account the fact that a defendant was registered in a tax haven, where it had no assets and no work was carried out.

In the case of *Powerscourt Estates* v. *Gallagher* [1984] ILRM 123, the defendant was a company within a group of companies. Most of the companies were located outside the State, so assets could easily be removed from the reach of the plaintiff. The Court noted the defendant's trade record and said a history of bad debts would be taken into consideration, as well as the trading history of any member or officer of the company.

A **draft order** for a Mareva injunction will:

1   restrain the defendant, his servants or agents, from removing from the jurisdiction, or disposing of, any assets (including any specific assets) worth more than a certain amount until trial or further order,
2   allow the defendant certain business, legal and living expenses, as notified to the plaintiff's solicitor,
3   direct the defendant to disclose full details of all his assets in the jurisdiction, by affidavit to the plaintiff's solicitor within a certain period and
4   give the plaintiff liberty to apply on 48 hours' notice to vary or set aside the order.

The order ends with the penal clause, threatening sequestration of assets or imprisonment for contempt.

ANTON PILLER ORDERS

An Anton Piller order is an interlocutory mandatory order aimed at preserving vital evidence which the defendant might otherwise destroy. (*EMI* v. *Pandit* [1975] 1 WLR 302 and *Anton Piller KG* v. *Manufacturing Process Ltd* [1976] Ch55)

In order to obtain an Anton Piller order, the plaintiff must be able to produce evidence to show:

1   a **strong** *prima facie* case,
2   **serious potential or actual damage** to the plaintiff, outweighing the potential damage to the defendant,
3   that the defendant has the items **in his possession** and
4   that there's a **real risk of destruction** of the items.

All material facts must be disclosed. The order will only be made *ex parte* against a defendant outside the jurisdiction if leave would be granted to serve the writ outside the jurisdiction, and the Court may require **security for costs** if the *plaintiff* is outside the jurisdiction. The plaintiff must undertake not to allow anyone else access to the items or evidence and must preserve them pending trial.

Procedure

The application is made *ex parte* but in *Microsoft Corporation* v. *Brightpoint Ireland Ltd* [2001] 1 ILRM 540, Thomas Smyth J said it was not of the essence that the application be heard *in camera*. He said that the Court might, however, limit publication of an order made in open court. A **plenary summons, grounding affidavit** and **draft order** are required. The grounding affidavit sets out:

1   the **background** to the claim,
2   the **justification** for an Anton Piller order,
3   the **reasons** for the *ex parte* application,
4   any **facts** known to the plaintiff which might result in the refusal of the order (including hearsay evidence).

The draft order should include undertakings:

1   to serve the notice of motion and exhibits on the defendant,
2   not to use any of the information obtained, except in legal proceedings,
3   in damages and
4   to inform anyone on whom the order is served that they face contempt proceedings if they fail to comply.

The plaintiff's solicitor will undertake:

1   to keep any documents/articles in safe custody until further order or until the defendant's solicitor has given a written undertaking to keep them safe (the plaintiff's solicitor can copy them before return),
2   to advise the defendant of his right to legal advice and
3   to advise the defendant in *plain language* of the effects of the order.

The order will restrain the defendant from:

1   parting with the goods, other than to the plaintiff's solicitor,
2   destroying, altering, selling or dealing with the goods,
3   disclosing the contents of the action to third parties or warning any third parties.

The order normally directs the defendant to:

1   allow up to two *named* people, plus a solicitor, to enter his premises on a particular date at a certain time, to allow them to search for and remove a specified list of items,

2   disclose the whereabouts of items,
3   identify everyone with whom he has dealt in relation to the goods, (on affidavit),
4   allow a search of other premises, and
5   deliver up any documents within 24 hours. Any information on computer should be printed out and delivered to the plaintiff's solicitor.

The document ends with the penal clause.

The plaintiff's solicitor can't force his way into the defendant's premises without the defendant's consent. Anything removed must be listed. The defendant has a right to legal advice *first*, but must not remove, hide or destroy any evidence. The defendant may make an *immediate* application to Court to discharge or vary the order if the plaintiff failed to:

1   disclose all facts,
2   show a strong *prima facie* case,
3   prove a risk of serious potential damage if the order were not granted, or
4   prove that the defendant had (or would destroy) the incriminating material.

SPECIFIC PERFORMANCE

Specific performance is "the equitable discretionary remedy by which a party to an agreement is compelled by order of the Court to perform his obligations according to the terms of that agreement."

An order for specific performance is like a mandatory injunction and is often sought where a vendor refuses to complete a contract for the sale of land. The order is served personally on the defendant, endorsed with a penal endorsement (O. 42 RSC), and calls on him to perform the contract within a reasonable specified time.

If the defendant fails to perform the contract, the plaintiff issues a motion on notice, grounded on an affidavit which refers to the:

1   **proceedings to date** and a copy of the pleadings when produced,
2   **copy of the order** for specific performance when produced,
3   **affidavit of personal service** of the order when produced,
4   **letter** sent to the defendant with the Court order and
5   defendant's **failure to perform the contract**.

The notice of motion and the affidavit are served on the defendant through his solicitors or personally, and an affidavit of service of both is required.

The Court will fix a time within which the defendant must perform the contract and will adjourn the motion pending performance. If the defendant still does not comply, on the adjourned date the Court will order that an officer of the Court execute the conveyance. The purchase money is paid into Court to the credit of the action and the defendant may seek a payment out. The plaintiff may also execute against the money for costs.

ATTACHMENT AND COMMITTAL

As a last resort, if a defendant fails to obey an order, a motion may be brought for attachment and committal to prison for contempt. The motion is brought in the earlier injunction proceedings, on notice to the defendant. It must be served personally on the party, with four clear days' notice (O. 44 RSC) and should also be served on the party's solicitor.

The motion seeks:

1 an **order** directed to the Commissioner and members of the Garda Síochána **to attach the defendant** (by name, address and occupation) and bring him before the Court at a time and date specified by the Court,
2 an **order committing the defendant to prison** for failing to obey the order of the Court on a certain date and
3 **costs**.

The motion is grounded on the:

1 **existing proceedings**,
2 **Court order** and **affidavit of personal service** of the order on the defendant (with penal endorsement),
3 **documents** and **exhibits** referred to therein and
4 **affidavit of service** of the notice of motion and grounding affidavit.

The **grounding affidavit** refers to the proceedings, to the pleadings when produced, to the nature of the order made and to the affidavit of personal service of the order (with the penal endorsement) on the defendant. It should specify that the defendant is in breach of the order (giving details of the breach) and seek the relief sought in the notice of motion.

The motion is heard on the return date after giving four clear days' notice. If the defendant appears and agrees to be bound by the order, the motion is adjourned generally, with liberty to re-enter. This saves having to serve the order and penal endorsement a second time.

If the defendant fails to appear, an order will be made directing the Commissioner to attach him and bring him to court – usually on the next motion day. The order of attachment (Appendix F No. 11 RSC), which issues in the Central Office on foot of the Court order, is similar to an arrest warrant and *must* be taken up and directed to the Garda Commissioner immediately. If the gardai fail to attach the defendant, they must attend court to explain why.

The order of attachment remains in force for a year and may be renewed (O. 42 rule 20 RSC). If the gardai subsequently manage to attach the defendant, they can bring him to court on reasonable notice to the plaintiff and the Court.

If the defendant does not give an explanation for his contempt and an undertaking not to repeat it, he will be sent to jail, either for a defined period or until he has purged his contempt. (If he wishes to purge his contempt, he may apply by **motion on notice** to the plaintiff to discharge the order. A time is fixed for a Court hearing to allow the defendant to apologise and agree to abide by the Court order.) If a body corporate is in contempt, the plaintiff should seek sequestration of its assets (O. 43 RSC).

9. Judicial Review

Judicial review relates to the review by a High Court judge of the actions (or failure to act) of an inferior Court or tribunal. In *Re Article 26 and the Illegal Immigrants (Trafficking) Bill 1999* [2000] IESC 19, Keane CJ said that judicial review provided for "a speedy and expeditious determination of the validity of administrative action, in contrast to the procedural complexities and delays common in the case of proceedings commenced by plenary summons."

An applicant for judicial review may be seeking orders of *certiorari*, prohibition, declaration, *mandamus, quo warranto*, an injunction or damages.

- **Certiorari** is used to quash the decision of a lower Court, tribunal or public body, where it is charged with public duties and its decision was made in excess of jurisdiction. The Court will only be concerned with the *legality* of a decision, not its merits (*Ryan v. Compensation Tribunal* [1997] 1 ILRM 194).
- **Prohibition** prevents or restrains a lower Court or body from doing a particular act.
- **Mandamus** compels a body to do a certain act.
- **Quo warranto** is an application brought against someone claiming to be a holder of an office, where a declaration is sought that that office has not been lawfully filled. This may be used, for example, to challenge the warrant of appointment of a District or Circuit Court judge.
- **A declaration** is a binding judicial affirmation of a person's rights

In *Todd* v. *Judge AG Murphy* [1999] 2 IR 6, Lynch J succinctly set out the function and purpose of judicial review. He said: "Judicial review is concerned in general with the manner in which proceedings are conducted by courts of limited jurisdiction, or by public bodies or persons with powers impinging on legally-recognised interests of citizens. The Superior Courts have an inherent supervisory jurisdiction over inferior courts and tribunals and such bodies. If such a body has exceeded or acted without jurisdiction or has failed to act fairly or in accordance with the rules of natural justice, or if it has made a determination exhibiting an error of law on the face of the record, its decision can be set aside.

"Judicial review is not another form of appeal from a decision of such a body with which a citizen does not agree. It follows that, by and large, judicial review is not concerned with whether the decision challenged is right or wrong, but with the manner in which, and the procedures by which, the decision was reached."

Evidential shortcomings may not generally be challenged by way of judicial review. In *Stokes* v. *O'Donnell* [1999] 3 IR 218, Laffoy J said that judicial review was confined to cases where reliance could be placed on want or excess of jurisdiction, some clear departure from fair and constitutional procedures, on bias, on fraud and perjury or on error on the face of the record. It was not available, except in the most extreme cases, where the only challenge was to the sufficiency of the evidence before the inferior tribunal.

In *Egan* v. *UCD* [1996] 1 IR 390, Shanley J said the matters to be taken into consideration when deciding whether a decision was subject to judicial review included:

1   whether the decision challenged had been made pursuant to statute,
2   whether the decision-maker, by his decision, was performing a duty relating to a matter of particular and immediate public concern, which would therefore come within the public domain,
3   where the decision affected a contract of employment, whether the employment had any statutory protection so the employee might rely on "public rights" and
4   whether the decision-maker's powers – though not based directly on statute – depended on the legislature or government for their continued exercise.

And in the planning case of *O'Reilly* v. *O'Sullivan*, High Court, 25 July 1996, Laffoy J said that, in any application for judicial review:

1   the decision must be fundamentally at variance with reason and common sense,
2   the decision must be so overwhelmingly unreasonable that no reasonable person could ever have come to it,
3   the Court cannot intervene just because it would have come to a different conclusion on the facts and
4   the onus is on the applicant to establish that the decision-making authority had no relevant material to support its conclusions.

In another planning case, *De Faoite* v. *An Bord Pleanála*, High Court, 2 May 2000, Laffoy J said that an applicant should not be granted leave for judicial review of a planning decision unless the High Court was satisfied that there were substantial grounds for contending that the decision was invalid or ought to be quashed.

The claim must have a public law dimension. In the case of *Rizk* v. *Royal College of Physicians of Ireland*, High Court, 27 August 1997, the applicant – a medical doctor living in England – had failed the examination for membership of the RCPI. He sought an order of *mandamus* in relation to his examination results and an order granting him the degree of MRCPI.

Laffoy J said that orders of *certiorari* or prohibition would not issue to a body which derived its jurisdiction solely from, or with the consent of, its members. In this case, the applicant had agreed to be bound by the regulations of the College in relation to his exams, so no public law dimension applied.

In *McEvoy* v. *Prison Officers' Association* [1999] 1 ILRM 445, the Court held that the internal management matters of a private body are not susceptible to judicial review, unless the body has acted with *mala fides*.

The Court may grant an order of *mandamus* wherever "just and convenient". It may be unconditional or on whatever terms the Court thinks just (O. 50 rule 6 RSC). If the Court grants an order of *mandamus* (or a mandatory order, injunction or judgment for specific performance) and the defendant fails to carry out the order, proceedings may be brought for contempt and the Court may also order that another person may perform the act required, at the expense of the defendant (O. 42 rule 31 RSC).

An order of *mandamus* may not be granted where it would be futile to do so. In *Brady* v. *Cavan County Council* [1999] 4 IR 99, Keane J said the Supreme Court would not make an order of *mandamus* against a public authority where the authority did not have the means to comply with the order.

The time limit for a judicial review application is three months or, in the case of *certiorari*, *six* months, but the High Court has the power to extend the time for good reason.

O. 84 rules 18–27 deal with judicial review applications. O. 84 rule 1 states that orders of *certiorari*, *mandamus*, prohibition and attachment shall be witnessed in the name of the Chief Justice or, in his absence, the President of the High Court, with the seal of the High Court, bearing the day and date.

Judicial review is a two-stage procedure. As Kelly J explained in *O'Leary* v. *The Minister for Transport, Energy and Communications, Michael Lowry, Ireland and the Attorney General* [2000] 1 ILRM 391: "The judicial review procedure is designed to ensure that cases which are frivolous, vexatious or of no substance cannot be begun. Hence the necessity for judicial screening at the stage where leave is sought. The procedure is also designed to ensure that a fair and expeditious trial takes place, and that such trial is focussed upon the issues in respect of which the judge, at the leave stage, felt ought to be argued – and those alone.

"The existence of the temporal limitation for the bringing of such claims is indicative of a desire to ensure that issues which touch upon the exercise of public authority, as judicial review applications do, ought to be brought on expeditiously, and not allowed to go stale."

The first stage is an *ex parte* application to the High Court for **leave to apply for judicial review**. Applications under O. 84 rule 20 of the RSC are made by motion ex parte on Mondays at 2pm to the judge presiding over the list.
　　Such application should be grounded on:

(a)　a verifying affidavit and
(b)　a notice in Appendix T Form No. 13 RSC containing a statement of:
　　　(i) the applicant's name, address and description,
　　　(ii) the relief sought and the grounds on which it's sought and
　　　(iii) the name and business address of the applicant's solicitor (if any) or the applicant's address for service within the jurisdiction if unrepresented.

The notice should be dated and signed. The verifying affidavit is entitled:

THE HIGH COURT

JUDICIAL REVIEW

Judicial Review No. 2001 / 432 JR

Between/

CATHERINE O'BRIEN

Applicant

and

THE ATTORNEY GENERAL

Respondent

Where a judge is the respondent, the Director of Public Prosecutions should be co-respondent, so costs can be awarded against the State. In

O'Connor v. *Carroll* [1999] 2 IR 160, the Supreme Court said it was not necessary to join as a party to the proceedings the judge whose decision was being challenged as he had no interest or function in supporting his decision. The High Court should not award costs against a District or Circuit Court judge where there was no bad faith or impropriety and where he had not opposed the proceedings.

The affidavit should refer to the grounding statement when produced, giving details, exhibiting any order or conviction and praying for the relief sought and costs. The affidavit is sworn, signed and filed in the Central Office with the original statement before the application is made. (Court fees are not payable on proceedings involving *habeas corpus*, extradition or bail, nor in criminal cases involving applications for orders of *certiorari*, *mandamus*, *quo warranto* or prohibition.)

The solicitor will produce for use in court a copy affidavit bearing the Central Office record number, certified as a *true copy* of the original affidavit, with the date of filing. A second copy of the statement should be provided to the Court registrar. The facts are then outlined to the judge.

If the application for leave to apply is granted, the Court may impose restrictions or conditions. In *Breathnach* v. *Government* [2001] IESC 13, the appellant had sought leave to apply for an order of *certiorari* quashing convictions, as well as a declaratory order dealing with his complaints. The High Court gave him leave to seek judicial review by way of *mandamus*. In the Supreme Court, Geoghegan J said it was entirely incorrect to suggest that the High Court was not entitled to limit the leave granted or alter the type of relief being sought.

Once leave has been granted, the judge will fix a return date for the hearing of the substantive motion. (Applications will now be heard every day of the week, not just on Mondays as was previously the case.)

At the first listing, there will be a short *inter partes* hearing at which the judge will give directions for the exchange of pre-trial documents. should be asked to:

1   direct who should be served,
2   extend time for the service of the notice of motion on the respondents (limited to 14 days in the Rules) for two to three weeks,
3   extend time for delivery of any statement of opposition,
4   grant a stay of execution on any conviction being challenged, and
5   reserve the costs.

Any stay of execution will lapse if the notice of motion is not served within the permitted time.

If the judge is unhappy about any aspect of the case, Counsel should consider withdrawing the application, amending the affidavit and making another application later to a different judge. A refusal to grant leave to apply may be appealed to the Supreme Court.

In stage two of the proceedings, the applicant's solicitor takes up the High Court order granting leave to apply. The solicitor then issues in the Central Office and serves on the defendant a **notice of motion**, returnable for the first motion day after *10 days from the date of service*, together with a copy of the High Court order, the statement grounding the application for judicial review and the grounding affidavit. A bound indexed book of documents is lodged with the registrar at least seven days before the hearing, comprising copies of the:

1 **notice of motion,**
2 **order giving leave** to apply for judicial review,
3 **statement** grounding the application,
4 **affidavit verifying the statement,**
5 **exhibits,**
6 **statement of opposition** (if any) and
7 **affidavit verifying any statement of opposition.**

The book should also contain an **affidavit of personal service** on all relevant parties of the motion, statement, affidavit and order giving leave. In applications for orders of *certiorari*, the book should contain a copy of any impugned decision or order, verified by affidavit.

Thereafter, in stage three of the proceedings, the respondent has *seven days* within which to serve any statement of opposition. In practice, this period is too short, so, on the return date, the respondent will probably seek more time to serve the statement of opposition. However, if the respondent doesn't intend to oppose the judicial review, the applicant may seek a hearing on the return date.

The statement of opposition will be supported by an affidavit, verifying the facts on which the respondent intends to rely. If there appears to be a dispute on facts, either side may serve a notice of intention to cross-examine. Both sides should file written submissions unless the Court orders otherwise.

Counsel for the applicant should attend at the Thursday callover the week before the case is due to come on, and indicate whether the case is proceeding and whether there has been compliance with the practice directions. Cases in which there is no appearance will be struck out.

10. Enforcement of Money Judgments

Where a person is ordered by a Court to pay money under a judgment, he is bound to pay the amount on service of the judgment or order, without any further demand (O. 41 rule 1 RSC). But that does not always happen. Obviously, the value of a right to a litigant is no greater than the available remedy: a Court judgment for a money debt is no use unless it can be enforced. But judgments may be difficult to enforce, especially against a party who has few resources or who is determined not to pay. The main Court enforcement mechanisms (O. 42 RSC) include

- a writ of execution (*fieri facias*) allowing the debtor's property to be seized and sold, with the proceeds going to the creditor
- appointment of an equitable receiver
- a garnishee order allowing the creditor to deduct all or part of the judgment debt from money owed to the debtor or from his bank account
- an instalment order
- an examination notice requiring a debtor to attend Court and be examined about his financial circumstances
- attachment and committal
- an order of sequestration
- an order of possession
- an order for delivery of property
- receivership or winding up, in the case of a company.

No execution order can be issued without production of the judgment (or attested copy) and the filing of a *praecipe* – and, in the case of a money judgment, a certificate – in the Central Office (O. 42 rules 10–11 RSC).

These enforcement mechanisms can be expensive, cumbersome, time-consuming and often ineffective. They usually involve the preparation, filing and service of additional Court documents and, in many cases, require further attendance at Court. Even then, it may still not be possible to obtain payment from someone who is determined not to pay.

Equally, an order for costs is valueless if the defendant has no money, so a plaintiff may wish to ensure, at an early stage of proceedings, that he will not have to meet the costs if he wins his case.

SECURITY FOR COSTS

One mechanism for ensuring that all or part of a costs order will be enforced is an order for security for costs (O. 29 RSC). A party may be ordered to pay money into Court or otherwise give security for payment of costs if he loses the action.

The purpose of this order is to ensure that litigants do not unreasonably or by artificial means avoid a costs order made against them, and to ensure that those who stand to benefit from the litigation also run the risk of its burdens – although, as Fitzgibbon J pointed out in *Perry* v. *Stratham* [1928] IR 580, security for costs is not intended as "an encouragement to luxurious litigation" by the respondent.

In practice, most orders for security for costs are made against the person who chooses to bring the action – that is the plaintiff. An order for security for costs also focuses the attention of the parties and the Court on the possible apportionment and expected amount of the costs of the litigation at an early stage of the proceedings.

When deciding whether to order security for costs, the Court must balance the risk of exposing an innocent defendant to the expense of defending the action against the risk of unnecessarily shutting out from relief a plaintiff whose case, if litigated, would result in the relief being granted. The discretion to order security must be exercised in light of all the circumstances, but relevant factors include:

* whether the plaintiff has a *bona fide* claim with good prospects of success
* whether a requirement for security would be oppressive or bring the action to an end
* the means of the plaintiff and of any persons who stand behind the litigation
* whether the wrongful conduct of the defendant might have contributed significantly to the plaintiff's impecunious condition
* whether the plaintiff is resident outside the EU
* whether there has been delay in applying for security and
* the amount of costs likely to be incurred.

In *Broadnet Ireland Ltd* v. *Director of Telecommunications Regulation* [2000] IEHC 46, Laffoy J said a Court would only exercise its discretion not to award security for costs in special circumstances, such as "matters connected with the alleged wrongdoing, and its contribution to the financial status of the plaintiff or applicant."

O'Neill J refused to order security for costs in *Ochre Ridge Ltd* v. *Cork Bonded Warehouses Ltd*, ITLR, 5 February 2001, because he said the financial status of the plaintiff – a shelf company – was inextricably linked to the merits of the its claims and to the outcome of the proceedings.

In the case of *Beauross* v. *Kennedy*, High Court, 18 October 1995, Morris J said that, if the plaintiff incurred additional costs because of the delay of the defendant in seeking an order for security of costs, the Court would not make the order.

In most cases, a natural person is not required to give security in the absence of special circumstances. An order for security for costs will not be made solely on the grounds that a plaintiff lives in Northern Ireland (O. 29 rule 2 RSC) and no defendant will be allowed security for costs on the grounds that the plaintiff lives abroad, unless he can show in an affidavit that he has a defence on the merits of the case (O. 29 rule 3 RSC).

In some cases, an order for costs may prevent a person exercising his Constitutional right of access to the Courts. But in *Salih* v. *General Accident* [1987] IR 628, O'Hanlon J recognised that the obstacle to access which an order for security for costs might cause was not unconstitutional.

In *Malone* v. *Brown Thomas & Co.* [1995] 1 ILRM 369, the defendants sought security for costs from the plaintiff, who lived in Australia. She lodged £7,500, but lost her case and was ordered to pay the defendant's costs. She appealed and the defendants sought a stay on her appeal pending the lodging of further security for costs. The Supreme Court refused.

Hamilton CJ said the Court had discretion whether to award security for costs. Residence outside the jurisdiction or the poverty of the plaintiff were not, in themselves, sufficient reason for ordering a lodgment. He said no unnecessary financial obstacle should be put in the way of those seeking access to the Courts, and it was up to the applicant to establish reasonable grounds for his entitlement to the order.

Residents of the EU would normally be treated in the same way as residents of Ireland. In *Maher* v. *Phelan* [1996] 1 ILRM 359, the plaintiff lived in England and had assets there and in Ireland. The defendant estimated the costs of the proceedings at £386,000 and sought security for costs. But Carroll J said that Article 7 of the EEC Treaty (re-numbered as Article 6 by the 1993 Maastricht Treaty) prohibited discrimination on the grounds of nationality. A plaintiff resident in this jurisdiction would not be required to give security for costs in any circumstances, so a resident of the EU must be treated in the same way.

And in *Proetta* v. *Neil* [1996] 1 ILRM 457, Murphy J refused to grant security for costs against a plaintiff who had dual Spanish and British citizenship, was resident in Spain and shared an apartment in Gibraltar, because it would be discriminatory under the EEC Treaty.

But in *Pitt* v. *Bolger* [1996] 2 ILRM 68, Keane J said the Court might make an order for security for costs against an EU resident where there was very cogent evidence of substantial difficulty in enforcing a judgment in the other member state.

The strength (or otherwise) of a party's case is not an appropriate consideration in an application for security for costs, unless the plaintiff's case is unanswerable (*Lismore Homes* v. *Bank of Ireland Finance* [1999] IR 501)

An order for costs may also be made against a company under s.390 of the Companies Act 1963 "if it appears by credible testimony that there is reason to believe that the company will be unable to pay the costs of the defendant". The Court may stay proceedings until such security is provided.

In *Bula (in receivership)* v. *Tara Mines (No. 3)* [1987] IR 494, Murphy J said the power to order security for costs was discretionary but, where a plaintiff company admitted that it could not meet the costs of a successful defendant, the onus was on the plaintiff to establish to the judge's satisfaction the special circumstances which would justify the refusal of an order.

But in the case of *Irish Press* v. *Warburg Pincus* [1997] 2 ILRM 263, McGuinness J said that, on balance, the Courts tended to lean against the making of orders for security for costs in such "David and Goliath" scenarios.

If the Court does order security for costs, it will remit the matter to the Master to decide the amount, the person to whom security should be given and the time, manner and form of payment (O. 29 rule 6 RSC).

If a party is ordered to provide security for costs and fails to do so within the time specified, the Court has a discretionary jurisdiction to strike out the proceedings. In *Lough Neagh Exploration Ltd* v. *Morrice* [1999] 4 IR 515, Hamilton CJ said that this "ultimate sanction" was to be used sparingly and only in extreme cases to secure compliance with the rules, rather than to punish the defaulter.

PROTECTIVE COSTS ORDER

An applicant who brings a case in the public interest may apply for a preemptive (or protective) costs order, directing that the applicant should not be responsible for the costs of any other party. Such an order is only available where the Court is satisfied that the public law issues raised are of general importance and the applicant has no private interest in the outcome of the case. The Court should consider the financial resources of the applicant and respondent and be satisfied that the respondent is more capable than the applicant of bearing the burden of legal costs and that, without a pre-emptive order, the applicant might reasonably discontinue the case (*R* v. *Lord Chancellor ex parte CPAG* [1998] 2 AER 755). The criteria for deciding whether a question of public law exists were set out by Morris J in *Lancefort* v. *An Bord Pleanala* [1998] 2 ILRM 401. He said the point had to be of such gravity and importance as to transcend the interests of the parties, and the interests of the common good had to require that the law be clarified for future cases.

In *Village Residents' Association* v. *An Bord Pleanala and McDonalds Restaurants* [2000] 1 IR 65, Laffoy J said a pre-emptive costs order had no place in ordinary *inter partes* litigation.

FIERI FACIAS

An order of *fieri facias* (literally, "cause to be made") may be obtained as soon as a judgment has been obtained – either in Court or in the Central Office in default of appearance or pursuant to an order of the Master giving liberty to enter final judgment (O. 42 rule 17 RSC).

The so-called *fi-fa* order (Appendix F Part II Form 1 RSC) is directed to the sheriff of the district in whose bailiwick the defendant has his personal assets (including leasehold property), requiring him to seize them and levy execution by selling them. At the same time, another *fi-fa* order may be directed to the sheriff of a neighbouring county, without waiting for a return on the first order (O. 42 rule 34 RSC). It is not necessary for the petitioner or his solicitor to inform the sheriff about the location of the respondent or his property. In *Mehigan* v. *Duignan* [1999] 2 IR 593, Laffoy J said it was up to the sheriff to use "due and reasonable diligence" to ascertain the property liable to execution.

The goods that may be seized must:

1   **belong** to the defendant (not be leased or on hire purchase)
2   not be necessary for his **domestic life** (such as bed, clothes, crockery) or **business** (for example tools or a computer).

Leaseholds (as personalty, rather than realty) *are* seizable by the sheriff, so before buying a leasehold property, a search should be performed in the sheriff's office for any *fi-fa* awaiting execution. If there are no goods seizable (which frequently happens), the sheriff returns the order marked *nulla bona* (no goods).

In *Mehigan* v. *Duignan*, the sheriff returned the order marked *nulla bona* without attending at the premises. Laffoy J said that, if there was no *bona fide* attempt at execution, the return *nulla bona* could be challenged, as it would not constitute a "return of no goods" within the meaning of the Bankruptcy Act 1988.

Where a judgment is obtained against a firm, it may be executed against any property of the partnership in the jurisdiction or against a partner (O. 14 rule 8 RSC). Other execution processes may depend upon the *fi-fa* being issued and returned *nulla bona* or yielding only part of the judgment.

In *Wymes* v. *Tehan* [1988] IR 717, the defendant, who was the Meath county registrar, had to execute a number of orders of *fieri facias* against the plaintiff in relation to judgments for more than £400,000. She seized 91 head of cattle and two tractors from the plaintiff's farm. He sought an injunction to prevent the sale of his goods. He claimed that the orders of *fieri facias* were invalid because they were out of date and that his Constitutional rights had been breached by the registrar entering his lands without notice or permission.

O'Hanlon J said an order of *fi-fa* could be renewed *ex parte* within one year of its issue. Alternatively, he said a new writ could be issued, even if there had been partial execution under the original writ. The judge said there was no legal requirement to forewarn a judgment debtor of a sheriff's impending execution of a writ, and any trespass on the lands did not invalidate the seizure. He refused the injunction.

In *National Irish Bank* v. *Graham* [1994] 1 ILRM 372, the plaintiffs had an order of *fieri facias*, but sought an order appointing a receiver over the defendants' milking herd under s. 28(8) of the Supreme Court of Judicature (Ireland) Act 1877 and O. 50 rule 6(1) of the RSC.

Keane J said the most frequent ground for the appointment of a receiver was the protection or preservation of property for the benefit of persons who had an interest in it. He said the bank had no interest in the milking herd and had already obtained an order of *fiera facias* based on a judgment for £3.5 million. Although the bank could seize and sell the herd on the basis of that order, it was not in their interests to do so. But, since the herd remained the exclusive property of the defendants and the bank had no vested or contingent interest in the herd, there were no grounds for the appointment of a receiver.

If the sheriff does manage to seize goods, as soon as the order of *fi-fa* is filed marked *fieri feci*, the applicant may issue an order of *venditioni exponas* (Appendix F Part II Form 4 RSC), directing the sheriff to sell the goods at the best price available. If the goods have been seized from a company, the sheriff must hold onto them for 14 days, in case a notice is served to wind up the company.

GARNISHEE ORDER

An **order of garnishee** (like the appointment of a **receiver by way of equitable execution**) is a preventative, non-punitive equitable remedy, which is discretionary and operates *in personam* (against a specific person). The remedy does not give the judgment creditor any security or prior charge over other creditors. Other judgment procedures should be tried first, as the Court may refuse a garnishee order if the ordinary methods of execution have not already been tried.

The relationship of debtor and creditor must exist between the judgment debtor and proposed garnishee; that is why the procedure is often referred to as **attachment of debts** (O. 45 RSC). The application is a two-stage process. First an *ex parte* **application** for a conditional order is brought. If that is successful, an **application on notice** (which does not require a notice of motion) is brought for the conditional *ex parte* order to be made absolute.

At any time after the plaintiff has obtained the original judgment (and has issued an order of *fi-fa* which has been returned *nulla bona*), an *ex parte* application may be made to satisfy the judgment by attaching a debt *currently* payable by a third party (the garnishee) to the defendant. If the money owed is a *periodic* or *future* debt, an application should instead be made for the appointment of an equitable receiver.

The application is normally brought in the Common Law *ex parte* list, but if delay would prejudice the plaintiff's efforts to attach the debt, he should apply immediately in any Court, explaining the facts in the grounding affidavit. If a *fi-fa* order has been issued but not yet executed, he should say that he believes the *fi-fa* will be returned *nulla bona*.

The application is brought in the original proceedings in which the judgment was recovered, so the heading and title are the same. (The garnishee's name does *not* feature in the title.) The affidavit is sworn by the plaintiff and refers to:

1 the nature of the **proceedings** and the **pleadings** when produced,
2 the amount of the **judgment**,
3 a **copy of the judgment** when produced (including whether it was in default of defence),
4 the **amount due** at the date of the affidavit (the judgment sum, plus interest, less any payment already made),
5 the *fi-fa* returned **nulla bona** and the **order of fi-fa** when produced,
6 grounds for the belief that the named garnishee **owes a lump sum** to the defendant,

7   the **amount owed** by the garnishee and
8   the garnishee's **address within the jurisdiction** of the Court.

Even where the original contract did not provide for the payment of interest, Courts Act interest runs on the amount from the date of judgment, so it should be calculated up to the date of the affidavit. (The Courts and Court Officers Bill, 2001, proposed that interest on legal costs should be only two per cent from the time of the judgment until the parties had agreed the costs, or a certificate of taxation had been issued. Thereafter, the interest rate applicable to judgment debts would apply to any outstanding costs).

If the garnishee is a bank, the affidavit should give the name and address of the branch where the debtor has his account. This affidavit is relied on at the next stage of proceedings, so the deponent should seek the full form of absolute order:

> *I therefore pray this honourable Court for an order attaching the debt due from N. to the defendant, or so much thereof as will satisfy the judgment and the costs of the proceedings, together with the measured costs of this application.*

As an *ex parte* application is *uberrimae fidei* (of the utmost good faith), the Court must be told of any authorities *against* the granting of the application, as well as in favour. If, at the next stage, the defendant or garnishee open authorities which should have been opened at the earlier hearing, the plaintiff may be refused this discretionary relief.

The Court will make an order that the debt (or enough to satisfy the judgment and costs) be attached, unless cause be shown on the return date for making the conditional order absolute. The garnishee and judgment debtor must be given seven days' clear notice of the date of hearing (O. 45 rule 1(2) RSC).

The order does not take effect until it is served *personally* on the garnishee. It should also be served on the defendant or his solicitor. If in doubt (for example, if there has been a lapse in time between the judgment and the conditional order), the order should be served on the defendant *personally*. Once the order has been served on the garnishee, he may not dispose of the money owed to the judgment debtor (O. 45 rule 2 RSC).

The application for an **order of garnishee** appears in the Common Law motion list under the heading *Garnishee*, and will be called at the close of **motions for the sitting of the Court**. There is no notice of motion in this case. A copy of the conditional order will have been sent by the registrar who drafted it to the registrar of the Common Law list, who will list it. (This is the only situation in which this happens. In other cases, such as an application for an interim injunction, the solicitor must issue and file the notice of motion in the Central Office and serve it, to ensure the case is listed).

The Court will require an **affidavit of service** of both the **conditional order** and the **grounding affidavit** on the garnishee *and* the defendant, either through his solicitor or personally. The proofs are:

1   the **grounding affidavit,**
2   the **certified copy of the conditional order** issued by the Central Office and
3   an **affidavit of service**.

If the garnishee disputes the conditional order, the Court may decide the matter summarily (O. 45, rule 4 RSC). But if the garnishee does not appear, the Court will order execution, attaching the debt and directing the garnishee to pay the money to the plaintiff, after deducting his own costs. The absolute order can only be discharged by consent, unless there is a suggestion of mistake. The costs of the plaintiff and the garnishee will usually be measured by the Court and paid out of the garnishee's funds.

EQUITABLE RECEIVER

A receiver by way of equitable execution may be appointed where *legal* execution (including a garnishee order) is not available, such as in the case of periodic payments, rents or a debt due in the future. The order gives the creditor a legal title which he may enforce at law if no other prior claim is proved. The jurisdiction of the Court derives from s.28(8) of the Supreme Court of Judicature (Ireland) Act 1877 which allows a judge to grant the order whenever "just and convenient".

Many judges believe that – except in cases of urgency – a receiver should not be appointed unless a fi-fa has been returned *nulla bona* or has been only partially successful, so a solicitor should issue a fi-fa immediately judgment is recovered.

In *National Irish Bank* v. *Graham* [1994] 1 ILRM 372, Keane J. said a receiver by way of equitable execution could only be appointed where a debtor had an *equitable* interest in property which could not be reached by legal process. In this case, the debtor had a legal, rather than equitable, interest in a milking herd. The plaintiff could execute a writ of *fi-fa* against the herd, so was not entitled to an order for an equitable receiver.

The *ex parte* application is made in the original proceedings and is grounded on an affidavit which, after the means of knowledge clause, refers to the:

1   **proceedings** and pleadings when produced,
2   **recovery of the judgment**, with a copy, when produced,
3   **amount outstanding**,
4   **issue of fi-fa** and its return *nulla bona*,
5   **reasons for the application** (such as the unavailability of a garnishee order),
6   details of the amount owed by the **third party** to the judgment debtor,
7   **name of the proposed receiver**,
8   receiver's **consent to act** if appointed,
9   **receiver's undertaking** to apply all money received in accordance with his receivership and
10 estimated **costs** of the receivership.

An **affidavit of fitness** of the receiver will also be required, sworn by someone who can vouch for his integrity. The deponent will say how long he has known the proposed receiver and why the candidate would make a good receiver.

The Court must consider:

1   the **amount of the debt** claimed,
2   the probable **amount to be obtained** by the receiver and
3   the likely **costs** of the receiver's appointment.

The Court has absolute discretion in deciding whom to appoint receiver. The order appointing the receiver is served on the defendant and on anyone due to make periodic or future payments to him. In the case of rental income, the receiver should be appointed receiver of the *property*, not the rents. He will be responsible for the property and all outgoings before handing over any money to the defendant. Before the receiver pays any money to the plaintiff, he must bring an application in the Master's Court, accounting for the money received, seeking liberty to pay the money to the plaintiff and seeking a discharge of the receivership. This is done by **notice of motion** to the defendant and the plaintiff, grounded on an **affidavit** sworn by the receiver setting out the background of the matter.

If the defendant claims the receiver has been improperly appointed, he may bring a notice of motion to have the appointment set aside.

BANKRUPTCY

The procedure for applying for an order of bankruptcy under the Bankruptcy Act 1988 is set out in Order 76 of the RSC. An order of bankruptcy should not be used simply to execute judgments – although it is often a very effective means of doing so. Bankruptcy proceedings may be used without a prior judgment in all debts for a liquidated sum over £1,500, where the act of bankruptcy (s.7 1988 Act) took place within the previous three months. But, unless the debt is undisputed, a judgment should first be obtained to avoid any suggestion of abuse of process.

The creditor must first serve a notice on the debtor in the form of Appendix O No. 4 RSC, demanding payment of the sum within four days. If the money is not paid, a copy of the notice, verifying affidavit and draft summons are lodged with the Examiner and an ex parte application is made to the bankruptcy judge for liberty to issue a debtor's summons (Appendix O No. 1 RSC). The summons must be personally served on the debtor within 28 days, with details of the sum demanded and a verifying affidavit.

Accuracy is essential in drawing up the papers and making calculations. In *Re Gerard Sherlock, a Bankrupt [1995] 2 ILRM 493*, the bankrupt applied to have the order set aside because of a miscalculation in the summons. Murphy J said a certain degree of precision was required in the documentation grounding an application for bankruptcy, because the code was penal in nature and should be strictly complied with. Where an amount on a summons exceeded the amount owed, this was a substantial defect rendering the summons defective, so the subsequent adjudication was void.

The affidavit (Appendix O No. 5 RSC) must state that no process of execution is outstanding (such as for a fi-fa or order of garnishee), otherwise liberty will not be given. The debtor summons will be returnable on a date fixed by the Court, when the proposed bankrupt can appear and show cause why he should not be made bankrupt.

In *O'Donoghue* v. *Ireland* [2000] 2 IR 168, a challenge to the constitutionality of the examination process was unsuccessful.

The Court then directs the advertising in *Iris Oifigiúil* of a statutory sitting at least ten days later, where other creditors of the proposed bankrupt can make their claims. The bankrupt must lodge a statement of affairs with the Official Assignee at least two days before the sitting. If he does not pay the sums due, he will be adjudicated bankrupt, all his property will vest in the Official Assignee to be sold to pay his debts, and he will be excluded from activities such as the formation of companies.

INSTALMENT ORDER

A judgment may be executed by requiring the defendant to pay the debt in weekly instalments. A District Judge will examine the defendant's means and then make an order directing him to pay an affordable weekly sum. Even if the defendant's means are extremely limited and the payment is a pittance, such an order is useful in keeping a judgment alive after the 12-year period specified by the Statute of Limitations.

WINDING UP

The High Court has jurisdiction to wind up any company (s.212 Companies Act 1963). The procedure for winding up is set out in Order 74 of the RSC. An application is made by **petition** (s.215) presented by the company, creditors or contributories. The forms of **petition** and **verifying affidavit** are set out in Appendix M of the RSC.

Every petition must be advertised (in the form of Appendix M No. 5) at least seven days before the hearing in *Iris Oifigiúil* and two Dublin daily papers (O. 74 rule 10 RSC). Any affidavit opposing the winding-up must be filed within seven days of the last advertisement, and notice given to the petitioner the same day. (O. 74 rule 17 RSC). Anyone who wants to appear at the hearing of a petition must serve notice of his intention to the petitioner or his solicitor by five o'clock the day before the hearing (O. 74 rule 15 RSC).

Any application to stay winding-up proceedings must be made by **motion on notice** to the plaintiff. But in *Truck and Machinery Sales* v. *Marubeni Komatsu* [1996] 1 IR 12, Keane J said the Court's power to restrain winding-up proceedings should be exercised only where the plaintiff has established at least a *prima facie* case that the petition constitutes an abuse of process.

When the **winding-up order** has been made, a certified copy must be left at the Examiner's Office within 10 days. A notice to proceed is then taken out and served on everyone who appeared at the hearing of the petition.

A certified copy of the **winding-up order** must also be delivered to the company or the registrar of companies (s.221). A statement of the company's affairs must then be filed in court (s.224) with a verifying affidavit. The statement (Appendix M No. 13 RSC) gives:

1   details of the company's **assets, debts and liabilities,**
2   names, addresses and occupations of the **creditors,**

3   the **securities** held by each creditor and
4   the **dates** when the securities were given.

The statement must be filed within 21 days by one or more of the directors and the secretary of the company – or such other persons as the Court may order (s.224(2)). The Court may appoint a provisional liquidator any time after the presentation of the winding-up petition (s.226). A winding-up order made by a Court in Britain or Northern Ireland may be enforced by the Irish High Court (s.250).

EXAMINERSHIP

The High Court may appoint an examiner where it appears that a company can't pay its debts and no winding-up order has been made (s.2 Companies (Amendment) Act 1990). The procedure for the appointment of an examiner is set out in Order 75A of the RSC.

A petition for an examiner (s.3) may be presented by:

1   the **company**,
2   the **directors**,
3   a **creditor** (including employees) or
4   **members** of the company holding at least 10% of the voting shares.

The petition must nominate a person to be appointed examiner (with a notice of consent from the person) and include evidence to show why an examiner should be appointed. If the petition is presented by the company or a director, it must include a statement of the company's assets and liabilities. (s.3(3)). Where the company's liabilities are under quarter of a million pounds, the matter may be remitted to the Circuit Court. Within three days of the presentation of the petition, it must be delivered to the registrar of companies.

An examiner must deliver a copy of his appointment to the registrar of companies within three days. He must also publish details of his appointment in at least two daily newspapers within three days and in *Iris Oifigiúil* within three weeks (s.12).

The examiner must deliver an interim report to the Court within 21 days (or longer, if the Court allows), stating whether he believes the company is capable of survival (ss.15–17). If it is, he has another three weeks in which to present a scheme of arrangement to shareholders and creditors and report back to the Court (ss.18–19).

FOREIGN JUDGMENTS

An application to enforce a foreign judgment, under s.7 of the Jurisdiction of Courts and Enforcement of Judgments Act 1998, is made ex parte to the Master of the High Court who is the central authority for the enforcement of foreign judgments (O. 47A RSC).

The application, by **motion on notice**, is grounded on an affidavit which states:

1   that the judgment (or part of it) has **not been satisfied,**
2   whether the judgment is a **money judgment,**
3   details of any **interest** allowed by the other State,
4   the **name and address** of the judgment debtor,
5   the **applicant's address** within the State and
6   the grounds for the applicant's **right to enforce the judgment**.

The grounding affidavit should exhibit:

1   the **judgment** (or a certified copy),
2   an affidavit of **service of the summons** (in the case of a default judgment),
3   documents establishing the **enforceability of the judgment** in the other State,
4   an affidavit of **service of the judgment** and
5   any document showing the applicant is receiving **legal aid** in the other State.

If documents are in a foreign language, translations should be provided, with an affidavit as to the competence and qualifications of the translator. Any **notice of enforcement** should be served personally (or as the Master directs) on the person against whom the enforcement order was made, with a copy of the order. The order must state the period of appeal (one month, or two months where the debtor is domiciled outside the State) and that execution will not issue until the appeal period has expired (O. 42A rule 8 RSC). The **notice of enforcement** must state:

1   full particulars of the **judgment** and the **order for enforcement,**
2   the name of the applicant,
3   the applicant's address for service within the State,
4   details of any **protective measures** granted against the property of the judgment debtor,

5   details of the debtor's **right to appeal** and
6   the **appeal period allowed**.

In *Paper Properties* v. *Power Corporation* [1996] 1 ILRM 475, the plaintiff
applied to the Master to enforce a judgment of the English Court of
Appeal but did not disclose that the defendant had appealed the
judgment. The Master granted a Mareva injunction and ordered that the
notice of judgment be served by post and fax on the office of the
defendant's solicitor. Service did not comply with the Master's order, but
Carroll J refused to set aside the order. She said the Master had been
informed orally of the appeal and ruled that service of an enforcement
order was sufficient where the party was served with the notice, even if
the manner of service specified by the Master was not followed exactly.

If the applicant wishes to enforce an Irish High Court judgment in
another contracting State, he should obtain a certificate from the High
Court registrar. The affidavit grounding the application for a certificate
must state:

1   the **nature of the proceedings,**
2   the **provisions of the 1968 Convention** applied,
3   the **date** on which the appeal period expires,
4   whether a **notice of appeal** or **notice to set aside the judgment**
     has been lodged and
5   whether the judgment is a **money judgment** and, if so, the **interest
     applicable**.

Two certified copies of the originating summons and one copy of any
proceedings should be annexed to the affidavit (O. 42A rule 19 RSC). If
the judgment is in default of appearance, the applicant should establish
that the debtor was served with the originating summons.

11. Mortgages

A mortgage (literally "dead pledge") is the conveyance of an interest in property (usually land) as security for a loan, on the understanding that the property will be returned when the loan is paid off. The mortgagor (the person who borrows the money) normally remains in possession of the land unless the debt is unpaid, when proceedings may be taken by the mortgagee (the lender) to recover the amount owed by selling the security. But the mortgagee cannot insist on the sale of the security immediately the debt falls due; even after the *legal* date of redemption, the mortgagor still has an *equitable* right to redeem the mortgage. There are three types of mortgage:

Legal mortgages, which convey the *legal* estate in the property to the mortgagee. The mortgagor must have the legal estate to begin with and must execute a legal conveyance to the mortgagee. If the land is registered, the owner *charges* the land. He remains the owner, but an *encumbrance* is registered on his folio in the Land Registry. This is the usual situation where someone buys a house through a financial institution.

Equitable mortgages, where

1   someone who has already created a legal mortgage thereafter mortgages his remaining interest (his *equity of redemption*), or
2   a person *undertakes* to execute a legal mortgage, or
3   the owner of the legal estate deposits his title deeds (or Land Registry certificate) with the mortgagee as security, creating *prima facie* an equitable mortgage by deposit of title deeds.

Judgment mortgages (or statute mortgages), whereby a Court judgment may be converted into a mortgage. An affidavit detailing the debt is lodged in the Land Registry (or Registry of Deeds if the land is unregistered). With a *joint tenancy*, registration of a judgment mortgage will sever the tenancy and attach to the defendant's moiety and an order will have to be sought under the Partition Acts for sale of the property *in lieu of partition*. If the debt is paid off, a memorandum of satisfaction is drawn up.

A mortgagee by deed (with a legal mortgage) has the right to sue for **breach of covenant** to recover the principal and interest, and has a right to:

- **Foreclosure** which extinguishes the mortgagor's equity of redemption by making the mortgagee the full owner of the property, even if it is worth more than the outstanding loan. Although this remedy is technically available in Ireland, the Courts here prefer that a property should be sold and the mortgage debt paid out of the proceeds.
- **Sale by the mortgagee:** the power of sale is exercisable once the date for redemption has passed on condition:

    1 the mortgagee has served notice on the mortgagor to repay the principal and it's not repaid within three months,
    2 the mortgage interest is two months in arrears, or
    3 there's been a breach of a condition in the mortgage deed (such as a requirement to insure or repair the property).

If the mortgagee is a building society, it is under a statutory duty to obtain the best possible price for the property. A buyer need only ensure the power of sale has arisen (by looking at the mortgage deed) to get good title. The proceeds of sale must be used, in order, to pay off:

1 prior mortgages,
2 sale costs and expenses,
3 the current mortgage with interest and costs and
4 subsequent mortgages.

The mortgagor then receives the balance (if any) of the proceeds.

- **Appointment of a receiver** (by statute or by agreement in the mortgage deed). The receiver, who is appointed in writing by the mortgagee, is deemed to be the agent of the *mortgagor*, so there is not the same liability as if the mortgagee went into possession. The receiver collects the rents and profits of the property, and must apply them in order towards:

    1 rents, taxes, rates and outgoings,
    2 annual payments and interest on prior mortgages,
    3 insurance and repairs of the property,
    4 receiver's commission,
    5 the interest of the mortgagee and
    6 the mortgagor.

- **Right to take possession**: a Common Law right (but the mortgagee has to account strictly to the mortgagor for all actual rents and profits, and for those he would have received but for his neglect). A legal mortgagee of unregistered land is entitled to possession as soon as the mortgage is created, unless otherwise agreed. An equitable mortgagee may apply to the Court for permission to go into possession – although this right is seldom, if ever, exercised.

- **Court order for sale**: where there is a judgment mortgage or equitable mortgage by deposit of title deeds. If the Court directs that the property be sold (O. 51 rule 1 RSC), it usually grants a stay of three months (or more) to allow the mortgagor to pay off the debt. If the debt is not repaid, the sale goes ahead by auction and the proceeds are paid into Court. It is the responsibility of the person who obtains the order for sale to ensure that the purchaser obtains vacant possession.

- **Court order for possession and sale out of Court**: any mortgagee can take out a summons for sale or possession, and any mortgagor can take out a summons for redemption of the mortgage, reconveyance or repossession. Since the case of *Irish Permanent Building Society* v. *Ryan* [1950] IR 12, the Courts have been willing to grant a mortgagee vacant possession. In that case, the plaintiffs had the right to enter into possession of the property if the mortgage was unpaid for three months. Although payments were outstanding for 12 months, the defendant refused to leave the property. The Court accepted that the property could be sold more easily and for a higher price if the mortgagee had vacant possession.

MORTGAGE SUITS

A mortgage suit is begun in the High Court by **special summons** (O. 3 rule 15 RSC). A **legal mortgage**, created by deed (or charge in the case of registered land) will usually have an express power of sale. Alternatively the power of sale of unregistered land may arise under the Conveyancing Act 1881 (or the Registration of Title Act 1964 and the Conveyancing Act 1881, in the case of registered land). The summons will seek an order for full vacant possession.

Depositing the title deeds of unregistered land will create an **equitable mortgage** (whereas, with registered land, deposit of the land certificate creates an **equitable charge**). Where a defendant has an interest in land (legal *or* equitable, sole, joint or as tenant-in-common), a duly-entered judgment may be executed by creating a **judgment mortgage** over that interest.

Because there is no power of sale in a **judgment mortgage** or **equitable mortgage**, *well charging proceedings* must be brought to realise the security.

The special summons is given a return date before the Master and must be served four clear days before that date. If the defendant or notice parties put in a replying affidavit, the function of the Master is only procedural and he will not consider whether there is any defence to the summons (unlike with the summary summons). Once any affidavits have been filed, the special summons is transferred to the judges' list: the *special* **special summons** list for mortgage suits.

The application comes into Court on a Monday and is usually dealt with if there is no defence. Because there is no express or statutory power of sale with an equitable or judgment mortgage, the summons seeks:

1. a declaration that the amount secured by the equitable deposit (or the amount of the judgment) stands **well charged** against the defendant's interest in the property,
2. an enquiry as to **other encumbrancers** and their priorities,
3. an order for **enforcement of the security by way of sale** and
4. **costs**.

The requirements in the Rules for proceedings to recover possession of land apply in all such cases, even those involving adverse possession or trespass.

The defendant will be the mortgagor, whether legal or equitable (or, in the case of a judgment mortgage, the judgment debtor). Notice of the proceedings must be served on *everyone* in possession or receipt of rents and profits from the property – not as defendants, but as parties whose rights could be prejudiced and who may wish to make submissions. In the case of a limited company, the directors are served with notice. If the property was let, the tenants and/or under-tenants would be notice parties. If the defendant lived with his family, they would also be served.

The summons is addressed to the defendant "and all persons concerned" (O. 4 rule 7 RSC). The affidavit of service must state that *everyone* in possession of the property, or in receipt of rents or profits from it, has been served with notice of the proceedings *and* that the deponent knows of no such person who has not been served. The solicitor must also swear an affidavit verifying the contents of the affidavit of service.

The **special summons** identifies the plaintiff and the defendant (with professions and addresses) and then sets out the facts establishing how the mortgage arises:

In the case of a **legal mortgage**, the summons might say

> *By deed of mortgage dated the___day of_____19__ made between the defendant and the plaintiff, the defendant mortgaged the property set out in the Schedule hereto on foot of money advanced by the plaintiff to the defendant by way of loan ...*

With an **equitable mortgage**, the summons might continue

> *The plaintiff advanced money to the defendant as banker (with particulars of the loan). The loan was secured by the defendant depositing with the plaintiff the title deeds to the property set out in the Schedule (or the land certificate to the property set out in the Schedule) thus creating an equitable mortgage by deposit of title deeds (or land certificate).*

In the case of a **judgment mortgage**, the wording might be

> *In proceedings entitled (set out the Court, record number and parties) the plaintiff was granted judgment against the defendant in the sum of £___ and costs, together with interest on the judgment at X%".*

The next paragraph, in the case of a legal or equitable mortgage, would say

> *The defendant has failed to make all payments due on foot of the mortgage (with details of the default).*

With a judgment mortgage, the wording would be

> *The entire (or remainder of the) judgment is outstanding and £____remains due.*

The fourth paragraph says

> *A demand has been made of the defendant for the repayment of the money due but the defendant has failed, refused or neglected to pay the said sum. (Set out the amount, including calculation of interest, if not already done).*

And the plaintiff claims (in the case of a **legal mortgage**):

1   an order directing the defendant to deliver up **possession of the property** set out in the schedule,
2   an order directing the defendant to **pay the sums due** and
3   **costs**.

With an **equitable** or **judgment mortgage**, the plaintiff claims an order:

1   declaring that the amount owed by the defendant stands **well charged** against the defendant's interest in the property in the schedule to the summons,
2   directing an enquiry as to **other encumbrancers** before the Examiner of the High Court (or *all necessary accounts, directions and enquiries*),
3   directing the defendant to **pay the sum due,**
4   for **possession** of the property,
5   directing enforcement of the security by **sale of the property,**
6   for **costs**.

The schedule contains a precise description of the property:

> *ALL THAT AND THOSE the dwelling house and premises known as ... (in the case of unregistered property) or the property comprised in folio number ... in the register of property for the County of* _____.

At the end of all special summonses, there is a schedule setting out the affidavits filed in support of the summons.

The **grounding affidavit** will verify the facts in the summons and exhibit all the documents necessary to ground the claim. With a legal mortgage, it will exhibit the mortgage deed or the land certificate (or a certified copy) in an envelope, saying: *I beg to refer to (the document) which I have placed in an envelope and sealed and upon which, marked with the letter "A", I have signed my name prior to the swearing hereof.*

In the case of a **legal mortgage**, the affidavit should set out how the power of sale arises under the mortgage deed. Usually the deed sets out the events which may lead to a power of sale and the affidavit should specify which of these events has occurred.

With an **equitable mortgage**, the title deeds or land certificate are exhibited with any memorandum of deposit and an averment that the title deeds or land certificate were deposited as an equitable security (and not, for example, for safekeeping).

The affidavit should state whether or not the dwelling is a family home for the purposes of the Family Home Protection Act 1976. If so, it must confirm that both spouses are on notice of the proceedings and exhibit the prior written consent of both spouses to the creation of the mortgage.

The Family Law Act 1995 defines a dwelling as "any building or part of a building occupied as a separate dwelling and includes any garden or other land usually occupied with the dwelling, being land that is subsidiary and ancillary to it, is required for amenity or convenience and is not being used or developed primarily for commercial purposes, and includes a structure that is not permanently attached to the ground and a vehicle, or vessel, whether mobile or not, occupied as a separate dwelling."

Under the Family Home Protection Act, if the family home is sold by one spouse – who may be the legal owner of the property – without the written consent of the other spouse, the transaction is void. But in *Nestor* v. *Murphy* [1979] IR 326 the Court decided that, where spouses were co-owners of the home and they both agreed to sell it, they could not avoid the contract just because the wife had not given her prior consent in writing.

In the case of *Bank of Ireland* v. *Smyth* [1995] 2 IR 459, the Supreme Court ruled that a person had to be properly informed in order to consent to a charge over the family home.

The effect of the absence of prior written consent of the spouse to a legal mortgage was considered in *Bank of Ireland* v. *Slevin* [1995] 2 IR 454. The deeds of Mr Slevin's farm were deposited with the bank as security for a loan, without Mrs Slevin's consent in writing. Mr Slevin therefore claimed the whole mortgage was void for lack of consent, but the Court ruled that the mortgage was only void in relation to the family home, and granted a charge over the rest of the farm.

In *AIB* v. *O'Neill* [1995] 2 IR 473, Mrs O'Neill deposited the land certificate for the family farm as an equitable mortgage, without the prior written consent of her husband. The bank accepted that it could not seize the couple's house – but claimed it had an equitable mortgage over the rest of the farm.

The High Court said the legislature clearly intended that the family home might form only part of a larger holding and the Act only required the prior written consent of the other spouse in relation to the home, not to the rest of the land. The Court ruled that the mortgage was valid against the farmlands, but not against the house and gardens.

In *Bank of Ireland* v. *Hanrahan*, High Court, 10 February 1987, a couple claimed that a mortgage was void because the wife had not given her consent until two hours *after* her husband deposited the title deeds with the bank. The Court said the mortgage was valid because there had been an implied agreement that the bank would only hold the deeds as custodian until the wife gave her consent.

In *O'Keeffe* v. *Russell and AIB* [1994] 1 ILRM 137, a land certificate was lodged as security for a loan to a farmer, despite the objections of his wife. The Supreme Court said the wife had not been party to the loan, so there was no equitable charge against her half of the farm.

Until 1996, anyone buying unregistered property had to check every conveyance of the land since the passing of the 1976 Act, but the Family Law Act 1995 says a conveyance will be valid unless declared void by a Court. Any proceedings to declare a conveyance void must be instituted within six years of the transaction. (This procedure is not necessary with registered land, as an entry in the register is regarded as conclusive proof of the title of the registered owner.)

The 1976 Act provides that, where a non-owning spouse can pay arrears or continue the mortgage payments, the mortgagee is obliged to accept such payments and the Court will not make a well-charging order.

The Family Law Act 1995 now allows a general written consent to all future loans. This may mean that, if one spouse gives such consent in writing, the other spouse may thereafter secure any future borrowings against the family home, effectively contracting out of the safeguards of the original legislation.

No such written consent is needed for a judgment mortgage. In *Containercare (Ireland)* v. *Wycherley* [1982] IR 143, a husband and wife were joint owners of the family home. A creditor obtained a judgment mortgage against the husband for outstanding debts. The Court ruled that a judgment mortgage was not a conveyance by the spouse involved, but the creation of a mortgage by operation of law. The judgment mortgage was registered against the husband's share of the home, so that the wife and the creditor effectively became joint owners of the property.

In the case of a **judgment mortgage**, the affidavit should refer to a copy of the judgment when produced and exhibit a certified copy of the judgment mortgage affidavit as registered in the Registry of Deeds or give details of the Land Registry folio number.

The deponent should then refer to the debt, how it arose and the amount due, ensuring that it matches the amount in the special endorsement of claim. He should refer to the demand for payment and exhibit it.

The affidavit should confirm that everyone in possession or in receipt of rents or profits has been served and should refer to the affidavit of service and the verifying affidavit when produced. The affidavit should verify that all the facts in the special summons are true and correct.

The affidavit is filed in the Central Office and a certified copy is returned to the plaintiff's solicitor. That copy *is* the judgment mortgage *(Re Flood's Estate [1865] 17 Ir Ch R 116)*. The certified copy is registered in the Registry of Deeds or Land Registry (depending on whether the land is registered or unregistered).

In *Irish Bank of Commerce* v. *O'Hara*, Supreme Court, 7 April 1992, the plaintiff bank obtained judgment against the defendant for £744,000 and costs. The bank swore an affidavit seeking a **judgment mortgage** over Mr O'Hara's lands in Killiney. He claimed the judgment mortgage was invalid because the affidavit did not specify the parish in which the lands were situated. The bank said failure to specify a parish in a **judgment mortgage** affidavit only invalidated the mortgage if the lands were in a town. Costello J said that, if the **affidavit** achieved the purpose which the legislature sought to achieve, there was no reason why the Court should construe the section as requiring strict compliance with its provisions, particularly in a case where to do so would be to offend against commonsense and justice.

The defendant also claimed that the bank had failed to file the **judgment mortgage affidavit** in the Central Office as well as the Registry of Deeds. Costello J said, once it was established that the affidavit had been filed in the Registry of Deeds and there was a sworn averment that the provisions of the Judgment Mortgage (Ireland) Act 1850 had been complied with, it was not necessary to prove that the affidavit had been filed in the Central Office, unless the defendants produced evidence to suggest this had not been done.

The date of registration of the judgment mortgage governs its priority over other encumbrances. A judgment mortgage is registered subject to *all* existing rights over the property, registered or unregistered, so a prior *deed* (even though unregistered) would take priority.

In the case of a **legal mortgage**, the Court will give an order for possession which the plaintiff may then enforce. The defendant may seek a stay on the order to try and pay the debt or to give him time to organise somewhere else to live.

In the case of **equitable** or **judgment mortgages** the Court will make an order deeming the sum claimed well charged against the defendant's interest in the property. It will fix a period (usually three months) within which the defendant may dispute the figures upon which the application is based – especially if he has not appeared. The Court will direct that an enquiry be made before the Examiner of the High Court, who will certify as to priorities (legal or equitable, first in time). Other encumbrancers will also put their claims. At this stage the Court will make an order for sale, but *not* for possession.

A motion is then issued in the same proceedings to bring the matter back before the Court on the basis of the Examiner's certificate, so that an order for possession may be made. The motion is again served on the defendant and all persons in possession or in receipt of rents and profits from the property, and a similar **affidavit of service** and **verifying affidavit** are required.

The Court will then grant an order for possession and the property will be sold under Court supervision. The Court will approve the contract and price, and the proceeds will be lodged in Court, to be paid out in accordance with the priorities laid down by the Examiner. (This is not required in the case of a **legal mortgage** where the mortgagee is exercising his power of sale under the deed or by statute.)

If both sides agree that the sale of the property out of Court would yield a better price, the Court should be asked to permit the sale outside the supervision of the Court. The proceeds, in the case of the **legal mortgage**, are paid out by the mortgagee on advice as to priorities.

The mortgagee is trustee of the proceeds of sale and may be sued for breach of trust if there is a wrongful payment. In *Murphy* v. *AIB* [1994] 2 ILRM 220, the plaintiff's mother created a charge over her house in favour of the defendant bank. When she died, the bank sold the house and, after deducting debts, put the balance of £1,980 in a demand deposit account. Although the bank contacted the woman's family on several occasions, the executors did not ask for the money. In 1984 the woman's son brought an action against the bank for failing to invest the surplus.

The judge said a mortgagee who retains surplus money after selling mortgaged property is obliged to pay interest on the sum, or to hand over the profits of a business carried on with the trust money. In this case, the rate of interest payable was that of a bank demand deposit account – or the Court rate of interest, where the bank rate was not identified. (But the judge said that the Statute of Limitations applied, so only six years' interest was payable in total.)

In the case of sale under Court supervision, the Examiner's office will pay out the money in accordance with the Examiner's certificate.

Mortgage proceedings can be very lengthy. Often with a **judgment mortgage**, the mortgagee will prefer to register his mortgage on the deeds of the property and recover his money when the property is sold.

12. Probate

The law and practice of probate is largely contained in the Succession Act 1965 and Order 79 and 80 of the Rules of the Superior Court. The law divides up into:

1.   **testate succession** – that is the execution and validity of wills, grants of probate and administration of an estate under a valid will and
2.   **intestate** (or **partially-testate**) **succession**, where a person dies without making a valid will, including the extraction of a grant of administration and distribution of the estate.

Probate law is divided into so-called contentious and non-contentious jurisdictions. The non-contentious jurisdiction (O. 79 RSC) covers issues such as the proving of a will in the Probate Office and the grant of probate (or letters of administration).

The contentious probate jurisdiction (properly called probate actions, which begin by originating summons) involves matters such as challenges to wills, disputes over administration of estates, and applications by children who claim their parents failed to make proper provision for them.

Most wills are proved in **common form** by application to the Probate Office, without any reference to Court. But even an order made by the Court in its non-contentious jurisdiction is still proof in common form. **Solemn form** of proof follows a full plenary hearing on the contentious side and is binding once and for all on everyone.

WILLS

The formal requirements for a valid will are set out in s.78 of the Succession Act:

1.   it must be **in writing** (oral wills for sailors or soldiers on military service are no longer permitted),
2.   it must be signed (or a mark made) **at the foot or end** by the testator, or by someone in his presence and by his direction,
3.   the signature must be made or acknowledged in the presence of **two witnesses, both present at the same time** and

4   the witnesses must **sign in the presence of the testator**, but not necessarily in each other's presence.

A witness may be an executor of the will (s.84), or even a child – although this may cause problems if he is called on to swear an affidavit while he is still a minor. The incompetence of a witness does not invalidate a will (s.81).

"Signature" can include the initials of the testator or, in the case of an illiterate or severely disabled person, a mark. In the case of *Glynn* v. *Glynn* [1987] ILRM 589, an X was accepted as a signature. In *In bonis Cook* [1960] 1WLR 353, the Court proved a will signed simply "Your loving mother". But with a feeble signature or a mark, the Probate Office will require an affidavit from the witnesses, confirming that the will was read over by (or to) the deceased before execution and that he was of sound mind, memory and understanding.

A will is not necessarily invalidated simply because the signature does not immediately follow the last word or is after the *witnesses'* signatures (s.78(4)). But any writing after the *testator's* signature is normally excluded as an unexecuted codicil – s.78(5). (A codicil is an addition to a will which changes the original document.) In the case of *In Re Beadle* [1974] 1WLR 417, the Court ruled that a document could not constitute a will where the testatrix signed at the top of the page.

A will which does not comply with these provisions will be valid (ss.102–3) if it complies with the law

1   of the **place** where the testator made it,
2   of the testator's **nationality**, either when he made the will or at his death,
3   of the place where the testator was **domiciled** or habitually resident when he made the will or died,
4   of the place where immovable **property** is situated or,
5   when a will is made on a ship or plane, where it had its most real **connexion**.

For a will to be valid, the testator must be:

1   **18 years old** or over, or be (or have been) married,
2   acting of his own **free will** and
3   of sound **mind, memory and understanding**

(A person who is entitled to appoint a guardian of a child may do so by will, even if he is under 18 and single.)

In *Banks* v. *Goodfellow* [1870] LR 5 QB 549, Cockburn CJ said a testator must:

1   **understand that he is making a will**, though he need not understand its precise legal effect,
2   **know the nature and extent of his property** (he must not bequeath property which he had sold earlier) *and*
3   be able to **recall the people who might be expected to benefit** from his bounty (or to call to mind those who might have a claim against, or expect to benefit from, his estate).

A will may be challenged on the basis that the testator did not have testamentary capacity but the deceased will be *presumed* to have had testamentary capacity, unless a reasonable doubt is raised. Testamentary capacity may be proved by an **affidavit** from a doctor or solicitor present when the will was made, stating that the testator was of sound mind.

But, in the last resort, testamentary capacity is a matter for the Court, as stressed by the Supreme Court in *Glynn* v. *Glynn* [1987] ILRM 589. In that case, the capacity of the testator was challenged by his sister after he left his residue to a cousin. He had already instructed a parish priest to draw up his will for him, but two months later he suffered a stroke which left him dumb. When the will was read back to him in hospital, he was only able to nod or shake his head. He marked an "X" at the end of the will. A doctor testified that the deceased did not have testamentary capacity at the time. The priest said he did. In the High Court, Hamilton P upheld the validity of the will. The Supreme Court upheld that decision on appeal, but Walsh J, in a dissenting judgment, said the incident in the hospital was a travesty of justice and that the deceased lacked testamentary capacity.

The testator must have testamentary capacity when the will is *executed*. In *In Re JR* [1993] ILRM 657 the deceased was of sound disposing mind when he executed the will. The Court held that he *did* have testamentary capacity – even though his condition later worsened. (While, in a criminal case, there is a *legal* burden on the defendant to rebut the presumption of sanity, in a probate case, the presumption of sanity can be rebutted by discharging merely an *evidential* burden.)

In *Blackall* v. *Blackall*, High Court, 28 June 1996, a 99-year-old woman made a will leaving her property equally between her four children. When her solicitor read the will over to her, the testatrix commented: "I think that's fair, one of them is a bit fiery". McCracken J said he was satisfied that was the comment of someone who knew what had been read to her, and that the testatrix had testamentary capacity.

In a case reported in the London *Times* on 23 October 1996, Judge Hazel Williamson QC overturned a will in which the testator left half his property to a man he had met in prison. Mrs Wanda Wisniewska had given half her home to her adopted son in 1990, in the belief he would survive her. He made a will in 1992 leaving everything to her. But in 1994, the son – who was by then a heroin addict and an alcoholic – changed his will to leave half his estate to a man he had met in prison 25 years earlier. The son died a month later.

Judge Williamson said the son had been extremely ill when he signed the later will, and lacked the testamentary capacity to do so.

A blind person can make a will, but the Probate Office will require an affidavit from one of the witnesses, confirming that, if the testator had been sighted, he could have seen them sign. But a blind person *cannot be a witness* as he is unable to see the testator sign.

A witness or his spouse cannot benefit under a will (s. 82). Even a *charging clause*, agreeing a fee for drawing up or executing the will, is void if the solicitor or a member of his firm (or their spouses) act as a witness. An executor who acts as a witness will lose any benefit.

A person who signs a will, not as a witness, but merely to show that he agrees with its contents, may benefit (although the will should indicate that this is the case). And a witness or spouse may benefit where the:

1 legacy is given as a **legal or moral duty** of the testator (such as a debt),
2 benefit is given **in trust** for someone else,
3 benefit arises from a **secret trust**,
4 beneficiary and the witness **married *after* the will** or
5 legacy is confirmed in a **subsequent codicil** witnessed by someone else.

CONTENTS OF A WILL

A will should contain:

1 the testator's **name and address**,
2 a **revocation clause**,
3 a clause appointing **executors** (preferably, but not necessarily, two or more),
4 details of general and specific **legacies** (gifts of money or goods),
5 details of **devises** (gifts of real property),

6   a **residuary clause**, disposing of the remainder of the estate,
7   the **date**,
8   the testator's **signature,**
9   the **attestation clause** or *testimonium* and
10 the **witnesses' signatures**.

The revocation clause must revoke all other codicils and earlier testamentary dispositions, as well as former wills. The executors, who should be likely to outlive the testator, should be clearly identified. "*I appoint AB and CD as my executors*" or "*I appoint AB as my executor or, if he dies before me, I appoint CD in his place*" are satisfactory, but "*I appoint AB or CD as my executor*" would be void for uncertainty.

But in *In Re Doran*, ITLR, 9 October 2000, the testatrix provided in her will for the appointment of A or B as executors. Herbert J ruled that the intention of the testatrix was to appoint A as original executor and B as substitute executor. He said the clause was not void for uncertainty, as it was possible to appoint the substitute executor.

If the will has no residuary clause, any property not specifically mentioned would pass according to the rules of intestacy in Part VI of the Succession Act. Also, if for any reason any of the other specific gifts should fail (for example, under the *doctrine of lapse*), the property involved would fall into the residue (s.91).

A will may contain only an executor clause and a residue clause, and still be valid if it expresses the wishes of the testator. If the executors have died or cannot (or will not) act, the person entitled to the residue can administer the estate.

The lack of a date on a will does not invalidate it, but the Probate Office will require an affidavit from one of the witnesses confirming that the document was executed before the testator died.

The *testimonium* might read: *Signed by the testator as and for his last will and testament in the presence of us, both present at the same time, and signed by us in the presence of the testator.* The witnesses normally sign under this clause, but the will is not invalid if they sign elsewhere on the document. If the will does not contain a testimonium, the Probate Office will require an affidavit from a subscribing witness (O. 79 rule 6).

Wills "speak from death", and are interpreted as if they had been executed immediately before the death of the testator, unless the will itself specifies otherwise. If any children of the testator die before him, property bequeathed to them will automatically pass to their children (s.98). If two or more people die together (for example in a car crash) and it is not possible to establish who died first, they are deemed to have died simultaneously (s.5).

If the will is in a foreign language, a translation may be admitted to proof. Any obliteration, insertion or alteration in a will after its execution is invalid unless:

- the testator and witnesses sign near the alteration,
- the changes are proved to have been in the will before its execution,
- the alterations are mentioned in the recital clause or
- there is a properly-executed codicil or memorandum referring to the alterations.

If the will refers to any documents which existed when the will was executed, they should be produced. If a will is written in pencil, a copy in red ink must be produced for the Probate Office. An official copy of any will or grant of administration may be obtained from the Probate Office or district probate registry.

If a testator is married, he or she must make proper provision for the other spouse and children (Part IX Succession Act 1965). If there are no children, a surviving spouse has an automatic right to half the estate, including the family home. In the case of *O'Dwyer* v. *Keegan* [1997] 2 IR 585, a testator had died leaving £2.4 million. His wife, who was in a coma at the time of her husband's death, died 12 hours later, leaving £370,000. The husband had not made provision for his wife in his will. The couple had no children and the wife had not renounced her legal right.

Kelly J ruled that s.111(1) of the 1965 Act did not give rise to an automatic transfer to the wife of half the husband's estate on his death. Rather, it was a right which she could exercise if she wished. On appeal, the Supreme Court reversed that decision.

If there are children, the surviving spouse has a right to one third of the estate (ss. 56, 111). If a testator has disposed of property within three years of death in an attempt to disinherit a spouse or children, the Court may rule the disposition void. The spouse's "legal right" has priority over any other bequests, although it may be renounced in writing at any time while the testator is still alive. The legal right may be extinguished following a judicial separation and disappears after a divorce. A spouse who has deserted or committed a serious offence against the testator or against the testator's children (s.120) loses any right to a share in the estate.

In *In Re Martin Glynn, deceased* [1992] 1 IR 361, the executor of a will murdered the testator's sister (to whom the testator had bequeathed his farm as a tenant for life, with the remainder to the executor). By the murder, the executor would have hastened the vesting of the farm in himself. The Court held that a grant of probate should not be made to the executor, and the Chief State Solicitor was given permission to apply for an unlimited grant of administration with the will annexed.

A husband and wife's mutual rights to succeed to each other's estates may also be extinguished by the Court at any time on or after a decree of judicial separation, under the Family Law Act 1995. (Succession rights are automatically extinguished after a divorce, as the couple are no longer man and wife. Where a marriage is void, the partners are not spouses and these provisions also do not apply.)

A simple will might read:

> *I, Catherine O'Brien of Ailesbury Road in the City of Dublin, declare this to be my last will and testament. I hereby revoke all former wills and testamentary dispositions made by me. I appoint my brother Al and my sister Sal as executors of this my will and direct them to pay my just debts, funeral and testamentary expenses.*
>
> *I leave £500 to my housekeeper Vera. I leave my James Joyce first editions to my chauffeur Brendan. I leave my house in Ailesbury Road to my brother Willy. I leave my house at Ballinteer to my brother Vinnie. I leave £1000 from my Anglo-Irish Building Society account to the Stephen's Green Cats' Home.*
>
> *All the residue and remainder of my property of whatsoever nature and description and wheresoever situate I leave in equal shares between my children, Bobbie and Barbie.*
>
> *Dated this___day of_____   200*
>
> *Signed*
>
> *Catherine O'Brien*
>
> *Signed by the testatrix as and for her last will and testament in the presence of us, both present at the same time, and signed by us in the presence of the testatrix*
>
> *Philip Watt*
> *Mike Parsley*

A legacy may fail where it:

1   **abates**, due to insufficient assets,
2   is **adeemed**,
3   **lapses**, because the beneficiary dies first, or
4   is **void for uncertainty.**

Abatement means the amount of the legacy is reduced because there are insufficient assets to cover all the dispositions. *Ademption* happens where the testator leaves a specific asset (for example a work of art) but disposes of it before death. A legacy which lapses falls into the residue unless:

1   the legatee is a child of the testator and leaves children of his own,
2   the will shows a different intention,
3   the legacy fulfils a moral or legal duty or
4   the legacy is a charitable gift.

In the case of a **demonstrative legacy** payable out of specific funds, such as the one from the building society account, if the *subject* of the legacy (that is the cats' home) does not exist at the date of death, the legacy will be extinguished or *adeemed*. If, on the other hand, the *source* of the legacy (that is the building society account) has been closed, the legacy may be paid out of the residue, if there are sufficient funds.

REVOCATION OF A WILL

A will may only be revoked (s.85 of the Succession Act 1965) by:

1   a **subsequent marriage** – unless the will is made in contemplation of *that* marriage,
2   a duly-executed **later will** or codicil which **expressly revokes** all earlier testamentary dispositions,
3   **declaring in writing** the intention to revoke the will, and executing the document in the same way as a will or
4   **burning, tearing or destruction** by the testator (or someone in his presence and by his direction), with the simultaneous *intention* of revocation.

A letter to a person who holds the will, asking him to destroy it, would revoke the will, whether or not it was actually destroyed. If no other will is executed, this would produce an intestacy. An earlier will is not revived by revocation of a later will; that may only be done by *re-execution* or a duly-executed codicil. There may be an implied revocation of an earlier will if the later will is clearly inconsistent with it – for example if the testator disposes of all his assets in the later will (*In Re Bonis Martin* [1968] IR 1).

The *presumption of revocation* by destruction may be rebutted by an **affidavit** from someone who saw the will after the testator's death. Revocation of a will may be conditional. For example, a testator may destroy a will with the intention of making a new will, in which case the Court may consider the doctrine of *dependent relative revocation.*

In *In bonis Hogan* [1980] ILRM 24, Eileen Hogan executed a will in her solicitor's office in 1977. She was given the original and the solicitor kept a copy. In 1979, she executed a second will in her solicitor's office and was told that, as the first will had been revoked, it should be destroyed. She took the original of the 1979 will and the solicitor kept a copy.

Two months later she burned some documents in front of her son. She died soon afterwards and the only will found among her papers was the 1977 version. Her daughter applied to have the photocopy of the 1979 will admitted to probate. Gannon J said it was correct to infer from the testatrix's behaviour that she intended to destroy the 1979 will by burning, that she intended to revive the 1977 will and that she did not intend to die intestate.

But the 1977 will had not been re-executed according to s.87 of the 1965 Act, so her intention to revive the will could not be carried out. The judge said the purported revocation of the 1979 will was based on the testatrix's mistaken view of the law, and the dependent relative revocation was not effective. The judge admitted the copy of the 1979 will to probate.

In *In bonis Coster,* Supreme Court, 19 January 1979, Hannah Coster had her will drawn up by a solicitor in 1971. Two years later, she took away the original will, leaving a copy. Three years later she died. A blank will form was found in her possessions, but the will was missing. She had left the residue of her estate to her sister, a nun, who had since died. The superior of the convent applied for an order declaring that Mrs Coster had died intestate.

Gannon J refused because the original will might have been mislaid and, even if it had been destroyed, the revocation was conditional on the execution of another will.

On appeal, the Supreme Court said that, if a person has made a will and it is missing when the person dies, there is a presumption that it was destroyed with the intention of revocation. But Kenny J said he did not believe the revocation by destruction was conditional on the making of another will. A mere intention to make a new will was not of itself enough to make the revocation conditional. Kenny J said the revocation by destruction was absolute, so the deceased died intestate.

GRANTS OF REPRESENTATION

When a person dies, his estate is administered by a personal representative who can be either an **executor** (nominated in a will or codicil) or an **administrator** (appointed by the Court).

A personal representative holds the entire estate (both real and personal) as trustee for anyone entitled to the property by law. Where someone dies without leaving a will (or executor), his estate vests in the President of the High Court as a corporation sole, until the Probate Office grants administration.

There is no legal requirement to extract a grant of representation to an estate but a grant is usually necessary to be able to sell property of the deceased or collect assets. Applications for a grant of probate or letters of administration may be made in person or though a solicitor 14 days or more after the death of the deceased (O. 79 rules 3, 33 RSC).

There are three types of primary grant of representation. A grant of **probate** *only* applies to the executors named in the will and simply confirms their authority, which is derived from the wishes of the testator expressed in the will.

A person named as executor does not have to act and is entitled to renounce his rights to administer the estate. If two or more executors are named in the will and one or more of them is willing to act, they may reserve the rights of the other executors, who may extract a grant of **double probate** while the existing executor is still alive, or a grant of **unadministered probate** where the acting executor has died. If an executor renounces probate, he has no further rights in relation to the estate. He can only withdraw the renunciation in exceptional circumstances, with the permission of the Court. But an executor cannot renounce his rights if he has *intermeddled* in the estate – such as instructing a solicitor to prove the will, or swearing documents to extract a grant.

A grant of **administration with the will annexed** is made where there is a valid will but the testator did not name an executor, or where the executor:

1   is not clearly identified,
2   is not willing to act,

3 dies before being granted probate,
4 fails to appear to a citation,
5 renounces probate,
6 is a minor or
7 is of unsound mind.

A grant of **administration intestate** is made where there is no valid will and the deceased died *wholly* intestate. Part VI of the 1965 Act sets out the rules for the distribution of an estate in the case of intestacy. Section 67 of the Act says that, if an intestate leaves a spouse and no children, the spouse takes the whole estate. If there are children, the spouse takes two thirds and the children share the remainder. If both spouses are dead, the children share the estate. If there is no surviving spouse and no issue, the estate goes to his parents or is divided according to ss.68–73 of the Act.

If an administrator or executor dies, leaving part of the estate unadministered, his successor will have to apply for a further grant *de bonis non administratis* (of goods not administered) through the Probate Office or the district probate registry (s.17 Succession Act 1965). The types of *de bonis non* grant are:

1 **administration with the will annexed** (where there is a full or partial testacy),
2 **administration intestate** (in the case of intestacy) or
3 **unadministered probate** where another executor is still willing to act.

But limited administration will not be granted unless everyone entitled to a *general* grant has consented, renounced or been cited and failed to appear (O. 79 rule 20 RSC).

The powers and duties of an administrator are set out in the Succession Act. A grant of administration will not normally be made jointly to more than three people, unless the Probate Officer directs. Administration may be granted to an attorney where a person is about to leave the country or is suffering from a severe continuing disability. Administration may also be granted to the guardian of an infant or the committee of a person of unsound mind. An administrator must provide a bond to the President of the High Court for twice the value of the estate, as a surety for its proper collection and administration.

If the testator was blind or illiterate, the Probate Officer will require evidence on affidavit that the will was read over to him before execution or that he knew its contents (O. 79 rule 63 RSC). If the testator died without any known relations, citations should be issued against anyone having a claim on the estate, but no grant may be issued without the direction of the Attorney General as the representative of the State, the ultimate intestate successor (O. 79 rules 65–6 RSC).

Most non-contentious matters are dealt with by the Probate Office, but only the Court may deal with:

1   **lost or mislaid wills,**
2   **special grants** under s.27(4) of the Succession Act 1965 or
3   **rival applicants** (which are regarded as non-contentious).

LOST WILLS

If the original will has been lost, advertisements should be placed in appropriate newspapers and the Law Society Gazette to try and find it. The Probate Office will not accept a copy will, in case the original was revoked by destruction. An application in relation to a lost will is by **motion on notice** in the non-contentious probate list, supported by affidavits:

1   of the **applicant,**
2   of the **attesting witness,**
3   of **service on anyone benefiting** under the will or on intestacy and
4   to establish the **other proofs**

If the beneficiaries agree to the application, their **written consents** should be exhibited, and they need not be served with notice.

The affidavit of the applicant must:

1   exhibit the testator's **death certificate,**
2   exhibit the **copy of the will** to be proved,
3   explain the **reasons** for the application,
4   list the **testator's assets,**
5   list the **persons entitled to inherit upon intestacy**, confirming that notice has been served on each of them, and
6   prove **service** on the notice parties (unless they appear).

At least one of the witnesses to the will must swear that it was properly executed – even if everything appears to be in order. If the witnesses are dead, their **death certificates** should be produced. If they are untraceable, the applicant should detail his efforts to find them. The

Court may then rely on the rebuttable presumption *omnia praesumuntur rite esse acta* (everything necessary is presumed to have been done).

The solicitor or person who made the copy will must swear that it is authentic. If no photocopy or carbon copy exists, someone with means of knowledge (such as the original on computer disk) may give evidence so the will can be reconstructed.

The application will normally be a **motion for the sitting of the Court**, as the claimants' solicitors are not on record. The **notice of motion**, headed "*The High Court, Probate*", sets out:

1   the date of the **will**,
2   the **date of death** of the deceased,
3   that the original will **existed unrevoked** at the time of death and
4   that the will is **lost or unavailable**

and prays that the Court will admit the copy to proof.

SPECIAL GRANTS

The Succession Act gives the High Court power to grant probate or administration to one or more persons, or to revoke, cancel or recall a grant. But in *Dunne* v. *Heffernan* [1997] 3 IR 431, the Supreme Court held that, once an executor had been appointed and had proved a will, he could only be removed if there were "serious grounds or weighty reasons" for overruling the wishes of the testator.

The executor was removed by the High Court in the case of *Flood* v. *Flood* [1999] 2 IR 234 because he had borrowed money from the testator and refused to repay it. Macken J said the Court should not remove an executor except in the case of "serious misconduct and/or serious special circumstances".

Section 27(4) allows the Court to grant administration to any person it thinks fit where *special circumstances* render it *necessary* or *expedient*. (Administration may be granted where, for example, distant relatives of the deceased wish to administer the will, because closer relations are untraceable.)

An application may be brought *ex parte* or on notice, depending on the circumstances. Notice should be given to any appropriate persons (such as the other branch of the family). Any question of fact may be tried by a jury, with the consent of both sides.

If the application is *ex parte*, it is grounded on a **motion paper**, which is lodged in the Probate Office with a copy of the will and any grounding affidavits at least two clear days before the hearing. The **motion paper** sets out:

1 the **names and descriptions** of the parties,
2 the **purpose** of the proceedings,
3 a short statement of the **facts**,
4 details of any **earlier proceedings**,
5 details of any **ruling** made by the Probate Office and
6 the **prayer**.

Before the hearing, the specially-assigned probate judge will consider:

1 the **grounding affidavit** giving the reasons for the application,
2 **other affidavits** (for example, where the next-of-kin is unknown, an affidavit of pedigree) and
3 the **affidavit of service** on any notice parties.

If the next-of-kin cannot be traced, the judge may appoint someone to represent his interests (O. 15 rule 22 RSC). If there is a problem proving the death of the deceased, the applicant may rely on a *rebuttable presumption of law* that, once a *basic* fact is proved, the Court must draw an inference as to the existence of the *presumed* fact unless there is evidence to the contrary. A presumption of death requires that the person be absent and unheard of for seven years by persons likely to have heard from him (that is close relations, rather than – for example – a separated spouse). The Court may presume death after a shorter time if the circumstances warrant it (for example, if someone appeared to have committed suicide or died in battle), although any motive for feigning death (such as a recent substantial life insurance policy) will be considered.

In *Re Phene's Trusts* [1870] 5 Ch App 139, a testator had bequeathed his residence equally between nephews and nieces. One nephew joined the US Navy in 1858 and deserted in 1860. The testator died the following year. In 1868 the nephew was advertised for but did not reply. If he had pre-deceased the testator, he would not have been entitled to a share in the estate.

The Court decided that the burden of proving survivorship was on the applicant whose claim was based on the testator dying before the nephew. But there is no *presumption of life* in law. On appeal, the claim failed as there was no evidence to show that the nephew had survived the testator. But a legatee may establish survivorship by using the presumption of death where the *testator* disappeared more than seven years before.

In *Re Bonis Doherty* [1961] IR 219, the defendant instructed stock-brokers in 1919 to buy £30-worth of shares. Nobody ever heard from him again. In 1961 the Minister for Finance applied to the High Court to declare the shares *bona vacantia*. The High Court presumed not only the defendant's death, but that he died without next-of-kin.

RIVAL APPLICANTS

The order of priority of entitlement to administer the estate in the case of a will or intestacy is laid down by the **Rules of the Superior Courts**.

In the case of intestacy (O. 79 rule 5(1) RSC), the order begins with the spouse and deceased's children and continues through great-grand-parents, next-of-kin, the State and creditors of the deceased. Where there is a will (O. 79 rule 5(6) RSC), the order is:

1   executors,
2   residuary legatee or devisee in trust,
3   residuary legatee or devisee for life (if any),
4   any other residuary legatee or devisee (or their personal representatives),
5   any residuary legatee or devisee for life with any ultimate residuary legatee or devisee on the consent of the remaining residuary legatees or devisees,
6   any legatee or devisee entitled to a share of the estate already disposed of,
7   anyone entitled to a grant on total intestacy and
8   any legatee or devisee or creditor (or their personal representatives).

The class of person entitled to administer the estate is established once and for all at the time of the testator's death. If a beneficiary inherits and then dies, his estate has to be dealt with before that of the testator. An applicant cannot move from one class to another. First of all, the persons in the previous class must be "cleared off" by death or renunciation. An administrator should word any oath in such a way that anyone with a prior right to the grant has been cleared off (O. 79 rule 28 RSC). If there is a complete testacy, but the residuary legatee is unable or unwilling to act – or untraceable – nobody can administer the defendant's estate except by application to Court under s.27(4).

The next-of-kin is the nearest blood relation, so there may be a number of equal class (such as two nephews making rival applications). The Probate Officer can adjudicate between rival applications if both sides agree to be bound by his decision. If not, he may refer the matter directly to the High Court

The application is brought by **motion on notice** to the other applicant. The notice of **motion will be a motion for the sitting of the Court**, even though the solicitor for the other applicant may have lodged the rival application in the Probate Office.

The applicant's grounding affidavit will set out why the Court should prefer his own application (for example, that most of the family prefer him, or the other applicant is claiming against the estate or he's an alcoholic, bankrupt or mentally unstable).

The applicant on notice puts in a **replying affidavit** and the Court decides on the basis of the affidavits. The order in which the applications are made is only relevant if there is nothing else to choose between one applicant and another. There is nothing to stop a grant being made to two persons in the same class, but rival applicants may refuse to co-operate in administration of the estate.

The application is heard on the non-contentious probate side as there is no substantive issue (such as testamentary capacity) involved.

CONTENTIOUS PROBATE APPLICATIONS

Contentious matters begin by **plenary summons** or by **administration suit**. This type of case may be tried by a judge and jury, although in practice it is almost always dealt with by a judge alone. The **plenary summons** is used where there is a challenge to the validity of a will. A **verifying affidavit** must be filed *before* the summons is issued and a warning notice or **caveat** lodged in the Probate Office (O. 5 rule 13 RSC) to stop anything being done in relation to the estate until the dispute has been resolved. The Central Office will not issue the **plenary summons** until the Probate Officer has noted on it that a **caveat** has been entered.

The **caveat**, in the form of Appendix Q Form 20 RSC, says: "*Let nothing be done in the estate of (name) who died on (date) at (address) unknown to me (name) of (address), having interest*". The **caveat** remains in force for six months and may be renewed (O. 79 rules 41–51 RSC).

Anyone seeking to prove the will then issues a **warning to caveat** to the caveator, requiring him to enter an appearance in the Probate Office within six days to state his interest in the estate. A will may only be challenged by someone who would be entitled to benefit if it was struck down. A caveator may, for instance, have been a beneficiary in an earlier will or, if the caveator is the testator's next-of-kin, it might be in his interests to create an intestacy.

If the person entering an appearance to the **warning to caveat** has no apparent interest in the estate, an application should be made to have the caveat set aside in the non-contentious probate list by **notice of motion** to the caveator *(In bonis Norris* IR 1 Eq 384).

In the case of *In bonis Nevin* ITLR 16 June 1997, Shanley J said the Court must consider the *bona fides* of the caveator, but would not set aside a caveat unless the applicant could show either that the caveator had no interest in the estate or that the caveat was lodged vexatiously.

If the caveator does not enter an appearance to the warning, the caveat may be cleared off by filing an affidavit of service of the warning and a certificate of non-appearance (O. 79 rule 51 RSC). But if the caveator *does* have an interest, the executor should issue a **plenary summons** to establish the will as the last will of the deceased. The executor may sue as representative of the estate, without joining any of the persons beneficially interested in the estate (O. 15 rule 8 RSC). An executor may also prove a will this way if he has any doubts about its validity – but he must first lodge a **caveat** in the Probate Office.

The executor's summons must be accompanied by an affidavit confirming that the contents of the **plenary summons** are correct. If the defendant is abroad, the Court may grant leave to serve the summons (or notice) out of the jurisdiction (O. 11 rule 4 RSC). If an appearance is not entered, judgment may be sought in default of appearance.

The **statement of claim** should state that:

1   the testator made a valid will and died,
2   the plaintiff is the executor of the will and
3   the defendant is the caveator.

The defence will normally include one or more of the statutory pleas, such as that the testator:

1   did not sign the will in the presence of two witnesses,
2   was not of sound mind, memory and understanding,
3   was not aged 18 (or married),
4   acted under duress or undue influence,
5   was persuaded to sign the will by fraud or
6   did not know the contents of the will.

If undue influence is alleged but not proved, costs will be awarded against the party making the allegation. Where a presumption of undue influence is established, the onus lies on the recipient of the legacy to prove that the gift was a free exercise of the will of the testator (*Carroll* v. *Carroll*, Supreme Court, 21 July 1999).

Full details must be given in the **defence** or **statement of claim** about any mental incapacity or claim of undue influence (O. 19 rule 6(1) and (2) RSC), including the names of anyone accused of exerting the influence, with the nature and dates of the alleged conduct. Evidence of other instances of undue influence or mental incapacity will not be allowed at the trial.

It is a matter for the caveator to establish the nature of any problems with testation, so the **statement of claim** should not presume the grounds on which the will may be challenged. There is a presumption of due execution and testamentary capacity (*per* McCracken J in *Blackall* v. *Blackall*, High Court, 28 June 1996), so if the will appears valid, it is presumed to be so. If no defence is filed, the action may still proceed (O. 27 rule 7 RSC) and the Master may fix the time and mode of trial.

If the caveator simply wishes to have the will proved in solemn form, and only intends to cross-examine the witnesses produced in support of the will, he may say so in a notice accompanying his defence. In that case, he will not be liable to pay the costs of the other side, unless the Court considers that the challenge was unreasonable (O. 21 rule 17 RSC).

After the **defence** has been filed, a **reply** is usually filed. When the pleadings are closed, a motion is brought in the Master's Court – generally by the plaintiff on notice to the defendant – to fix the time and mode of trial and the issues arising on the pleadings or questions to be answered (O. 36 rule 4 RSC).

The issues are fixed in the form of questions, such as:

1 Was the will properly executed according to the requirements of the Succession Act 1965?
2 Is the will the last valid will of the deceased?
3 At the date of execution of the will, was the deceased of sound mind, memory and understanding?
4 Did the deceased understand and approve of the contents of the will?
5 Was the deceased acting under duress or under the undue influence of the defendant?

and such other issues as the trial judge may deem appropriate.

The Master may make any ancillary order relating to pleadings, particulars, discovery, or settlement of issues. Within eight days of the defendant's entry of appearance, *both* sides must file an **affidavit of scripts**. This is similar to an **affidavit of discovery**, but is mandatory

(O. 12 rules 27-29 RSC). The plaintiff should then deliver a **statement of claim** within eight days of the defendant filing his **affidavit of scripts**.

Any scripts in the defendant's custody must be annexed to the affidavit and deposited in the Central Office. A script is any document such as a will, codicil, draft will or codicil, written instructions for a testamentary document or attendance notes taken when the document was executed. The deponent details what scripts he has (or may have had but passed on to someone else) and avers that he has not suppressed, destroyed or cancelled any other scripts. No-one may inspect any affidavit of scripts until he has filed his own affidavit.

Parties may also seek general discovery and other interested parties may be joined by motion if they are not already represented.

These proceedings prove the will in **solemn form** and put it beyond any subsequent challenge (unlike proof in **common form** of law, which still leaves the will susceptible to challenge). In order for the judgment to be binding on everyone concerned, leave might be sought from the Master to issue a **citation to see the proceedings** (O. 15 rule 12 RSC). This is a notice issued by the Central Office and directed to anyone who may be prejudiced by the Court order, and includes a copy of the proceedings. It does not make the person on whom it is served a party to the proceedings, but puts him on notice so he will be bound by the eventual Court order.

The proceedings – a full plenary hearing with oral evidence – are heard in the non-jury list (or, in exceptional circumstances, in the jury list). If the executor proves proper execution of the will, the Court will presume the testator was sane and that there was no undue influence.

Even if the challenge to the will is withdrawn, the executor may still ask the Court to prove it in solemn form of law, to protect himself. The Court may be asked to fix a date to hear oral evidence, after which the Court may establish the document as the testator's last will. The Court order should confirm that oral evidence was heard, otherwise the Probate Officer will not act on it.

If the Court believes that there were reasonable grounds for opposing the will, it may award costs from the estate (O. 21 rule 17 and O. 99 rule 3 RSC). In *Vella* v. *Morelli* [1968] IR 11, the High Court held that, where there were sufficient circumstances to arouse suspicion, the Court had jurisdiction to award costs out of the estate, despite the failure of an allegation of undue influence. The requirements of public policy – to have wills scrutinised where there were valid reasons for doing so – allowed the Court to depart from the general rule that costs follow the event.

SPECIAL SUMMONS

If the will is valid, but its terms are uncertain or ambiguous, the administrator may seek protection from allegations of wrongdoing by instituting an administration suit by **special summons** (O. 3 rule 7 RSC).

The **special summons** is used for:

1   construction of a will (O. 83 RSC),
2   issues arising during administration,
3   directions to executors or administrators (for example where an estate is insolvent),
4   payment of money into Court by the executors or
5   s.117 applications.

The **special endorsement of claim** should state whether the plaintiff claims as creditor, executor, administrator, residuary legatee, legatee, next-of-kin, heir-at-law, devisee or in some other capacity (O. 4 rule 10 RSC). The correct defendant in such an action is established by O. 54 rule 2 RSC.

The judge in Chancery 1 or 2 is asked a series of questions on the face of the summons about the construction of the will (or of part of it). Since a will speaks from death, it is seldom possible to construe one will by reference to the construction of similar words in another will. The intention of every testator will be different – or, in the words of Carroll J in *Re Howell* [1992] ILRM 518, "no will has a twin brother".

Extrinsic evidence is admissible to show the intention of the testator (s.90) and an operative interpretation of a bequest is preferred to a non-operative interpretation (s.99). In the case of *Lindsay* v. *Tomlinson*, High Court, 13 February 1996, the testatrix left £25,000 to a non-existent charity, the "National Society for the Prevention of Cruelty to Animals (Dogs and Cats Home), 1 Grand Canal Quay in the city of Dublin". To confuse matters further, the Dublin Society for the Prevention of Cruelty to Animals and the Irish Society for the Prevention of Cruelty to Animals had formerly shared premises at 1 Grand Canal Quay. Carroll J admitted extrinsic evidence that the testatrix was a dog-lover, that she subscribed annually to the Dublin Society and that the Dublin Society operated the "Dogs and Cats Home" when it was situated at Grand Canal Quay. On the balance of probabilities, the judge said the scales came down in favour of the Dublin Society.

But if the terms of a will are *unambiguous*, extrinsic evidence may not be adduced as to its construction. In *O'Connell* v. *Bank of Ireland* [1998] 2 IR 596, a widow told several people that she had left her house and contents to the plaintiffs. But the will only mentioned the contents, not the house. Barron J said he was quite satisfied on the evidence he had heard that the testatrix *had* intended to leave her house to the plaintiffs, but there was no ground for construing the will other than in accordance with its terms. The decision was upheld by the Supreme Court in May 1998.

Occasionally, a testator's intention may be frustrated by circumstances beyond his control. In *Kelly* v. *Cahill* [2001] IEHC 2, the testator had changed his will, intending to leave all his property to his wife, rather than his nephew. Due to a mistake by his solicitor, certain lands were excluded from the revised will and would have been inherited by the nephew. Barr J said that, in such circumstances, a 'new model' constructive trust could be presumed which was "an equitable remedy intended to restore to the plaintiff the benefit of which she has been deprived". The judge said that such a trust – the purpose of which was to prevent unjust enrichment – was an equitable concept which deserved recognition in Irish law.

Questions of construction are decided on the facts of each case. If all parties involved agree on one construction and sign a deed to that effect, the administrator will be protected. If it's alleged that an estate is being wrongly administered, either the administrator or beneficiary may apply to the Court for directions or for the estate to be administered under the supervision of the Court.

SECTION 117 APPLICATIONS

If the testator died wholly or partly testate, any of his children may bring an application under s. 117 of the Succession Act claiming that he failed in the moral duty to make proper provision for the applicant. This action may be brought by a child of any age, whether adopted or not, whether born inside or outside the marriage and whether dependent or not.

In *EB* v. *SS* [1998] 2 ILRM 141, Keane J said: "(S)ince the legislature, no doubt for good reasons, declined to impose any age ceiling which would preclude middle-aged or even elderly offspring from obtaining relief, the Courts must give effect to the provision, irrespective of the age which the child has attained."

The proceedings are by **special summons**, grounded on an **affidavit** which sets out the circumstances of the alleged failure. The Court will consider the application *in camera*, from the point of view of a "prudent and just parent", taking into account any payments made during the testator's lifetime (s.63) and the situation of any other children, but disregarding the testator's attitude to the applicant.

In the case of *Re GM* [1972] 106 ILTR 82, Kenny J said the Court would consider:

1   the amount left to the surviving spouse (or the value of the legal right),
2   the number of the testator's children,
3   the ages and positions in life of the children at the testator's death,
4   the means of the testator,
5   the age of the applicant,
6   the financial position and prospects of the applicant and
7   any other provision already made by the testator for the applicant.

In *IAC: C&F* v. *WC & TC* [1989] ILRM 815, the Chief Justice said a "positive failure in moral duty" must also be established.

In *McDonald* v. *Norris* [1999] 4 IR 301, McCracken J ruled that a Court could also take into account a plaintiff's behaviour towards his parent when assessing whether or not the parent had fulfilled his or her moral duty.

In *Browne* v. *Sweeney* [1998] 4 IR 527, the plaintiff's mother bequeathed £5,000 to each of her grandchildren and divided the residue of her estate, worth about £1.3 million, between five charities. The plaintiff and his three siblings had each received about £275,000 five years before their mother's death. The plaintiff suffered from drink and drug addiction and had dissipated the money. Lavan J said that, in the circumstances of the case, the testatrix had discharged her moral duty and he dismissed the claim.

A child who has been found guilty of an offence against the deceased (or against any spouse or child of the deceased) punishable by two years' imprisonment or more, may not make a s.117 application.

In *PMcD* v. *MN* [1999] 4 IR 301, the Supreme Court said that the behaviour of a child towards his parent was a factor to be taken into account in deciding whether the moral obligation of the testator had been extinguished or diminished.

In *EB* v. *SS*, Lavan J said the time for considering whether the testator had failed in his moral duty was at the date of his death, not the date of the making of the will.

An application may be made where a person dies testate but the will is inoperative and the estate would otherwise be distributed according to the rules of intestacy (*RG* v. *PSG* [1980] ILRM 225)

Under s.46 of the Family Law (Divorce) Act 1996, which amends s. 117 (6) of the Succession Act, the application must be made within six months from the first taking out of representation of the estate. Unlike other limitation periods where an extension of time may be granted, it seems the s.117 limitation period cannot be extended by the Court. In

MPD v. *MD* [1981] ILRM 179, Carroll J decided that the strict time limit in s.117 went to the jurisdiction of the Court, and would operate whether or not it was raised as a defence.

(Limitation periods are calculated differently under English and Irish law. In *McCann* v. *An Bord Pleanala* [1997] 1 ILRM 314, Lavan J said that, under s.11 of the Interpretation Act 1937, where a period of time is reckonable from a certain day, that day is *included* in the limitation period unless a contrary intention appears. So, if the six month limitation period begins on 1 January, it ends on 30 June, not 1 July.)

13.   Statute of Limitations

The Statute of Limitations 1957 applies only to Common Law reliefs, not to equitable claims (except to equitable estates in land). In the case of *Murphy* v. *Ireland* [1996] 3 IR 307, Carroll J ruled that, where a plaintiff could sue in tort, the Statute applied, but if he had to sue directly for a breach of a Constitutional right, the statutory limitation period did not apply (although the doctrine of *laches* might be relevant).

In negligence claims, where there is no personal injury, the limit is six years. Where there *is* personal injury, the limit is three years. In a fatal injury case, it's three years from the date of death. In a claim involving breach of a simple contract (not under seal), the limit is six years. With personal injury arising from breach of contract, it's three years (or three years from the date of death). With a specialty contract (under seal), the period's 12 years, as it is for actions involving land. The period for recovery of arrears of rent is six years.

The three year limit for personal injuries is reduced to two years where the injury is sustained on board an aircraft, or while embarking or disembarking. In *Burke* v. *Aer Lingus* [1997] 1 ILRM 150, where a passenger was injured on a shuttle bus taking her from the aircraft to the terminal, Barr J ruled that the bus journey was an "air-related risk" and any action had to be brought within two years, under the terms of Article 29(1) of the Warsaw Convention.

s. 126 of the Succession Act 1965 amends s. 45 of the Statute of Limitations in relation to the estate of a deceased person. Before January 1 1967 (the operative date of the Succession Act), the limitation period for a beneficiary claiming a share in an estate was 12 years. Where a person claimed interest or damages in relation to a share, the period was six years. To speed up the administration of estates and extinguish stale claims, s.126 halved those times (12 years became six, and six years became three).

In *Drohan* v. *Drohan* [1981] ILRM 473, the son and personal representative of James Drohan, who died intestate in 1966, brought an action to recover land in the possession of other relatives for eight years. The squatter claimed to be in adverse possession and relied on s.126. McMahon J said the deceased had died before January 1 1967, so s.126 did not apply. He said *obiter* that, even if it had applied, s.126 did not contain the appropriate limitation period. The case had been brought to recover land for the estate, so it wasn't a claim brought by a beneficiary claiming a share. The appropriate period was therefore 12 years – for recovery of land. (But if the personal representative *had* recovered the land and kept it for himself, the beneficiary's claim might not have been statute-barred.)

In *Gleeson* v. *Feehan and O'Meara* [1991] ILRM 783, the Supreme Court upheld the view of McMahon J, so s.126 *only* applies to claims brought by beneficiaries against the estate.

The limitation periods for spouses to claim against the estates of deceased spouses (or ex-spouses) are governed by the Succession Act 1965 and the Family Law (Divorce) Act 1996. s.56 of the 1965 Act says that a spouse who wishes to claim the dwelling or chattels of a deceased spouse must do so within six months of being notified of the right by the personal representatives, or within a year of representation being taken out on the deceased's estate, whichever is the later.

s. 115 says spouses seeking to take either a legal right under a will or a bequest must also make up their minds within six months of being notified of the right by the personal representatives, or within a year of representation being taken out, whichever is later.

s.18(1) of the 1996 Act says a divorced spouse seeking a share of an ex-spouse's estate must do so within six months of the grant of probate. A spouse who has been informed about the death of an ex-spouse has one month in which to inform the personal representative of any intention to claim against the estate.

The limitation period for a s.117 application, by a child seeking a share in a deceased parent's estate, has been reduced from 12 months to six by s.46 of the 1996 Act.

Where a proposed defendant dies while an action is pending, his personal representative may be sued in his place (s.48 Succession Act 1965). But s.9(2)(b) of the Civil Liability Act 1961 lays down a *maximum* period of two years for the institution of a cause of action against the estate of the deceased. An action must be instituted either within two years of the date of death or within the *relevant period*, which runs from the date of *accrual* of the cause of action (which may be before the person died), whichever is sooner.

For example, if an act of negligence committed in 1998 resulted in a personal injury, but the defendant died in 2000, the action would have to be instituted by 2001 (that is the normal three year limitation period.) But if the act resulted in loss and damages, rather than personal injury (in which case the usual limitation period would be six years), the action would have to be instituted by 2002 (that is two years after death). This restriction does *not* apply to equitable relief.

Counsel should ensure that all appropriate parties are joined in any action before the expiry of any statutory time limit. In *Allied Irish Coal*

Supplies Ltd v. *Powell Duffryn International Fuels Ltd* [1998] 2 IR 519, the High Court refused to allow the joinder of the defendant's parent company as a co-defendant because the claim against that company was statute-barred.

If a proposed defendant dies, his legal personal representative should be sued in his place. If there is a will which names an executor, he may be sued even though no grant of probate has been issued, as he derives his authority from the will, not from the grant of probate.

But if someone dies intestate or does not name an executor or the named executor dies, nobody can be sued until letters of administration have been granted. The limitation period continues to run, so an application should be made in the Probate Office to have a citation issued to the person who is entitled to a grant of administration, commanding him to extract the grant. An affidavit must be filed grounding the facts in the citation and, if the person to be served lives abroad, stating whether he is an Irish citizen (O. 79 rules 52–3 RSC). If the person lives abroad and is not an Irish citizen, notice of the citation is served on him.

The citation is signed and sealed by the Probate Office, and a copy lodged there. If the person cited fails to appear within 14 days, his non-appearance is taken as a renunciation of his right to probate or administration (O. 79 rule 57 RSC). An application should then be brought before the probate judge under s.27(4) of the Succession Act 1965.

(If the proceedings are *already in being* at this stage, an *ex parte* application may be brought under O. 15 rule 37 to have someone appointed to represent the estate of the deceased. A temporary administrator may be appointed under s.27(7) of the 1965 Act.)

An action will not become abated because of the death of any of the parties (O. 17 rule 1 RSC). If a *defendant* dies during the course of proceedings, an application should be made to substitute a new defendant. If a *plaintiff* dies during proceedings, the action must be reconstituted by applying to have the legal personal representative substituted as plaintiff. This is done in the Master's Court by **motion on notice** grounded on an **affidavit** setting out the date of death, the issue of the grant and the necessity to continue the proceedings. The grant of probate or administration should be produced to the Master.

ACCRUAL

A cause of action **accrues** when a right of action comes into existence. In the case of negligence, for example, the cause of action may accrue as soon as the act is committed. But if the effects of the negligence are not realised at the time, it would be unfair to expect a plaintiff to bring an action before the effects become manifest, so the cause of action accrues on the date when it becomes apparent that there are grounds for an action.

For example, in *Murphy* v. *Minister for the Marine* [1996] 2 ILRM 297, the plaintiff, a fisherman, had applied in 1988 for a sea-fishing licence. He decided not to buy a fishing boat until he had received the licence. Department officials advised him in June 1989 to buy the boat, as the licence would be issued "within a very short period". He bought a boat for £120,000, but in November 1991, he was refused a licence.

He sued in 1991 for negligence, but his claim of negligent misrepresentation was not filed until November 1995, more than six years after the date of the alleged misrepresentation. The defendants said the claim was statute-barred but Morris J said the date of accrual was the date of the breach of the assurances, not the date on which they were made, so the claim was not statute-barred.

In *Morgan* v. *Park Developments Ltd* [1983] ILRM 156, concerning a latent defect in a house, Carroll J said a cause of action would not accrue until the latent defect could reasonably have been discovered.

But in *Irish Equine Foundation Ltd* v. *Robinson* [1999] 2 IR 443, Geoghegan J said that, in contract, the limitation period began on the date of the breach of contract. The defendants had designed and built an equine centre which was completed in November 1987. Water started leaking through the ceiling in 1991 and proceedings were issued in January 1996. The plaintiff said the limitation period ran from the first appearance of the leak, but Geoghegan J said the defective design of the roof would have been manifest to an expert at any time, so the action was statute-barred.

The plaintiff in *Hegarty* v. *O'Loughran* [1990] 1 IR 148 wanted to extend Carroll J's discoverability test to cover latent personal injuries (such as in medical negligence cases). In 1973 and 1974, the plaintiff had undergone two operations on her nose, both of which failed. She began proceedings against the two surgeons in 1982. They said the claim was statute-barred under s.11(2)(b) of the Statute of Limitations 1957.

Barron J said determination of that issue depended on the date of accrual. The defendants said it was when the operations were performed. The plaintiff said it was when a reasonable man exercising reasonable diligence about his own affairs could have discovered the manifestation of the damage. Barron J agreed with Carroll J's discoverability test but said that, historically, the accrual of a cause of action for damages for negligence was the date of the act causing the damage. It was a matter for the Oireachtas to change the law if it wished.

On appeal, the Supreme Court agreed that the Statute of Limitations did not permit such an extension. McCarthy J said he recognised the "unfairness, harshness and obscurantism" underlying the rule, and suggested that the legislature might make special provision for medical malpractice cases. As a result, the Statute of Limitations (Amendment) Act 1991 was passed, extending the discoverability test to personal injury actions.

In *Bolger* v. *O'Brien* [1999] 2 IR 431, the Supreme Court ruled that the test for determining a plaintiff's date of knowledge was to assess when he knew, or ought reasonably to have known from facts observable or ascertainable by him, that he had suffered a significant injury. This introduced an objective element into a test that was primarily subjective.

In cases involving adverse possession of land, the cause of action accrues when the possession becomes adverse.

Fraud or mistake postpones the date of accrual. Sections 71 and 72 of the Statute of Limitations say the cause of action will not accrue until the plaintiff has discovered the fraud or mistake (or could have discovered it, with reasonable diligence).

Where a plaintiff is under a disability (such as an infant, a convict or a person of unsound mind), the time is extended for six years from the end of the incapacity, except in slander or personal injury cases, where the extension is three years, and joint tortfeasors, where it's two years. In cases involving land, there is an upper limit of 30 years extension of time (that is 12 years after the age of majority), after which any action is statute-barred, even if the incapacity continues.

Section 49(2)(a)(ii) of the Statute of Limitations did not permit an extension of time where an infant's parent or guardian could have brought an action on his behalf. But the Supreme Court ruled this section unconstitutional in *O'Brien* v. *Keogh* [1972] IR 144. An 11-year-old boy was injured while a passenger in a car driven by his father, and the boy's mother instituted proceedings four and a half years later. The Court said the infant's rights would not be vindicated if the section was allowed to stand (for example where a child was injured in a car crash due to his parents' negligence, but they failed to bring an action on his behalf).

Under s.56 and s.65 of the Statute of Limitations, time runs afresh following any written acknowledgement or part-payment of a debt during *or after* the limitation period. But in cases of adverse possession of land, once the statutory period has expired, written acknowledgement will not give rise to a fresh accrual, as the original title to the land will have been extinguished. Anyone in adverse possession of land should avoid acknowledging the owner's title (for example, by offering to buy the land) during the limitation period.

14. Supreme Court Appeals

The procedure governing appeals to the Supreme Court is laid down in Order 58 of the Rules of the Superior Courts. All appeals to the Supreme Court are by way of re-hearing.

The first question to be asked is whether an appeal lies at all. There is an almost universal and untrammelled right of appeal to the Supreme Court in relation to civil cases which originated in the High Court. Article 34.4.3 of the Constitution provides that "the Supreme Court shall, with such exceptions and subject to such regulations as may be prescribed by law, have appellate jurisdiction from all decisions of the High Court ... "

However, a High Court decision may sometimes be final (s. 6 Courts Act 1964, s. 14(4) of the Mergers, Takeover and Monopolies (Control) Act 1968, s. 31 Courts Act 1981, s. 86(6) of the Central Bank Act 1989 and s. 32(1) Courts and Court Officers Act 1995). There is also no appeal from a decision of the High Court in the case of an appeal from the Circuit Court (*Prendergast* v. *Carlow County Council* [1990] 2 IR 482).

Some statutes require the leave of the High Court to bring an appeal, including s. 108(7) Patents Act, 1992; s. 82 Local Government (Planning and Development) Act, 1963 (as amended); s. 132(6) Electoral Act, 1992 and s. 57(8) Presidential Elections Act, 1993.

According to s.6(4) of the Roads (Amendment) Act 1998, the decision of the High Court in a judicial review brought under the Roads Acts is final unless the High Court grants a certificate that the decision involves a point of law of exceptional public importance and an appeal is desirable in the public interest. It is not necessary to obtain a certificate to challenge the constitutionality of any provisions of the Roads Acts. But in *Jackson Way Properties Ltd* v. *Minister for the Environment* [1999] 4 IR 608, Geoghegan J said that a certificate was required to appeal on those grounds which were unrelated to the Constitution, otherwise would-be appellants would simply add a constitutional challenge to their grounds of appeal.

A case may be stated from the Circuit Court to the Supreme Court where oral evidence is given (ss. 37 and 38 Courts of Justice Act, 1936). In the case of a consultative case stated from the District Court to the High Court, an appeal may only be brought to the Supreme Court with the leave of the High Court (s. 52 Courts (Supplemental Provisions) Act, 1961).

An appeal should not normally be brought until the High Court action has been finally determined. In *Superwood Holdings plc* v. *Sun*

Alliance plc (No. 2) [1999] 4 IR 531, Hamilton CJ said appeals should not be made to the Supreme Court against orders or rulings made by a trial judge during the course of an action.

It is not always necessary to involve all parties in the appeal. Sometimes the trial judge grants one of the parties a non-suit or other form of dismissal. Just because that party may have been involved in the litigation in the High Court does not mean that he need be a party to the appeal. If no relief is sought against him, there is no point in involving him in the appeal.

Order 58, rule 4 RSC provides that the notice of appeal shall "in every case state the grounds of appeal and the relief sought, or the order (if any) in lieu of the judgment or order appealed from sought by the appellant … " A claim that "the trial judge was wrong in law and in fact in the judgment and order made" is not a ground of appeal. The use of the word "perverse" in relation to any finding of a trial judge or jury should also be avoided, unless the claim can be substantiated.

In *Fagan* v. *Wong*, Supreme Court, 7 May 1997, Lynch J rejected a claim that a High Court judge had been uneven or unfair. He said: "Judges have a large measure of discretion as to how they conduct their Courts and the trials which they hear in them, provided always that all parties are allowed to present their respective cases fully and fairly."

At the drafting stage, care should be taken to spell out succinctly the essential grounds of the appeal. The first question to be asked is: why should the judgment and order of the Court of trial be reversed or varied?

In *Lopes* v. *Galvin*, Supreme Court, 25 November 1996, O'Flaherty J said that the powers of the Supreme Court on hearing an appeal were rather limited where a judge had made findings of fact about the credibility of witnesses or about the course of events. He stressed that, in such a case, "We have no jurisdiction to substitute our views for what the trial judge has expressly found."

But in the case of *Superwood Holdings* v. *Sun Alliance* [1995] 3 IR 303, O'Flaherty J accepted that the Supreme Court could substitute its own inference of fact for that of the High Court judge where the inference had been drawn from circumstantial evidence.

In *Foran* v. *Cobbe and Kelly*, Supreme Court, 13 June 1996, the Supreme Court allowed a plaintiff to introduce additional evidence under O. 8 rule 8 RSC. The Court said the evidence was relevant and of sufficient weight that it might have influenced the decision of the trial judge. But in *Blehein* v. *Murphy* [2000] 2 IR 231, Denham J reiterated that only in exceptional circumstances would an appellant be allowed to amend a notice of appeal to include a ground not argued in the High Court.

O. 58 rule 8 of the RSC says that the Supreme Court has the power to receive further evidence on questions of fact without special leave on "any appeal from an interlocutory judgment or order". On appeal from a final judgment, further evidence may only be admitted "on special grounds" by way of notice of motion. The thorny distinction between final and interlocutory judgments was teased out by Hardiman J in *Minister for Agriculture, Food and Forestry* v. *Alte Leipziger* [2000] IESC 13.

Final drafting of the grounds of appeal should not be left until the transcript has been trawled for possible grounds (or additional grounds). If the original grounds have to be elaborated for justice to be done, an application should be made to the Supreme Court as early as practicable for leave to adduce additional grounds. If the parties agree on the matter, the Court will generally allow the additional grounds to be argued.

The notice of appeal must be served within 21 days of the perfection of the High Court order. The conditions for allowing an appeal which is out of time were laid down in *Eire Continental* v. *Clonmel Foods* [1955] IR 170, a decision which has been applied in many cases since. The three conditions are:

1   a *bona fide* intention to appeal, formed within the permitted time,
2   the existence of something akin to mistake, and
3   an arguable ground of appeal.

Of course, the Court still has a full discretion to admit a late appeal (*Carroll* v. *McManus*, Supreme Court, 15 April 1964, and *Hughes* v. *O'Rourke* [1986] ILRM 538).

If, for example, the person is only marginally out of time due to a mistake, the other side should be asked in writing to consent to an extension of time. Such consent should readily be given, without having to apply to the Court. The Court will not allow costs to a party resisting such an application on unmeritorious grounds. (Indeed, costs may be awarded against such a party!)

The circumstances governing the admission of additional evidence on appeal are set out in the case of *Lynagh* v. *Mackin* [1970] IR 180. A notice of motion will be required, seeking leave to adduce the new evidence which should initially be set out in an affidavit. Subject to the Court's overriding discretion, it is necessary to show that the additional evidence:

1   could not have been obtained with reasonable diligence for use at the trial,

2   would probably have had an important influence on the result of the case and

3   was apparently credible.

In the first instance, it is necessary to file the original notice of appeal, endorsed as to service, and an attested copy of the High Court order. Five (or three – rule 2) books of appeal should be lodged "without delay" (O. 58 rule 12 RSC). They must include:

1   the pleadings,
2   all relevant affidavits
3   all relevant interlocutory orders,
4   the transcript of evidence and
5   the judgment. (A written judgment should be approved by the trial judge or else the note of the *ex tempore* judgment should be agreed).

Both sides should agree on the precise exhibits which were produced at the trial of the action, and clear copies should be available for the Supreme Court hearing – including albums of photographs and maps. If a document does not copy well, a fresh and clear copy must be produced.

Failure to have identical books of appeal leads to unnecessary delay and confusion, so the appellant must serve a copy of the index of the books on the other side. Both sides should collaborate in advance, so that everyone in Court will be reading from the same books with the same pagination.

The appellant's solicitor must certify when the documentation (including all exhibits) has been lodged. It is the responsibility of the parties – not the staff of the Supreme Court office – to make sure everything is in order.

Practitioners must attend the Friday morning callover in the Hugh Kennedy Court if their case is listed for the following Monday to confirm that listed appeals will be proceeding and that all written submissions have been filed. Without such confirmation, the appeal will not go ahead.

If papers are not lodged within a reasonable time, the other side may bring a **motion to dismiss for want of prosecution**. Such a motion should not be brought if there are genuine reasons for the delay, but the party in default runs the risk of having the appeal struck out, or the Court may make what is known as a *Conlon* v. *Meade* order (cf. *Conlon* v. *Meade*, Supreme Court, 17 June 1965) – that if the relevant papers are not lodged by a specified date, the appeal will be dismissed.

Once the certificate of readiness is issued, the case will appear in the Legal Diary. A number of appeals will be listed for each Friday during term so the Court can:

1   check whether the appeal is proceeding,
2   assess the time realistically required for the hearing,
3   decide whether written submissions are required and
4   fix a date for the hearing in a particular term.

In *Capital Radio Productions* v. *Radio 2000*, 26 May 1998, the Supreme Court held that it had an obligation to give priority to any matter that required urgent attention, such as family law matters or *habeas corpus* applications. It said there could be crisis situations which required the Court to drop everything and attend to the matter.

Once a date has been allocated for the hearing, the appellant must lodge written submissions in the Supreme Court office not later than three weeks before the date of the hearing. The respondent's submissions must be lodged in the office within one week of the appellant's submissions.

In long trials, signposts throughout the transcripts are helpful to the Court. Any "dead issues" should be indicated, to save members of the Court unnecessary reading on issues which are no longer relevant. In some cases, it is unnecessary to lodge any transcripts in relation to spent issues. If, for example, liability is no longer an issue in a personal injuries case, there is no need to copy books of transcripts which relate exclusively to liability.

Before the hearing, the parties should exchange among themselves (and submit to the Supreme Court office) a list of authorities to be relied upon. If possible, there should be an agreed book of authorities, rather than each party presenting a separate book with many of the same cases. If one party wants to rely on a particular case or authority to which the other party does not wish to refer, the case may be added onto a separate list.

The Court will appreciate having clear copies of cases and authorities to be relied upon – especially old, rare or unusual reports. If, during the appeal, it becomes apparent that further cases or authorities may be helpful or relevant, Counsel will be allowed to refer to them.

If possible, the parties should meet before the hearing, so that neither side is taken by surprise at the appeal. If Counsel is relying on a point not made at the trial, he should say so as early as possible. The Court will decide whether to permit the new point to be argued.

Counsel for the appellant should assume that the Court will have read the original judgment and the written submission, so it is not necessary to read them out verbatim. In general, Counsel should get straight to the heart of the appeal and the judgment under appeal should occupy a central position in the written and oral presentations.

It may be assumed that the Court is aware of decisions such as *State (Healy)* v. *Donoghue* [1976] IR 325 and *Hay* v. *O'Grady* [1992] 1 IR 210 – although an occasional, apposite passage from such judgments may be cited.

The Court sets great store by the oral presentation, and so does not impose time constraints, as in other jurisdictions. But that does not mean the oral presentation may be verbose, repetitive and circumlocutory. It should be concise and precise and should be a submission in the true sense, rather than a speech. Ideally the oral submission should complement the written one. The advocate must be in a position to listen to and answer questions from the members of the Court. If the advocate needs to look up a point – particularly as a result of interventions from the Bench – he may seek time to do so.

In reply, it is not necessary to repeat arguments made at the original submission. And – subject to the ruling of the Court – it is not generally permissible to introduce a fresh argument at this stage. The reply (if required at all) should be strictly confined to rebutting the case made by the opposite party and should be concise and to the point.

Index